RELIGION
in the
NEW RUSSIA

RELIGION
in the
NEW RUSSIA

The Impact of Perestroika on the Varieties of Religious Life in the Soviet Union

JIM FOREST

CROSSROAD • NEW YORK

1990

The Crossroad Publishing Company
370 Lexington Avenue, New York, NY 10017

© 1990 by James Hendrickson Forest

Printed in the United States of America

Library of Congress Cataloging-in-Publication Data

Forest, James H.
   Religion in the new Russia : the impact of perestroika on the
varieties of religious life in the Soviet Union / Jim Forest.
     p.   cm.
   Includes index.
   ISBN 0-8245-1040-2
   1. Soviet Union—Church history—1917–   . 2. Soviet Union—Religion.
I. Title.
BR936.F67 1990
291'.0947'09048—dc20   90-36546
                                        CIP

TO
JANET DOUGLAS INGLIS
"RISE AND SHINE"

"Blessed are you
when men revile you and persecute you
and utter all kinds of evil against you falsely
on my account.
Rejoice and be glad,
for your reward is great in heaven,
for so men persecuted the prophets
who were before you."

—Matthew 5:11–12—

Contents

Preface

STANDING IN FRONT OF ME was Father Mikhail Zhakov, a monk with a reddish beard that was long and rather wild. His uncut hair was tied in a knot. Though with difficulty, he spoke in English. "Will you tell the truth in your book?" I doubt I will stand before a stricter face even at the Last Judgment. Father Mikhail was a living outpost of uncombed, God-centered old Russia. "It isn't easy to know the truth," I answered, "and even harder to tell it, but I will try to know it and to tell it." With the gaze of an icon, he charged me, "Truth, truth, but only truth!"

His words have come back to me again and again in the months since we met during Easter week in Petrozavodsk. The pages that follow are my attempt to tell the truth about the current state of religious life in the Soviet Union.

The undertaking is, nonetheless, the work of a blind man feeling an elephant. The Soviet elephant is eleven time zones wide. I have done my best to explore as much of the elephant as I could, travelling from Russia's Orthodox north to the Islamic south, from Catholic Lithuania in the west to a Buddhist *datsan* near the Mongolian border in the far east.

Much of the book is an account of conversations with a wide range of Soviet citizens whose lives center on their faith. I have also talked with state officials who still decide many matters affecting religious life. I have watched Soviet television to see what the religious content was — there has been quite a lot — and been attentive to the Soviet press.

Belonging to the Russian Orthodox Church gives me an intimate feeling for religious life in the Soviet Union, and not only for Orthodoxy. I also have the blessing of two decades of work in interfaith organizations, especially the International Fellowship of Reconciliation and the World Council of Churches.

xi

Another great advantage for such a project is that the Russian elephant has become much more talkative. When I first started writing about religious life in the USSR six years ago, the possibility of someone like Gorbachev coming to power hadn't entered anyone's imagination. The words *perestroika* and *glasnost* meant nothing. Except for a few brave dissidents who felt they had little to lose and perhaps something to gain by candor with strangers from the West, Soviet citizens discussed the more important subjects only with their most trusted friends. It was rare to hear Stalin's name and rarer still to hear anyone mention the Great Terror. Everyone knew where certain churches, synagogues, and mosques had once stood but no one pointed to those empty spaces. Every family had its large helping of tragedy but talked only of those losses caused by war, not purges. Many believed in God but few were willing to say so. Many hated the political order and its values but kept silence or even said it wasn't so bad.

Especially in the past year or two, one commonly hears complete and honest answers, whether talking to a *babushka*, a student, a priest, or even someone in a government job. It isn't only that the answers are honest; the present climate encourages questions a journalist might once have hesitated to ask out of compassion for the person being interviewed.

A key word in many conversations is *dukhovnost*, a term that should be added to our growing Russian vocabulary in the West. *Dukhovnost* has profound significance for anyone wishing to understand current events in the USSR. Literally the word means "quality of Spirit." Unfortunately "spirituality," its English equivalent, although it is identical in actual meaning, is usually understood to mean either the private relationship between the individual and God or a method of prayer. It has lost its social and its ethical dimensions.

Dukhovnost, while referring to the intimate life of prayer, also suggests moral capacity, courage, wisdom, mercy, social responsibility, a readiness to forgive, a way of life centered in love. Used by believers, it means all that happens in your life when God is the central point of reference.

The word also has a significant place in the vocabulary of nonbelievers. For them *dukhovnost* means whatever it is that draws one toward a moral life, a life of integrity and courage. Georgi Arbatov, addressing the Communist Party Conference in Moscow in June 1988, commented that the first three years of *perestroika*, while not resulting in significant economic progress, had created the "political, spiritual and moral preconditions for economic reform."[1] In few other countries would the spiritual element of economic life be stressed, or even mentioned, in political debate. To many Russians, even those who seem estranged from religious belief, the idea of a nonspiritual life is incomprehensible.

My children ask me why I spend so much time in the Soviet Union and why I write so much about religion. The answer is that I am drawn by the intensity of spiritual life I encounter among Soviet believers. I have never experienced anything like it and didn't dream such communities of prayer existed, East or West. I wanted to know how it was possible.

I was more than half afraid the answer was persecution — bad news, if true, as it would mean the main blessing for religious life is a government hostile to religion.

It is true that persecution has done much to purify religion in the Soviet Union, especially by driving out those who were drawn into the local church or synagogue by family pressure or peer expectations. Persecution has also graced the church with many martyrs. But I have learned that *dukhovnost* gains its strength not from enemies but from God. In fact one of the great discoveries of spiritual life is that one needn't look to the KGB to find the adversary. The enemy is much closer. As Alexander Solzhenitsyn has written of his conversion while in the *gulag:*

> It was granted to me to carry away from my prison years on my bent back, which nearly broke under its load, this essential experience: *how* a human being becomes evil and *how* good.... Gradually it was disclosed to me that the line separating good and evil passes not through states, nor between classes, nor between political parties either — but right through every human heart — and through all human hearts. This line shifts. Inside us, it oscillates with the years. And even within hearts overwhelmed by evil, one small bridgehead of good is retained. And even in the best of hearts, there remains... an unuprooted small corner of evil."[2]

I have learned from Soviet believers how important it is to love one's enemies, and that it is possible. Though this hard teaching is

[1] *International Herald Tribune,* June 30, 1988, p. 1.
[2] Alexander Solzhenitsyn, *The Gulag Archipelago* (London: Fontana, 1975), "The Ascent," volume two, part four, pp. 597–98.

common to both Judaism and Christianity, in the West we seem to have put it on some remote upper shelf and forgotten about it.

In the Book of Exodus we are instructed, "If you meet your enemy's ox or his donkey going astray, you shall bring it back to him. If you see the donkey of one who hates you lying under a burden, you shall refrain from leaving him with it" (23:4–5). In Paul's letter to the Romans, he wrote, "Bless those who persecute you; bless and do not curse them.... Repay no one evil for evil, but take thought for what is noble in the sight of all. If possible, so far as it depends upon you, live peaceably with all. Beloved, never avenge yourselves, but leave it to the wrath of God; for it is written, Vengeance is mine, I will repay, says the Lord. No, if your enemy is hungry, feed him; if he is thirsty, give him drink" (Rom. 12:14; 17–20).

Such biblical love has been widely practiced by many Soviet believers, love not in the sentimental sense but rather the rejection of revenge and the will to do good to an adversary, hoping always for the adversary's conversion. The person "on the way" — a typical Russian phrase for someone living the life of the Spirit — realizes that spiritual purification is never a private event but involves even one's enemies.[3]

Such love is linked to a readiness to forgive. "I must forgive," a Russian Christian told me. "Otherwise I am in hell and I am not permitted to receive Christ."

I have discovered that underneath the political and economic surface of Soviet life is an intense but largely invisible spiritual life. Believers waiting in line are often people at prayer. I have also come to realize that the strength of soul that has empowered people to retain their faith despite so many heavy blows has much to do with what the Russian Orthodox call *bytovoe blagochestie:* the art of ritual living. Nicolas Zernov wrote about this:

The way people greeted each other, or expressed their sorrow or joy, the various kinds of meals they ate at different seasons, the decoration of their houses, and the architecture of their churches — all these were used [and are still used] by the Russians as parts of their corporal effort to transform this world into the temple of the Holy Spirit. The material and the spiritual were treated as two sides of the same reality, and for this rea-

---

[3]For a more detailed treatment, see my earlier book, *Making Friends of Enemies* (New York: Crossroad, 1988).

son the smallest details of daily life were charged with religious significance."[4]

Most believers in the Soviet Union, whatever their nationality and faith, have preserved their particular variety of the art of ritual living, not only retaining ancient rituals of worship but maintaining an intense sense of sacred time and space.

"Why change the way we pray?" asked a woman in a Moscow church. "Beauty takes many generations. And why hurry at prayer? All good things take time and are best done slowly."

•

About the structure of this book: My last book, *Pilgrim to the Russian Church*, was organized as a journal as that seemed the best way to present a gradual process of discovery. While some elements of a journal are preserved in this volume, I have chosen a more thematic structure. The first chapter considers the repressive context in which Soviet believers were living in 1987. The second chapter is a detailed account of some of the events connected with the Millennium celebration in 1988. The following chapters are organized under confessional headings: Orthodox, Old Believers, Catholics, Protestants, Jews, Moslems, and Buddhists. There is a chapter on the Council for Religious Affairs. The final chapter considers the expected content of the new Soviet law on freedom of conscience and what is still lacking.

In the chapters about particular religious traditions, I have let believers speak for themselves. They do so eagerly now without fear of reprisal.

For all the voices that are contained in this book, I am painfully aware of those that are missing. In the section on Soviet Protestants, there are interviews only with Baptists, Lutherans, and Seventh-Day Adventists, but there are many other churches as well, including Jehovah's Witnesses, Methodists, Mennonites, and Dukhobors. There appear to be the seeds in Moscow of a Quaker Meeting. In the Catholic section, I wish that I had had more extensive contact with members of the Ukrainian Catholic Church and been able to visit the western Ukraine. The only visa I have sought and not received in the USSR was one to Lvov. I hope some day to write about this subject at length. In the Jewish section, I regret the lack of contact with members of the synagogue in Moscow. An appointment I had made with one of those

---

[4]Nicolas Zernov, *The Russians and Their Church*, 3d ed. (Crestwood, N.Y.: Saint Vladimir's Seminary Press, 1978), p. 106.

working there fell through, and I had to fly back to Holland the next day. The miracle of this book is that so many important meetings happened, but I miss that one, especially as a Jewish cultural center, museum, and library is opening in Moscow.

"Missing something gives you good reasons to come back," as my colleague Sergei put it when seeing me off.

●

Naming a book is sometimes harder than naming a child. In the end, the U.S. edition is going to press as *Religion in the New Russia*, a title that may suggest insensitivity on the author's part to the fact that much of the book concerns events occurring within the old Russian (now Soviet) empire but outside Russia.

While Russia is the largest Soviet Republic, there are fourteen others: the three Baltic states, Estonia, Latvia, and Lithuania; the two republics most closely linked by history and language to Russia, Byelorussia and the Ukraine; then Moldavia, Georgia, Armenia, and Azerbaijan in the Soviet Union's southwest corner; and finally Turkmenistan, Uzbekistan, Tajikistan, Kazakhstan, and Kirghizia filling a huge area in central Asia. Nor does that end the story. Within the borders of the vast Russian federation are a number of "autonomous" republics, two of which feature in this book: Karelia and Buryat. Despite all the press attention in recent years to the various Soviet nationalities, it still comes as a surprise to many to learn that there are a hundred non-Russian nationalities living in the USSR and to discover that Moslems are the second-largest Soviet ethnic group, a population presently growing at four times the rate of the Soviet population as a whole. The fact is that "Russia" isn't so Russian.

Yet in the last analysis, the publisher found none of the proposed alternative titles as engaging as the one that has ended up on the cover. Just as Holland (two provinces among twelve) equals the Netherlands for many people, so does Russia equal the Soviet Union in Western headlines. Our apologies to any who are annoyed. Please don't judge the book by its title.

●

Many of the same people who helped with *Pilgrim to the Russian Church* have assisted with this book as well: Metropolitan Pitirim of Volokolamsk, head of the publishing department of the Moscow patriarchate, and members of his staff, especially Tatiana Volgina and Vyacheslav Ovsyannikov; and Georgi Derevianchenko of the Department of External Church Affairs.

This book owes much to the staff of Keston College, a British institution founded by an Anglican priest, Michael Bourdeaux. For many years Keston has studied the situation of religious believers in countries under Communist rule, publishing books and pamphlets as well as producing two magazines and running a news service, all the while campaigning for the release of religious prisoners. The staff members who were most generous in helping me were Jane Ellis, Helen Bell, Suzanne Oliver, and John Anderson.

Among others outside the USSR who have given advice or helped in other ways I especially wish to mention Frans Van Agt, former Dutch ambassador to the Soviet Union; William van den Bercken of the Interuniversity Institute for Missiological and Ecumenical Research in Utrecht; Peter Jarman of Quaker Peace and Service; Metropolitan Anthony in London; Father Matthew Stadniouk, secretary to Patriarch Pimen; Father Alexis and Tatiana Voogd of the Saint Nicholas Russian Orthodox Church in Amsterdam; Father Amvrosi of Our Lady of Tikvin Center in Oregon; Richard Deats and Virginia Baron of the Fellowship of Reconciliation; also Maya and Rudolph Bitter, Boris Chapchal, Jacob Corret, Jane Floyd, Hannes de Graaf, Nico van de Kamer, Father Feodor Kovalchuk, Jim Larrick, Walter Lesiuk, Father John Meyendorff, Margot Muntz, Jan Nattier, Donald Nicholl, Father Henri Nouwen, Father Basil Osborne, Joseph Peacock, Mariquita Platov, Patrick and Helena Radley, Walter Sawatsky, Ivan Sewter, Sister Mary Catherine Shambour, Lee Weingarten, and the staff of the bookshop of the Russian Orthodox Cathedral at Ennismore Gardens in London.

The book would have been impossible without encouragement and financial help from a number of people: Gene Knudsen-Hoffman, Eleanor Detiger, Jim Henson, Roshi Bob Aitken, Dom John Eudes Bamberger, Elise and Kenneth Boulding, Elizabeth Cattell, Lambrecht J. J. van Eekelen, W. H. Ferry, Rabbi Everett Gendler, Morgan Gibson, and Sister Mary Luke Tobin.

My thanks to Jay Higginbotham, who first suggested this book, and to Alexander Avelichev, director of Progress Publishers in Moscow, who welcomed the proposal. I am also grateful to the officers and staff of the International Fellowship of Reconciliation who made it possible for me to be in the USSR for the Millennium events in 1988.

I owe much to my two editors: Michael Leach of Crossroad in New York, and to the editor I married, Nancy Forest-Flier.

•

Sergei Afonin, senior editor of Progress Publishers, was my companion in travels in the USSR in January and May 1989. His enthusiasm and hard work laid the foundation for this book. Though he appears only occasionally in the narrative, he merits an introduction.

Sergei is a balding former athlete turned heavy smoker and linguist. Besides being an almost tireless translator and enthusiast for this project, he frequently pulled genies out of bottles, again and again getting us to the remote places I wanted to go, no easy thing in a country where even a phone call is not so simple and where one gets a seat on a plane only by good luck, close friendship, or major battle.

Having in common a love of books, we rarely went past a bookshop without slipping in. In Leningrad in May, on a side street off Nevsky Prospekt we discovered a black market in books. Even Sergei, well used to the Soviet Union's shadow economy, was shocked by the high prices. An illustrated children's Bible of about a hundred pages was one hundred rubles — most of a month's pay for many people.

What most attracted Sergei was a recently published book about Vladimir Vysotsky, a Soviet poet-singer, now dead, who has become a secular saint. "He was more than a singer," said Sergei. "He was an actor, a poet, a great human being — and so was disliked by officialdom in Brezhnev's era. But he was loved by the people. His popularity cut across generational lines. He lived intensely, drank dangerously, and at age forty-two died of a heart attack. It was a terrible loss. His wife, the French film star Marina Vladi, wrote a book that was published in France. Now finally it will be published here." The book Sergei had picked up, a photo-biography of the singer, was forty rubles, ten times what it had been sold for when published a few months before. It was too much for Sergei. He reluctantly gave it back to the seller.

Sergei remembered when good books were plentiful and cheap. "As a kid with my small allowance, I could buy one or two classics every week and have enough left over to go to the movies. Now books are a luxury — not only much more expensive, but good books, especially classics, are very hard to find."

Afterward we sat for a long while on the embankment looking across the Neva to the Fortress of Peter and Paul, water slapping against the stone wall. It was a sparkling day with a huge lapus lazuli sky and a few creamy clouds.

"If you could have lived at another time," I asked him, "when would it have been and what would you have done?" He thought for quite a while. "I would rather have lived here in Saint Petersburg in the second half of the nineteenth century. There was a sustained burst of creative energy in Russia at that time. If I had my choice, I would have been an artist, musician, or composer — something in the arts."

Like most Russians, he is deeply troubled by what has happened in his homeland, not least to words. "After the Revolution," he said, "many words lost their former significance — for example, the word 'mercy.' We hardly know what it means. We destroyed mercy. We also destroyed courtesy. In Pushkin's time a letter began with some term of respect, not just 'comrade,' but 'Respected, distinguished Alexei Alexyevich.' It might close, 'and now I am always your obedient and most devoted servant.' Now we have 'efficient' letters that sound like a machine talking to a machine. The atmosphere for real communication is profoundly damaged."

He pointed out the religious content that still survives in certain words. "The word for 'thanks,' *spasiba*, means 'God save you.' The word for 'Sunday' means 'the day of the Resurrection.' We still refer to a person doing good — someone who is always near by, always blessing, whose example gives you courage — as an angel of mercy."

One of our main foes in the course of our travels was Aeroflot, the world's largest but possibly least humane airline. It treats its ordinary Soviet passengers like cattle and, despite efforts to handle foreigners with velvet gloves, domestic Aeroflot flights often have much in common with travel by rural bus in India. Like many Soviet citizens with language skills, Sergei had once worked for Aeroflot.

"Its problem, as in so many Soviet institutions, is a total absence of a sense of co-responsibility. Everyone does his own segment of a job and nothing more. Aeroflot has been severely criticized in the news media. New instructions are issued periodically by Volkov, the minister of civil aviation. Improvements are announced. But nothing changes."

Of the places we travelled together, he suffered most in the country where many visitors would have been most comfortable, Lithuania. Every hour he was reminded of injustice done to Lithuania by the imperial Russia that became the imperial Soviet Union — a feeling not unknown to Americans too, especially those living or travelling abroad.

"There is radical disagreement within me about being Russian," he said on our last day in Vilnius. "Sometimes I agree with Dostoyevsky that Russia will save the world. Other times I am convinced that Russia is lost forever. Sometimes I am proud to be Russian, sometimes miserable and deeply ashamed. Sometimes I would rather belong to any people in the world except this one. Other times I can't imagine being anything else. But it impresses me when I remember the priest who said that no Russian priest sent to serve in another country has chosen to remain abroad."

Though not engaged in the church, he is fascinated by religion and drawn to Orthodoxy. One of the more intimate moments we shared was a priest's blessing of a small icon he had purchased in May in Petrozavodsk — a story told in the chapter on Orthodoxy.

Sergei is at home in an Orthodox church but often uncomfortable among Protestants. After a Baptist service one day, I remember an old woman from the congregation scolding Sergei for smoking on the dirt road in front of the church. "She was right," he told me later. "I know I shouldn't smoke, especially near a church, but I needed that cigarette. I felt uncomfortable in that atmosphere. I don't like that way of preaching. It's like political speeches. It makes me feel irritated and indignant. The pastor's topic was love. What a way to teach love!"

Sergei smoked more than usual that day. The next morning at breakfast he had a headache, which he attributed to too many cigarettes the day before, but he declined my offer of aspirin: "The headache is a penance. I should mobilize my inner forces."

We occasionally shared our dreams. In one of these Sergei was visited by his father, dead many years. "He was a military officer, medical doctor, and Communist party member," Sergei said. "Though baptized as a child, he had abandoned religious ideas early in his life and, so far as I know, never thought about God. Yet in the dream my father said, 'What you must do is repent and forgive.'"

Sergei was deeply impressed, regarding the dream as a word from heaven. We talked about it for days afterward.

When I last saw Sergei he told me that helping me with the book had been good for him. "I was thinking recently about the seven deadly sins," he told me. "I found that I am guilty of three of them, maybe three and a half. But it used to be seven so I feel I am on the right way."

JIM FOREST

The Feast of Saint Sergius of Radonezh
October 8, 1989
Alkmaar, Holland

Chapter 1

A Spring Breeze

WHILE IN LENINGRAD IN FEBRUARY 1987, I met Nikolai Preobra-
jenski, a nuclear physicist who had become a priest of the Russian
Orthodox Church. He was serving as assistant rector of the Leningrad
Theological Academy. It was just four years since Brezhnev's death.
Andropov and Chernienko had in turn briefly reigned in the Kremlin, neither having exhibited any vital life signs between election and
burial. It was only twenty-three months since Gorbachev had become head of the Soviet Communist party. The words *glasnost* and
perestroika still needed to be translated as 'openness' and 'restructuring.' President Reagan was still describing the Soviet Union as the
evil empire. After Father Nikolai and I had talked about his decision
to leave a prestigious civil position to become a priest, I asked him
what impact Gorbachev and *perestroika* were having on church life.
"A new wind is blowing," he told me. "It hasn't yet touched religion
but we believe it will and we are beginning to live as if it had already
touched us."[1]

"*A new wind is blowing...and we are beginning to live as if it had
already touched us.*" Despite all the blows believers had received in
the past, in 1987 a remarkable sense of expectation had begun to flour-
ish within Soviet churches. While Gorbachev had as yet said nothing
about a new religious policy, something fundamental had changed.
One smelled it rather than touched it. What used to be unsaid was
being said, what used to be hidden was on the screen, what used to
be unprintable was being published, and what used to be thought
hopeless was being eagerly awaited.

---

[1] Jim Forest, *Pilgrim to the Russian Church* (New York: Crossroad, 1988), pp. 37–39.

1

But the rules and institutions governing religious life were exactly as before. The actual situation for religious life was still appalling. The Law on Religious Associations, signed April 8, 1929, revised in 1932 and 1975, remained in force, as did the structures of enforcement.[2] Under the law religious associations lacked a juridical personality and could operate legally only if registered. Local authorities were required to impede or prevent registrations. (Especially among Protestant churches, there was often a principled refusal to seek registration, while some other churches had no possibility of registration, most notably the Eastern-rite Ukrainian Catholic Church.)

Many obstacles were erected to make application for registration unlikely, including the rule that at least twenty persons must make a collective application. Those applying were well aware that a variety of costly actions might be taken against them — investigations, a job lost, a permit not given, even false criminal charges filed.

Associations of believers, having no legal standing as such, had no right to own property. Buildings used for worship were leased to believers by the Council for Religious Affairs. (The dining hall of a Russian monastery was officially listed as a restaurant by local authorities, the monks paying a monthly rent for its use.)

Religious rites could be performed only in places designated for worship. Religious associations had no right to sign contracts or to take action in court. Religious education of children and young people was forbidden. Neither could there be any special program of any kind for minors — no social activities, no excursions, no participation in choirs, no playgrounds. Libraries were banned from religious premises. The only books permitted were those recognized by state authorities as essential for ritual purposes.

The role of priests, ministers, rabbis, imams, and Buddhist lamas ("cult servants" in Marxist terminology) had been greatly diminished. A decree of March 1961 deprived clergy of any direct control over the functions of the local church, reducing them to the status of employees of the church council. Those employed in pastoral positions were placed in the highest tax bracket, paying far more than other members of society.

All religious bodies were under the administrative control of the Council for Religious Affairs, whose role went far beyond the reg-

---

[2]For a general overview of Soviet legislation on religion, see Trevor Beeson, *Discretion and Valour: Religious Conditions in Russia and Eastern Europe*, 2d ed. (London: Collins; Philadelphia: Fortress Press, 1982), pp. 22–50. For a study of the revisions of 1975, see Walter Sawatsky, "The New Soviet Law on Religion," *Religion in Communist Lands*, vol. 4, no. 2, pp. 5–10.

istration of religious communities and the leasing of buildings for religious use. The 1961 decree permitted state authorities to remove individual members from the executive body of churches and install "nonfanatical persons who sincerely fulfill Soviet laws." At times the "nonfanatical person" — in fact someone actively hostile to religion — might be inserted as chairman of a local church council. The same decree urged that "priests, choir directors, church watchmen...and other persons working for the church should not be included" in the membership of the parish council.

Religious associations had only the most limited possibilities for publishing. On the rare occasions when Bibles were published, the print runs were pitifully small. Neither were religious associations permitted to import religious books from abroad. Bibles, Korans, and prayer books brought to the USSR by visitors were confiscated at the border during gruelling searches at points of entry.

Only a few institutions of religious education were permitted. The Russian Orthodox Church, with its many million members, had three seminaries. The Old Believers and the various Protestant churches had none. The Catholics had one. The Moslems, the country's second biggest religion, had two. The Jews and Buddhists had none. Nor could the seminaries freely accept whomever they wished. The total number of students allowed was decided by the state. No applicant could be accepted without specific approval from the Council for Religious Affairs, which in turn had the KGB check every name.

While the 1929 law did not explicitly ban religious engagement in charitable service, in practice believers were excluded. In addition they were forbidden to operate hospitals, old-age homes, orphanages, day care centers, and other social service agencies, or to assist public institutions involved in meeting human needs. Religious life was defined exclusively in terms of worship activity.

Despite these and other oppressive regulations, religious associations were required to signal their support of the political establishment in a variety of ways. It was expected that a substantial portion of church income would be contributed to the Soviet Peace Fund. It was anticipated that religious associations, at the national level, would play an active role in supporting the Soviet Union's foreign policy, in any event never opposing the government's actions. No Soviet religious body protested the invasions of Hungary, Czechoslovakia, or Afghanistan, nor was there ever any public protest made by religious leaders of actions taken against believers, though a number of courageous individuals spoke out at the cost of arrest and imprisonment. Bishops and their counterparts in other religions often praised the state for its attitude toward believers.

A huge establishment of state-sponsored atheist education was operating at full steam. Members of the Communist party were required "to wage a decisive struggle against religious prejudices." There were obligatory courses on atheism in every school and university as well as atheist lectures at places of employment. In addition there were frequent articles in the press and programs on television, not so much making the case for atheism as attacking religion. Atheist posters were commonplace. Atheist museums were to be found in every city, normally in some former cathedral that had been confiscated. Perhaps this last form of atheist education, the museums, was the most impressive, with their vivid displays of heretics being tortured and a highly selective exposition of history that sought to show that religious associations were led by greedy hypocrites while the institutions they led were a central part of the machinery of oppression.

While it had been years since clerics and lay believers were arrested *en masse*, imprisonment remained a distinct possibility for anyone daring the slightest resistance. While the exact numbers at a given moment were never known, in 1986 Keston College had reported nearly three hundred imprisoned for reasons that had a religious basis. Though arrests were declining in early 1987, individuals like Alexander Ogorodnikov, founder of the Christian Seminar in Moscow, remained in labor camps.

There had been more than a thousand Orthodox monasteries and convents in 1914 in Russia and its territories; in 1987 there were eighteen, most of them near the country's western border. The others were in ruins — many churches and monasteries had been dynamited in the thirties — or were being used for other purposes. Some had been made into prisons or reformatories.

Once a land renowned for its countless churches and bell towers, in 1987 thousands of towns and even whole cities lacked any building in which prayer was permitted. Many Christians were hundreds of miles from a living church, while for Jews, Moslems, and Buddhists the distances could be even greater. Occasionally believers gathered in cemeteries to pray. In the whole of eastern Siberia and the Soviet far east churches were "as rare as pigs with gold feathers."

This was the situation in the USSR in 1987, one year before Christians were to celebrate the Millennium — the thousand-year anniversary of the baptism of the people of Kiev.

And yet Father Nikolai, with countless other believers, felt some softening of the frozen earth. I felt it too, though it wasn't until the Millennium events in June 1988 that the spring breeze could be really felt.

Chapter 2

Millennium

WHILE HE LET IT BE KNOWN THAT HE HAD BEEN BAPTIZED AS A CHILD, during his first three years as general secretary Mikhail Gorbachev seemed to ignore the churches. He had been preoccupied with strengthening his leadership position within the Politburo, inaugurating positive relations with the United States and other Western countries, promoting disarmament, launching programs to revive the stagnant Soviet economy, and coping with the consequences of the Chernobyl disaster. His main gesture to believers had been the release of numerous prisoners.[1]

Then on April 29, 1988, five weeks before the Millennium celebration was to begin, Gorbachev received Patriarch Pimen and five Orthodox metropolitans in the Kremlin. Apart from Gorbachev and the clerics, two others were present: Gorbachev's friend, the philosopher Ivan Frolov, and the chairman of the Council for Religious Affairs, Konstantin Kharchev.[2]

---

[1]On February 5, 1989, Leonid Sizov, first deputy minister of internal affairs, stated that 356 persons regarded in the West as "prisoners of conscience," including those convicted of religious activity, had been released in the past two years. Other prisoners remained, however. In March 1989 Keston College reported 86 religious prisoners of conscience in the USSR; many were convicted for refusing military service.

[2]Speaking at the Higher School of the Communist party in Moscow a few weeks before the Kremlin meeting, Kharchev said: "Remember the Leninist idea, that politics begins when you start to talk in terms of millions.... The church has survived, and has not only survived but has rejuvenated herself. And the question arises, which is more useful to the party — someone who believes in God, or someone who believes in nothing at all, or someone who believes in both God and communism? I think we should choose the lesser evil." He went on to advocate "the training of a new type of priest" whose placement would be "a matter for the party." The underlying argument for the new policy toward religion, for Kharchev at least, was that it would make believers collaborators in achieving goals set by the Communist party.

That night Soviet television viewers witnessed Gorbachev's warm welcome to the patriarch, saw the bishops sitting with him around a circular conference table in the ornate Saint Catherine Hall, and heard Gorbachev express regret for past "mistakes made with regard to the church and believers" in violation of the constitution and socialist principle. He cited the recent return to the Orthodox Church of several monasteries and said a new law was being drafted to protect freedom of conscience.

Patriarch Pimen responded: "Esteemed Mikhail Sergeyevich, I pledge support to you, the architect of *perestroika* and the herald of new political thinking.... We pray for the success of this process and are doing everything we can to promote it."

While most of what he said was unremarkable, the patriarch used the occasion to say that, though much had improved, "not all the problems of church life are being resolved or duly attended to." The comment, despite its brevity, was as unprecedented as the meeting. In the past church leaders routinely denied troubles existed even when the situation they faced was much worse.

The informal exchange that followed was not broadcast, but press articles reported that the bishops raised "a number of specific questions connected with guaranteeing the normal activity of the Orthodox Church." According to an interview with Konstantin Kharchev published late that year in *Ogonyok*, the bishops expressed their desire to open new seminaries in Byelorussia and in other republics of the Union, to reestablish nine dioceses suppressed in the sixties, and to reopen religious associations closed in the same period. They also raised a group of questions relating to publication work. Gorbachev promised he would "pass on the requests and considerations to the government, which would carefully examine them and make appropriate decisions."

It was the second time that religious leaders had been received by the head of state since the Bolshevik revolution. The other occasion was on September 4, 1943, two years after the German invasion. Realizing that a change in policy toward religion would be a positive factor in the war with Hitler, Stalin had met with Metropolitan Sergei (soon after elected patriarch) and two other Orthodox bishops. But it was a private meeting. No photo was published. The image of Stalin and the metropolitan together was never communicated to the public. Accounts of what occurred vary. All that is certain is that the situation for the church changed drastically. A Council for the Affairs of the Orthodox Church (later the Council for Religious Affairs) was set up. Many churches were reopened and antireligious propaganda sharply curtailed. The patriarch, formerly exiled to a log cabin on the outskirts of Moscow, was given a mansion in the Arbat district of central Moscow, a residence previously occupied by the German ambassador. The Holy Trinity–Saint Sergius Monastery forty miles north of Moscow became a living monastery again, and a seminary was opened within its walls. During the fifteen-year period that followed, religious life was partially restored in many parts of the USSR. It wasn't until Khrushchev's antichurch campaign, launched in 1959, that the Soviet state resumed full-scale war with religion.

"Until Gorbachev received the patriarch," an official of the Council for Religious Affairs told me in May 1989, "it was B.C. Afterward it was A.D."

When I arrived in Moscow on June 2, 1988 — the fifth week of this new A.D. — it was immediately evident that the state was celebrating the Millennium of the baptism of Kievan Rus'[3] nearly as much as the faithful. At Moscow's Sheremetyevo Airport Millennium guests were taken directly to the VIP lounge and served a cup of coffee while awaiting delivery of their baggage. There was no border guard comparing and recomparing my visa photo with my face, no long wait by the baggage carousel, no searching of luggage. I felt more like a visiting prime minister than a religious journalist poking around in a society where God's obituary had been published long ago.

At the Ukraina Hotel, where most Millennium guests were housed, an exhibition of church photography had been mounted in the lobby. One flight up, in front of the hotel's hard-currency store, a large stand was set up for the sale in rubles of icon reproductions, crosses, church badges, and other religious articles manufactured by the Moscow patriarchate. (It proved even more popular with the hotel staff than with the Millennium guests. For every bishop in line, there seemed to be at least two cleaning women.)

---

[3] A thousand years ago Rus' centered on Kiev, whose Prince in 988 was Vladimir. Extending from territory north of Novgorod to lands well below Kiev, Rus' was ruled collectively by the family of Rurik, whose most senior member had the throne of Kiev. In the thirteenth century Tatar forces destroyed Kiev, forcing the center of Russian culture to the north. Moscow was only a small river settlement in the days of Grand Prince Vladimir. First mentioned in the Chronicle in 1147, it became the seat of the Metropolitan of All Russia in the fourteenth century, the same period when the prince of Moscow, Ivan at that time, became the Grand Prince of All Russia. In the fifteenth century the Russian Church became self-governing. In 1589 Patriarch Jeremiah of Constantinople enthroned Metropolitan Job as the first Patriarch of Moscow and All Russia. In 1593, a meeting of the four patriarchs in Constantinople recognized Moscow as the fifth ranking patriarchate.

In Moscow the center of Millennium celebration was the Danilov Monastery, located in an industrial district a mile south of the Kremlin. Founded in the thirteenth century, the monastery had been closed in stages between 1929 and 1932 until all that was left to the monks was the Resurrection Church outside the walls, and finally that was taken away as well. The monastery became a prison for juvenile delinquents. Then in 1983 the badly-damaged monastery was returned along with the Resurrection Church and several adjacent buildings including a former umbrella factory.

After five years of restoration work in which many believers volunteered their labor, the monastery no longer showed any trace of political vandalism. Walls, bell towers, churches, and other buildings — everything looked as good as new. Several new buildings were still under construction, including a hotel-sized hostel for church guests.

Metropolitan Pitirim and his staff at the church's publishing department had set up a press center within the former Resurrection Church. On June 4 it was packed with reporters and TV film crews, most of them still recovering from the just-ended Moscow summit meeting.

Metropolitan Filaret, exarch of the Ukraine, announced the major news item: the return of part of the Monastery of the Caves in Kiev, the oldest monastic community in the Russian Orthodox Church. Founded in 1051, it was closed in 1929 and reopened in 1941 during the German occupation. In 1961 the monks, having been limited to a small section of the monastery, were ordered out altogether on the grounds that the buildings were in danger of falling down. Given the neglect the structures suffered afterward, it is a wonder that the pretext didn't turn into a prophecy. The section being given back was the Far Caves, consisting of two churches and the caves beneath, a bell tower, and various buildings. "We are on the verge of resuming monastic life after a pause of twenty-five years," said the metropolitan. The keys were to be turned over at a ceremony June 7 in Kiev.

Konstantin Kharchev of the Council for Religious Affairs, a participant in the press conference, was asked about new legislation being drafted that would protect religious rights. All he would say was that the law would be published soon, depending on "the relevant parliamentary commissions." When asked by a reporter about how an atheist state can undertake such positive actions on behalf of churches, Kharchev insisted that the changes occurring did not mean that the government was giving up its "materialistic outlook."

The changes only indicate "that constitutional guarantees of religious rights will be fully protected."[4]

As there were no more Millennium events that day, I drove out to Peredelkino, a village on the edge of Moscow made famous by the writers who lived there, among them Boris Pasternak. His grave is in the cemetery near the Transfiguration Church. Three women were sitting on a bench at the foot of Pasternak's grave. One of them pointed out the branch of pale lavender orchids lying in front of the tombstone. "Nancy Reagan put them there. I saw her do it with my own eyes." She asked what I was eating at my hotel. I mentioned the various kinds of meat and fish. "Well, that's not real Moscow food. You should go into one of the local *produckti* [food stores] and buy two rubles' worth of sausages. Cook that and see how you like it! There was an article in the press recently about sausages. They found insects, hair, paper, and many other things — everything but meat." She had a copy of the Russian edition of *Moscow News*. She pointed out a back-page interview with a young village priest. "We never used to see anything like that in our press. I only wish they would do to the sausage what they are doing in the press."

The Millennium celebration began the following day with the celebration of the Holy Liturgy in Moscow's Epiphany Cathedral. The chief celebrant was Patriarch Pimen, who stood more easily than when I had last seen him sixteen months before. At that time I doubted he would live another year. After the Liturgy he placed a wreath on the tomb of the unknown soldier next to the Kremlin wall.

The main Millennium event for the Russian Orthodox Church was to be the *Pomestny Sobor* — the local council — set to start the next day, June 6. The only others in this century had been in 1917, in the midst of the Revolution at which time the first patriarch was elected since the time of Czar Peter the Great; in 1945, after Patriarch Sergei's meeting with Stalin; in 1961, when Khrushchev wanted the priest's parish role restricted; and in 1971, in the midst of Brezhnev's "years of stagnation."

The day turned out to be fiercely sunny and hot, Moscow's hottest weather in 109 years. I was reminded of New York in August.

We were received at the Holy Trinity–Saint Sergius Monastery by

---

[4]At the party conference in June 1988, Gorbachev spoke briefly about the rights of believers: "We do not conceal our view that the religious world is unmaterialstic and unscientific, yet this is no reason for disrespect toward those who believe in the spiritual world and still less a reason to use administrative means to advance materialistic views....All believers, no matter what their religious views, are citizens of the USSR with full rights....The draft Law on Freedom of Conscience which is in preparation in based on Leninist principles and takes into account all present day realities."

large crowds and the constant ringing of bells in the monastery belfry.
For years church bell-ringing had been suppressed by Soviet officials
but the skill survived. Russians again were ringing bells with the
joyous abandon of children skipping rope.

The council meeting place was the monastery's colorful refectory,
normally used as a winter church. The light in the large room was
nearly blinding. While the church's last council in 1971, also held
in this hall, was completely ignored by Soviet television, this time
television crews were not only present but had set up five camera
platforms around the hall and had installed klieg lights as well.

From additional TV platforms outside cameras followed the parade of church leaders whom the bells were welcoming: heads of other
branches of the Orthodox Church, several Roman Catholic cardinals,
the archbishop of Canterbury, representatives of the World Council of
Churches, leaders of national councils of churches from many countries, and bishops and lay people from the various dioceses of the
Russian Orthodox Church.

Gogol wrote in *Dead Souls*, "Russia likes to assume large dimensions: mountains, woods, steppes, faces, lips, and feet." This applied
to Millennium celebrations as well. With its cast of thousands, the
event could have been designed by Cecil B. De Mille.

The last to arrive was Patriarch Pimen, walking slowly and with
the support of two young, sturdy clerics. The council began in sung
prayer, the sound of the monastic choir bursting on us with the re-
freshing force of sudden rain.

Sitting at the side of Patriarch Pimen was Konstantin Kharchev of
the Council for Religious Affairs, conspicuous in his grey suit amid
all the ecclesiastical raiment. One also was struck by the stillness
of his hands when, during the opening prayers, all around him were
crossing themselves. One of the first to address the council, Kharchev
spoke of the state's responsibility "to protect the rights of all citizens,
whether believers or unbelievers."

Patriarch Pimen expressed his satisfaction with the meeting a few
days earlier of Gorbachev and Reagan. Supporting *perestroika*, he
called on "all the children of our church to be honest in labor and
pure, humble and loving in their service to others."

One of the council's first items of business was to review the
past. Metropolitan Filaret of Kiev said that many participants in
the church council held in Moscow in 1917 were "closely bound up
with" the czarist and economic system and "were altogether alien-
ated from the real socio-political questions affecting the life of the
people." Thus "the majority of the council members did not under-

stand the real meaning of the fundamental changes which took place in our homeland and the positive effect they had on life." Proceeding to describe initial church resistance to the Bolsheviks, Filaret referred to the "hostile actions undertaken by the council with regard to the newly-established people's power." These "led to tension and even confrontation between church and state which became especially strong during the civil war and made a dramatic and lasting imprint on their relations." With the separation of church and state established by the Revolution, "the Orthodox Church lost the privileged position she had enjoyed," a separation begun under the conditions of "famine, economic dislocation, antigovernment conspiracies and civil war." Filaret described the unfolding tragedy: confrontation between believers and atheists, the mass closure and destruction of churches and monasteries, the killing of many believers, lay and clerical. In the early years of the Revolution "the clergy often supported the adversaries of Soviet power." At the same time Soviet laws on religion were often and brutally ignored. He concluded that "every departure from democratic principles...dealt a blow to the common cause of building and developing our socialist society."

Among other speakers at the morning session was Cardinal Johannes Willebrands, head of the Vatican's Secretariat for Christian Unity. He rejoiced in "the holy act of God" that had brought the people of Kiev to the Christian faith, from whom it "rapidly spread across huge territories." A thousand years ago, he recalled, Christians of East and West, despite dissension, were still in communion with one another. But estrangement reached the breaking point. "Catholic and Orthodox fought each other in word and with sword. It is time to overcome division, to develop a sense of being together as church." He mentioned various ways in which dialogue between Catholics and Orthodox has developed and deepened in recent years, becoming a "dialogue of charity." One consequence of the encounter was the "struggle of churches for disarmament and peace to prevent the catastrophe of nuclear war." He pointed out that several points of division still remain, especially questions of church structure — an allusion to Orthodox criticism of the lack of conciliarity (the Russian word is *sobornost*) in the Catholic Church. Common reflection was needed on the special role in the church of the bishop of Rome, understanding that "unity does not mean conformity of one group to another but the recovery of unity around the eucharistic table." Moving on to a more controversial subject, he expressed regret that there was still no recognition of the Ukrainian Catholic Church. "Nonetheless," he said, "a new climate has been created in which we can heal old wounds." He extended to the council and the entire Russian Orthodox Church "the greetings and blessing of His Holiness John Paul II."

The archbishop of Canterbury, Robert Runcie, described the Russian Church as "an icon of the Resurrection." Despite severe persecution, it has risen from the tomb to celebrate its millennium. "The martyrs have been the seed of new church life. We honor the suffering that you have borne, we honor those who have testified to the faith that was in them with their own lives both during the time of the 'cult of personality' [as the Stalin years are called] and in more recent times." Russia offers a witness that "when we take God from the center of our lives, the god-substitutes are deadly."

The main event of the afternoon session was the addition of nine names to the calendar of saints. The most renowned name was Andrei Rublev, the fifteenth-century monk whose icons of the Holy Trinity and the Savior have made their way to churches and homes throughout the world. Also canonized was Father Amvrosi, *staretz* (holy elder) of Optina Pustyn, a monastery south of Moscow recently returned to the church. Amvrosi's wisdom and holiness were so renowned in nineteenth-century Russia that pilgrims walked hundreds of miles to seek his advice and guidance. Among the pilgrims was Dostoyevsky, who used Amvrosi as the model for Father Zosima in *The Brothers Karamazov.*

The Russian Church has always given special attention to *iurodivii:* fools for Christ's sake, people in whom Christ wears the guise of madness. These are ascetic Christians living outside of the borders of conventional social behavior. At the beginning of the seventeenth century there was even one holy fool who ruled Holy Russia, Czar Theodore, the son of Ivan the Terrible. Regarded by Western diplomats sent to Moscow as a weakling and idiot, he was adored by the Russian people. Brought up in an environment of brutality, disliked by his father, regarded with scorn by courtiers, he took shelter in simplicity, prayer, and devotion to his wife. Much of his time was spent in church. Throughout his fourteen years as czar he never lost his playfulness or love of beauty. A gifted bell-ringer, he often woke the people of Moscow in the hours before dawn by sounding the great bells of the Kremlin, a summons to prayer. "He was small of stature," according to a contemporary account, "and bore the marks of fasting. He was humble, given to the things of the soul, constant in prayer, liberal in alms. He did not care for the things of this world, only for the salvation of the soul."

"This simpleton," writes Nicolas Zernov, "robed in gorgeous vestments, was determined that bloodshed, cruelty, and oppression must be stopped, and it was stopped as long as he occupied the throne of his ancestors."[5]

The best known of the *iurodivii* beyond Russia, if only by name, is Saint Basil, from whom the cathedral on Red Square takes its name. Basil walked the streets of Moscow naked and dared to condemn the behavior of Ivan the Terrible.

The council canonized one of the more recent *iurodivii*, Xenia of Saint Petersburg, who had lived in a cemetery, worn the clothing of her dead husband, and answered only to his name. To the irritation of Leningrad officialdom, her grave continued to be a place of pilgrimage and prayer in the Soviet period.

After each canonization was solemnly declared, a newly made icon of the particular saint was used by the patriarch to bless all those present.

So ended the council's first day.

While the council continued at Zagorsk, during the second and third day nondelegates were invited to visit local churches. I joined a busload of people heading south. Our first stop was the town of Maloyaraslavets, seventy-five miles from Moscow. At least a thousand people were waiting outside the church with their young pastor, Father Vladimir Makheev, red-bearded and with grey-blue eyes. After being welcomed by bells, bread, and salt, we went into the church, also full of people, the kind of crowd that the church might contain on Easter when, as they say, "not an apple can drop."

Father Vladimir told us something of the town and church's history, recalling that Gogol had once stayed in a local house and pointing out that the church is a replica, though on a smaller scale, of Moscow's Cathedral of the Savior.[6]

"Thanks to local believers," said Father Vladimir, "our church is being restored — in fact now the restoration is nearly completed. Not long ago this church was in danger of falling down." Gifts were

---

[5]"A brief description of the Moscow Czars, of their appearance, age, habits and disposition," quoted by Nicolas Zernov in *The Russians and Their Church*, 3d ed. (Crestwood, N.Y.: Saint Vladimir's Seminary Press, 1978), pp. 66–67.

[6]The Cathedral of the Savior, on the south side of the Moscva River across from the Kremlin, was Moscow's largest church. Built late in the nineteenth century, it was blown up on Stalin's order on December 5, 1931. He intended it to be the location for a towering Palace of Soviets to be crowned by a seventy-five-meter-high statue of Lenin. In the end all that was built was an outdoor swimming pool. In 1989 many Muscovites signed a petition calling for the reconstruction of the cathedral.

distributed. I received an Easter egg with a painting of the restored church.

As we stood on the church steps in the intense sun to have our picture taken, a lean middle-aged man who hadn't shaved in several days asked me where I was from. "America," I said, skipping the part about living in Holland. "You are the first person I have met from America. Our countries have been enemies but I want to tell you that I have never been your enemy." He said he had read Mark Twain and John Steinbeck. I told him I read Dostoyevsky and Gogol. He gave me a scratchy embrace, kissing me on the cheek.

In the city of Kaluga, another fifty miles to the south, I had lunch with Father Vladimir. I asked him if *perestroika* was having much impact outside of Moscow.

"Yes," he said, "finally the parish priest is being allowed to play an important role in society. Also *perestroika* is happening in the church. Take our church in Maloyaraslavets. Because of the structure of church control imposed in the time of Khrushchev, the head of our parish council was a government appointee, a man named Vasili Osimin, an atheist who had no respect for the church. He was typical of the period of stagnation [the standard phrase used for the Brezhnev period]. All he wanted to do was scratch the backs of the local authorities. The parish priest's word meant nothing — he was simply considered an employee whose job was to stand at the altar. The head of the parish council was doing all he could to cause the death of our church, and having such a head of the parish council isn't rare. Many churches have this problem. But now we can be sure that this situation will be put right. In our case money raised for the preservation of our church, eighteen thousand rubles, simply disappeared. I wrote to the bishop and also to the head of the local Council for Religious Affairs. Still the man wouldn't resign.

"Finally, because of the new processes in our society, I was able to summon a parish meeting and 216 people turned up. All but sixteen voted to kick him out. That was December 13, 1987, a day I will never forget. On that day a real believer was elected to head the parish council. And since then we have repaired the church and restored our parish community. It is a period of restoration, at least the beginning of it. Since that day in December, I feel I have wings on my back. We are celebrating not only our church's millennium but the resurrection of Christianity in the Kaluga region. There are many times in these months when I have cried for joy. There are many times when I couldn't believe what was happening in front of my eyes."

It so happened that, as we talked, new church legislation making the priest the head of the parish was being submitted to the council in Zagorsk. But already its norms were being taken up locally.

I asked him what led him to become a priest.

"It was, I think, mainly my godfather. He was always watching me, caring about me. He was a priest. He celebrated the last Holy Liturgy at the Cathedral of the Savior in Moscow before it was destroyed. More than anyone, he inspired me to belief. He taught me to believe, to hope, to love. Because of him I came to realize that, when you believe from the depth of your heart, there are no obstacles in life."

The next morning we joined in the Holy Liturgy at a church near our hotel, the large building packed to capacity and the church itself embraced by huge crowds.

Afterward we were taken to meet the local political leadership. After a long review of Kaluga's history and economy, the chairman of the city council mentioned the recent return of three local churches as well as the famous Optina Pustyn monastery elsewhere in the Kaluga district, now undergoing restoration. Inviting responses from us, he was probably as surprised as I at the passion and depth of what was said by some in the audience. Speaking with a shaking voice, a woman from Australia said she had been born in this district but left as a child in 1925.

"I will not tell you what our life was like," she said, "or why we left, only say that we knew much suffering. Now I see things happening here which I thought I would never live to see. Every time I go into a church, I find myself crying."

Father Vladimir expressed regret that the bishop of Kaluga could not be here, as he was today at the church council. In his absence, he thought it might be appropriate to appeal to city authorities to authorize an apartment for the bishop.

A woman representing the Russian Orthodox Church in Paris gave the city council a small, finely made "travelling" icon cast from brass of Saint Vladimir. "The gift of icons to political leaders," a neighbor commented drily, "is not traditional. New times!"

In the hotel restaurant afterward, Allan Boesak of the World Alliance of Reformed Churches and the South Africa Council of Churches gave a brief, impromptu speech. "Christian love and Christian solidarity," he said, "recognize no limits in time or space. We have no borders. Apart from the ties of Christian love, there is another bond between my people and the people of Russia — your solidarity with our struggle for freedom in South Africa. My church thanks you for a thousand years of grace and mercy."

Driving back to Moscow, we stopped in a village lucky enough to have its own church. It appeared that every local inhabitant was there to receive us. At the door of the church stood a *babushka* offering the traditional Russian sign of welcome, bread and salt. Inside the church, Dr. Fairy von Lilienfeld from West Germany, a professor of Slavic studies, spoke to the villagers. Her roots are Russian, she said. Her family fled to the West after the Revolution. One of the great gifts of Orthodoxy, she said, was its emphasis on repentance and forgiveness. She said it was her prayer that German repentance would insure that never again would another war come from Germany.

"The Russians have an extraordinary capacity to forgive," she told me on the bus afterward. "They understand that you should never receive Communion until you have forgiven everyone. First you forgive, only then do you come to the altar. This is one of the reasons why receiving Communion is infrequent in the Russian Church. Believers prepare for it, sometimes for weeks or months. In a Russian village, it is understood that once someone has gone to confession and received Communion, there will never again be the renewal of an old enmity. This is part of what we Christians in the West have to receive from the Christians in the East."

I recalled how, in 1943, when German prisoners of war were marched across Red Square, Russian women broke through police lines to give food to German soldiers, an astonishing scene that the poet Yevgeni Yevtushenko describes in his autobiography.[7] At the time Moscow was hungry and many of the sons and husbands of the women in Moscow were dead in the war. But when the women saw the pathetic condition of the German soldiers, compassion took precedence over grief and hatred. I cannot imagine such a thing happening in any other country.

Back in Moscow, Boris Chapchal, one of the two Dutch participants in the council, told me about what had happened at the council during our two days away.

The highlight was acceptance of the new Statute of the Russian Orthodox Church. The existing church law, said Archbishop Kyrill of Smolensk, head of the drafting commission, was completely inadequate. It was written in 1945 while the war was still being fought, then amended in 1961 under pressure from the Khrushchev government.

"One can say with conviction," Archbishop Kirill declared, "that the amendments to the [church's] Regulations of 1961 were provoked not by the internal needs of the church but by the complicated ex-

---

[7]Yevgeni Yevtushenko, *A Precocious Autobiography* (New York: Dutton, 1963), pp. 24–27.

ternal situation in which our church lived in the late fifties and early sixties. . . . The regulations the government forced on the church were provoked by social ideas which can no longer be tolerated in today's society since they are in principle in opposition to the process of democratization, the growth of *glasnost*, and the struggle for *perestroika*." The 1961 amendments "separated the clergy not only from parish administration but from the parish itself. The relation of the clergy and the parish was based upon a contract which formally fixed the nonparticipation of the clergy in the life of the parish in which they celebrated the worship."

The new statute assumed that *sobornost* (conciliarity) must be the basis of church administration "from top to bottom." While the new statute was far from perfect, still it provided "a realistic organization of church administration and a system that corresponds fully to Orthodox ecclesiology and canon law."

After several hours of discussion, the Statute was adopted without dissent. "Still," one Orthodox priest told me, "there must have been some not happy with it. Now the parish priest is going to have to work much harder. Most are eager to do so, but there are still too many who like to take it easy. The priest can no longer say, 'It isn't my job.'"

Another highlight was a speech by Metropolitan Anthony from London: "The Millennium is a glorious feast," he said, "but when we speak of the triumph of Orthodoxy, we must realize that it is the triumph of God over the Orthodox, of truth and light over our sinfulness and our lack of understanding. We must approach the Millennium with a sense of wonder and gratitude. Also we must offer to God and to the people around us both historical and personal repentance for the fact that, historically, the Russian Church failed the Russian nation throughout ten centuries, because otherwise millions of people would not have fallen away from their faith in Christ at the first challenge. This was because baptism was given but education was not."

Arriving at Zagorsk the next morning, I joined the procession into the Cathedral of the Holy Trinity to venerate the body of Saint Sergius, the monastery's founder, who taught that contemplation of the Trinity would dissolve all discord.

Among events at the council's final day was a call by the head of the Orthodox Church in America, an independent church that grew out of the Russian Orthodox Church, for the canonization of Tikhon, elected to lead the Russian Orthodox Church just as the Revolution was occurring in 1917. While opposing the Bolsheviks, he also refused to give his blessing to those who went to war against Red rule. Eventually he became a prisoner before deciding that the church should provide the same degree of cooperation to the Communists that it had offered the state when it was led by the czars. His name is linked with the severe persecutions Russian Christians have suffered.[8]

The morning session ended with a *panikhida* (memorial service) for soldiers who had died in Afghanistan. They had, said Metropolitan Filaret of Kiev, "fulfilled their civil and patriotic duty and had given witness to the teaching of Jesus that there is no greater love than to lay down one's life for another." It is true, as Filaret said, that "thousands of mothers are left in grief." No doubt it is hard to say to those mothers that their sons fought in an unjust war forced on the population by a handful of old men far from the battlefield. One longs for the day when the Russian Orthodox Church will grieve for all who fall in war, cry out against military interventions by the Soviet army, and support those who refuse to fight such wars.

After lunch in the seminary, I wandered around the grounds of the Holy Trinity Monastery, a "city of churches" that has never ceased to be a place of pilgrimage even in those years when the monks had been driven out. "There are still those who walk here even if it is a walk of thousands of miles," a Russian friend told me. But the main body of pilgrims could have stepped off the Moscow Metro, people of every age and condition of life, including many teenagers and young adults.

The council ended with a closing service of thanksgiving and a brief speech by Patriarch Pimen in which he expressed confidence that the Russian Orthodox Church would continue to develop and grow stronger in its task of "sanctifying her children."

The next day Millennium events shifted to the Bolshoi Theater. When the curtain opened about a hundred people were sitting in tiers on the stage. In the center of the first row was Patriarch Pimen. Raisa Gorbachev was sitting a few places to his right, next to Metropolitan Filaret of Minsk, head of the External Church Affairs Department of the Russian Orthodox Church. During some of the more tedious speeches they took to conversation. I counted eight whispered exchanges between them during the four-hour meeting.

Among those on stage was Georgi Arbatov, a member of the Central Committee of the Communist Party and an architect of Soviet foreign policy. He had recently told a *Time* reporter, "We are going

---

[8]On October 10, 1989, in connection with the celebration of the four-hundredth anniversary of the founding of the Moscow patriarchate, Patriarch Tikhon was canonized.

to do something terrible to you. We are going to deprive you of an enemy."

The main speech was by Metropolitan Yuvenali of Krutitsky and Kolomensky. I have warm feelings for him. In 1986 we exchanged rosaries — he gave me the one he wore on his wrist, and I gave him one I had received from Pope John Paul II.

Talking about the cultural impact of Christianity, Yuvenali spoke of the improvement in the status and security of women, the introduction of book publishing, the Russian Church's contribution to the spread of Christianity, the commitment to the poor, and the church's role both in the defense of the nation and as a peacemaker. He reaffirmed the church's hope that the celebration of the start of Christianity's third millennium in the year 2000 would be a celebration of the "elimination of all weapons of mass destruction." He said the ecumenical commitment of the Russian Orthodox Church "is inseparable from its peacemaking responsibility."

The speech lacked the triumphal note one might have expected. Yuvenali noted that the church has also contributed to division in the world, adding, "We ask God and the people to forgive us for our imperfections."

It was the first speech by a Russian Orthodox leader providing statistics about the church's population. Yuvenali estimated that 50 million Soviet citizens were active in the Russian Orthodox Church (out of a population of 285 million) and reported that 30 million Russians have been baptized since 1971. It may be the figure was not provided in the past because the state required that baptisms be officially registered. Many of the 30 million were not. A few months ago the requirement was dropped.

Stressing the connection of faith to social responsibility, Yuvenali quoted Dostoyevsky: "Our church should be in us, not merely in our words but in our entire life."

Metropolitan Filaret of Kiev spoke of the trials the church had passed through, all the while sharing the fate of the people. "As a result of *perestroika* and *glasnost,* we have a much better relationship with the state." He hoped the new developments could help overcome historic divisions among Russian Christians. "The longing for unity is a characteristic quality of our people."

No doubt responding to widespread disappointment that the council had not canonized any of the martyrs who had perished in the period of Communist rule, Metropolitan Mefodi of Veronezh said that "the times were not ripe" — suggesting by implication that the church anticipates a time when such canonizations will occur.

Cardinal Casaroli, secretary of state for the Vatican, said that "Christianity is an undisputed fact of reality, one that cannot be ignored in any country without ill effect." In every society, Christianity offers, even to those without specific religious belief, certain ethical standards. "For many difficult questions, it is impossible to find a solution without morals." Noting the "new winds blowing here," he called for "new legislation to safeguard freedom of conscience." (Sitting next to Cardinal Casaroli was Cardinal Glemp, primate of the Polish Church. A Vatican adviser on the Russian Orthodox Church told me in 1987 that Glemp's visit should precede that of the pope.)

Arie Brouwer of the National Council of Churches in the United States gave thanks to God "for the victory of the resurrected Christ witnessed in the thousand-year history of the Russian Orthodox Church. We remember those who have lived and died in the Lord, especially those who have given witness with their blood." He had learned that the destinies of Americans and Russians "are bound up with one another" and was glad that the Millennium celebration was providing the occasion "for American Christians to learn more about Christianity in the Soviet Union." One consequence was a campaign of young people in American churches to send birthday greetings to Christians in the USSR. Of the tens of thousands of hand-made cards that have been sent so far, Brouwer presented Patriarch Pimen with a birthday card six yards long, filled with crayon-drawings of a thousand burning candles made by many young hands.

Among the other American speakers was Billy Graham. "I had many letters from people in the United States who were praying in support of the meeting of President Reagan and Secretary Gorbachev in Moscow," he said. "Most people never dreamed a person of such conservative convictions as President Reagan would participate in a breakthrough like this. We have been too isolated from each other." The Baptist paid his respects to Orthodoxy: "The Russian Orthodox Church has much to teach us. One of the great experiences of my life has been getting to know Russian Orthodox Christians. They have deepened my life, made me more aware of the power of the Resurrection, and that the crucifixion and Resurrection are the central facts of history."

The day ended with a Millennium concert at the Bolshoi with Patriarch Pimen seated in a box adjacent to the stage. Raisa Gorbachev again was present. The event was broadcast live throughout the USSR and in several other countries. While many famous choirs and orchestras took part, the most sustained applause was given to the nonprofessional choir of monks and seminarians from the Holy

Trinity Monastery at Zagorsk. No choir of believers had ever sung on the stage of the Bolshoi Theater since at least 1917. The next night the event was repeated in the presence of Mikhail Gorbachev.

The next day, June 11, police cars shepherded our buses through one of the gates in the Kremlin walls where we were taken to the Presidium of the Supreme Soviet near the Kremlin's Savior Tower. The main hall is a high, windowless chamber of clinical white marble with gold trim decorated only with the gilded emblem of the USSR.

Our host was Andrei Gromyko, chairman of the Supreme Soviet and president of the Council of Ministers of the USSR — in other words head of state, but in a country where it is the head of the party who is really in charge. Patriarch Pimen was sitting at his side. On the other side was Konstantin Kharchev of the Council for Religious Affairs. Gromyko, as poker-faced live as on film, gave a welcoming address in which he recognized the celebration of the Millennium of the baptism of Kievan Rus' as having universal significance. Christianity has influenced "every aspect of life — economics, education, and social care." The church had played a crucial role in periods of crisis and had contributed to the unity of the nation. It had shaped the nation's spiritual values and given birth to new art, sculpture, architecture, music, and literature. While church and state were separated after 1917, they had found a meeting point in their common concern for peace in the world. "We want a world without war, a world without violence. We want policies based on the integrity and interdependence of the world. All of us, whether believer or unbeliever, have to ask what the coming generation will inherit from us."

In the question period that followed, Gromyko said he could offer few details about the new legislation being written on freedom of religion. "The draft is being developed and I hope will be ready before long." The separation of church and state, a basic constitutional principle, will remain, but religious organizations will be permitted to engage in charitable public service. Bibles and other religious literature can be imported into the country. In cooperation with local authorities, religious bodies will be able to play a role in the conservation of historical monuments (these are mainly churches which, everyone realizes, will eventually be used for the purposes for which they were originally built).

Cardinal Johannes Willebrands, noting appreciatively what had been achieved already, expressed his hope that "under *perestroika* there will be further developments" in the protection of religious rights. In particular "we are concerned about our church in the USSR, in the Baltic states, White Russia, and the Ukraine. It would be a great help in promoting friendship and unity if we could resolve the question about the organization of our church in your country and find the way to form priests and maintain church structures."

The Vatican secretary of state, Cardinal Casaroli, asked if representatives of the different confessions could present comments to the new religious law while it was still in draft form. "It would be quite logical to know the view of the churches in the preparation process," Gromyko said. Casaroli added that never before had the Vatican sent such a delegation to the Soviet Union. "It is unprecedented, a sign of special respect for the Russian Orthodox Church and the people of the Soviet Union." Casaroli spoke of Moscow as the "third Rome," referring to the Russian idea that the mantle of religious leadership moved from Rome to Constantinople, and from Constantinople, after the Moslem conquest, to Moscow. While one assumes Casaroli sees no need for a second or third Rome, it was striking that he admitted religious leadership has more than one address.

Patriarch Pimen, the last to speak, expressed his joy that such a meeting could occur in the Kremlin. There had been nothing like it since Lenin came to power. He pledged to do "everything we can to encourage Soviet and American cooperation in disarmament."

At the end of the meeting Gromyko invited us to a meal. This turned out to be a sumptuous buffet in the most handsome of all Kremlin locations, the majestic Saint George Hall, last used for a reception honoring President Reagan. While we ate, a priest described the Russian family. "The husband is like the government, and the wife is like the party." So far in Russia, he said, the government has all the honor while the party makes the decisions. "The government and party will be renegotiating the terms of their not entirely happy marriage at the coming special meeting of the Communist party."

I talked briefly with Cardinal John O'Connor from New York. He was in a fairly hot state, annoyed that the car, driver, and translator he had been promised were in fact rarely to be found. "This isn't how they are taking care of Cardinal Casaroli," he said. "You can bet he has a car and translator when he wants them!"

One of the high points of the Millennium happened that night. It occurred neither in a church nor monastery but on Soviet television screens with the nationwide broadcast of a film about Russian Orthodoxy called *Church.*

The sixty-minute film began with scenes of the reconstruction of a village church. "Everybody is happy about our church," said a member of the parish council, "and everyone is helping, even the elderly and the sick. A lot of people are giving money to help — ten or twenty kopeks, even a ruble."

A priest in Vladimir, Father Dimitri, spoke about religious life in his large family. "My wife is in charge of the spiritual upbringing of the children. She starts reading the Bible to them the moment they are able to understand." There were scenes of a name-day celebration for two of the children, Olga and Vladimir. "After the Revolution," he said, "many things changed, but moral principles remain always the same. The question is still what is the point of departure in your life. For us it is God."

There were black-and-white film clips about the campaign against churches and believers in the twenties and thirties: icons being thrown into bonfires, church crosses being cut down, onion domes and bells being pulled off church tops and smashed, the dynamiting of the Savior Cathedral in Moscow: scene after scene of cultural barbarism.

The longest interview was with Father Nicholai, a priest who seemed as old as Russian Orthodoxy. He sat at the kitchen table in his small wooden house holding a cup of tea in his hand, his face shining with unaffected love.

"The time goes fast," he said. "Hour after hour — it goes and you can't get it back. Be thrifty about time! You only get so many hours. It is like sand pouring through your fingers. I stand near the doors of death. I am seventy-eight. Not bad. I have been a priest for many years. I love my work. I love God." He paused to cross himself. "With God a person is able to do a lot."

He serves an island church on Chudskoye Lake northwest of Pskov. "Our fishermen work hard. They go out even in bad weather. They do good work. We pray and ask God to save us from calamity, sickness, and war. Save us, Lord!" The camera showed a woman standing under grey skies at the water's edge, a chapel nearby.

"The old people die and the young people leave. Not so many of the young go to church any more." He paused and gazed out the window, speechless with grief.

The screen faded from him to kids on motorbikes roaring through a cemetery. The adjacent church had been turned into a youth club. Hard rock pounded in the former sanctuary. The din gave way to a solo male voice singing a hymn of mourning. The night club was replaced by birds flying in the cupola of a church crumbling into ruin.

The camera returned to Father Nicholai. "My father died in 1914," he said. "I stayed with my brothers. They went to war and

never came back. But we are still alive." He crossed himself. "For
this I thank the heavenly Father. We live in abundance. We have
bread and sugar, work and rest. For this I thank God. I give money
to the Peace Fund. By doing it I hope all acts of war will end. I hope
it helps. War shocks young people. Life is just beginning for them
and then suddenly it is over."

As he spoke about war, the screen shifted to a Leningrad cemetery
where those who died in the siege are buried. A young mother was
showing her child how to cross himself.

Father Nicholai's gentle face returned. He offered tea to the interviewer and the cameraman. "Please! Don't be embarrassed. But it's
probably cold."

In another interview a young woman said, "You have to believe
in God. Without God, you are dead. Religious faith is life itself."

A nun was shown praying while making bread. She explained,
"Human work that isn't framed by prayer has no meaning. Prayer
is the only answer to the industrial age. Otherwise the machine will
destroy us."

Father Zinon of the Monastery of the Caves near Pskov was ques-
tioned about icons. Those he paints are already regarded as treasures
of Orthodoxy. "Icons aren't meant for museums," he said. "The
Vladimirskaya [the most famous of Russian icons, now part of the
Tretyakov Gallery collection] isn't for a museum! It is nonsense to
call them a cultural expression. Icons are an expression of the spiritual life. They relate us to love and peace and mercy. The creation
of God is beauty itself. In the icon the beautiful is seen in the light
of holiness. Icons should be returned to the places for which they
were blessed."

"I am amazed they showed it," said a friend watching the film
with me. "It was shown in a few cinemas but millions will have seen
it on television who could never have seen it in the theater. A few
months ago there was an article about whether it was safe for atheists
to see it!"[9]

The next day, Sunday, was cool and windy, not ideal for an
outdoor Liturgy, but the rain that threatened never came. A specially erected platform in the courtyard of the Danilov Monastery

---

[9]"Under Merciful Protection," a two-hour history of the Russian Orthodox Church,
was distributed in video cassette form to council participants and guests. In addition to
scenes of the destruction of churches and monasteries, it includes photos of some of the
human casualties. "The church had to suffer persecution and lose many faithful," said
the narrator before a series of photos were shown of bishops, abbots, and priests who
perished. Each martyr's name was recited as his photo receded slowly into darkness.

held both the altar and the more prominent church representatives, including nine Catholic cardinals, more than I had ever seen in one place before. "Actually there are nine and a half cardinals," Etienne De Jonghe, general secretary of Pax Christi International, pointed out. "The archbishop from Hungary is soon to get the red hat."

Presiding at the Liturgy with Patriarch Pimen were the heads of other Orthodox Churches: Patriarch Diodorus I of Jerusalem, Patriarch Ignatios IV of Antioch, Patriarch Iliya of Georgia, Patriarch Teoctist of Romania, and Patriarch Maxim of Bulgaria.

Communion was distributed at ten points among the crowd — estimated at ten thousand — that filled a large area within the Danilov walls. While there are long lines for everything in Russia, usually the Communion lines are short, but not on this occasion. I had never seen so many people receiving Communion in Russia, where a profound awe for the presence of Christ in the Eucharist inspires preparation involving days or even weeks of prayer, searching out any trace of enmity in one's life, and finally confession.

The body language for receiving Communion is quite special: both arms folded crosswise on the chest, a simple gesture that suggests both submission and presence with Christ on the cross. Orthodoxy has not given up the body language of prayer: crossing oneself, kneeling, bowing down to the ground, kissing icons, and many other gestures in which body and soul are knit together. Communion is given slowly and by name: "The servant of God, [name], partakes of the holy precious body and blood of our Lord and God and Savior Jesus Christ, unto remission of sins and everlasting life." To receive Communion anywhere in the world is immensely significant, but for it to happen for an American in a monastery in Moscow within a long line of Russians, it is — as Thomas Merton once said about a certain ancient monk on Mount Athos — "to be kissed by God."

Speaking after the Liturgy, Poland's Cardinal Glemp welcomed the newly canonized Orthodox saints, a suitable stress as it was the Feast of All the Saints Who Illumined Russia. "How wonderful that these new saints are added to your iconostasis, and such a variety of people." He drew attention to one of the most recently canonized Catholic saints, Maximillian Kolbe, the Polish priest who gave his life to save a Jew when they were both prisoners in Auschwitz. "Father Kolbe went to a place of suffering to bring God's love, to pray, and to offer his service." The cardinal expressed his special feelings for "the people of this land, who have experienced so much suffering yet have always overcome their difficulties."

At a meal afterward in the Praga Restaurant at the end of Arbat Street, Patriarch Pimen expressed gratitude. "From all our hearts we thank the leaders of our country for their understanding of the needs of believers.... One can hardly overestimate the importance of what has been done by the state to help our church conduct this celebration in the proper way."

Over the meal a young Russian translator asked, "Please explain God to me." She told me about the joy of having a child and her longing to have another despite the numerous obstacles to family life and parenthood in Moscow. After a little while we were talking about the words from John: "God is love, and he who abides in love, abides in God, and God in him." She copied down the verse, entirely new to her. "I don't know if I am Orthodox," she said, "but I know I am a believer. I have so much to learn."

The next day, Monday, was the groundbreaking ceremony for what will be the first new church in Moscow since 1917. Just as important is the fact that it is in a modern part of the city on the city's southeast edge where there are no churches. Though dedicated to the Holy Trinity, perhaps it will be nicknamed Perestroika Cathedral. The word was used over and over again as we stood around the church's huge cornerstone. Konstantin Kharchev, speaking on behalf of the government, said that the new church will be "a symbol of *perestroika* and a symbol of the right of religious believers to have the churches they need." Patriarch Pimen said that the new church represents the fulfillment of his life's hopes. "Thanks to *perestroika*, relations between church and state are changing for the better, as this cathedral will bear witness."

Archbishop Desmond Tutu from South Africa rejoiced in the new church and all it stands for. "It is a sign that Christianity has a contribution to make in each society, especially in affirming the infinite worth of each person."

The location of the new church is stunning. The site is within a large park, just above Tsaritsino Ponds. The ground is high — the church will be visible for miles in every direction. "The sound of its bells will carry far," a priest standing at my side said with satisfaction. "Even more important," said one of the translators, "it is near a Metro station [the Orechovo stop]."

The Americans taking part in the Millennium celebration were invited to Spaso House, the residence of the U.S. Ambassador, where we discovered not only the embassy staff and trays of hot pizza awaiting us but several prominent dissidents, among them Father Gleb Yakunin.

Father Gleb had been among the most outspoken opponents of state interference in church life and church compliance with state direction. In 1965 he wrote an open letter to the former patriarch, Alexi, describing the Russian Orthodox Church as dangerously ill largely because the bishops were compromised by their obedience to atheist directives. Soon afterward the patriarch suspended him. In 1975 he co-authored an appeal to the World Council of Churches asking it to increase its attention to Christians suffering for their faith. In 1976 he was a founder of the Christian Committee for the Defense of Believers' Rights, sending reports west about violations of the human rights of believers. In 1979, arrested on the charge of anti-Soviet agitation, he was condemned to five years at a strict-regime labor camp. Internal exile in Siberia followed.

Freed in 1987 and permitted to return to the capital, he was assigned a parish north of Moscow near Zagorsk by the Orthodox Church. In April he had signed an open letter urging Patriarch Pimen to retire so that a younger person could lead the church "more energetically." (One priest in Moscow said that this proposal saddened him. "The patriarch's legs and kidneys may not be well but his mind and heart are strong. Does your father have to be healthy to be your father?")

A few days before Father Gleb had been one of three people invited to address Reagan at a meeting in Spaso House. Afterward he told reporters, "It is only after meeting the president that you realize how deep is his commitment to human rights." Reading this, I hoped that Father Gleb would one day have the chance to look at the U.S. from the perspective of those whose human rights were a matter of slight concern in the White House. But talking with him in the ambassador's residence, our conversation was instead entirely about the situation in the Soviet Union. He described recent events in the USSR as "miraculous." At the same time he was worried that "the celebration will screen awareness of the problems that remain to be solved."

"There is much vitality at the parish level," he said. "Last Sunday we had twenty baptisms. The church is attracting many people, but there is a desperate need for religious education. We don't have religious literature. The church has recently published a new edition of the Bible but it is very expensive and there are not nearly enough copies."

At the airport waiting for our flight to Kiev, I asked Billy Graham what had led him to undertake his first trip to the USSR in 1982 despite advice from Vice President Bush not to go. "I had been briefed at the Pentagon about what would happen if there was a nuclear war," he replied. "I had been to Auschwitz and seen how limitless is our capacity for evil. And I was thinking about Paul saying in his first letter to the Corinthians that he was called to be all things to all people. I realized I had closed myself to the people in the Soviet Union. So I felt I had to say yes to the invitation I received from the Russian Orthodox Church inviting me to take part in a peace conference they were preparing in Moscow."

We arrived in Kiev the night of June 13. At the hotel where we were staying I found some of the birthday cards American children had sent for the Millennium via the National Council of Churches. Shawn White in Anderson, South Carolina, wrote, "I am interested in knowing if you are a Christian. Happy 1000th birthday, Russian, whoever you are!" Kristi Matochi in El Campo, Texas, wrote in white letters on heavy black paper: "Hi, I'm Kristi, 13 years old, a girl! I like Heavy Metal and boys and my favorite color is black. Please write to me. Happy birthday."

The next morning there was a meeting in the Kiev Opera House that was similar to the one held a few days before at the Bolshoi. By choosing a back row seat, I was able to read Gogol's *Dead Souls* during some of the more repetitive speeches. Gogol seemed to have in mind the face of a local official of the Council for Religious Affairs when he wrote: "There was absolutely nothing in him: neither wickedness nor goodness, and there was something terrifying in this absence of anything." What was most striking about the official's face was his utter lack of enthusiasm. One assumed he had received word from on high that he must now do all sorts of things that previously it was his job not to do. More impressive were the entirely benevolent faces of Metropolitan Filaret of Kiev and Metropolitan Yuvenali, who could easily be turning victor's grins toward those officials who for so many years blocked the way.

Cardinal Willebrands was among the speakers, an important moment for the Catholics in the Ukraine. "The feast we are celebrating is an occasion for dialogue," he said, "a requirement that unfortunately is very often neglected. We need a dialogue between the believer and the nonbeliever, between faith and atheism. The state has tried to humiliate religion, to reduce it to a pathology. Now it offers signs of respect and a readiness to engage in dialogue." He noted that often believer and nonbeliever interpret the same facts differently, for human understanding often centers on oneself rather than on others. "*Glasnost*, the clarity of words expressing faith and wisdom, is the basis of a healthy culture. A new epoch is emerging in our world, an epoch that admits that it has not got all the answers but has the courage to hear the answers."

Vespers was at Saint Vladimir's Cathedral. The streets around were crowded. Inside, the huge church was filled to bursting and only those with invitations were being allowed to join the congregation. Even showing my plastic-encased Millennium identity card, I was told, "Nyet, nyet, nyet!" With all the authority I could muster, I said, "Da, da, da!" Then the gate opened enough for me to slip inside. I was lucky to find a bit of space right against the iconostasis. The television lights made it painful to look toward the congregation.

Billy Graham was invited to speak. Metropolitan Filaret stood at his side. It was a vintage Graham sermon: "My grandfather never dreamed of the changes that have happened in our world — space travel, color television, travel from continent to continent in a few hours by jet airplane. But some things never change. Interest in religion never changes. The nature of God never changes." He spoke about God's love for each person, a love we cannot damage by our sins. Graham recalled a Moscow lady who told him, "I am a great sinner." He responded, "I too am a great sinner, but we have a great savior." He recalled Prince Vladimir and his conversion. "He turned away from idols and destroyed them, opening a new path in life not only for himself but for millions of others right down to our own time. God never changes, but you and I must change just as Prince Vladimir changed a thousand years ago." He ended his sermon saying, "In the name of the Father and of the Son and of the Holy Spirit." The congregation replied in one voice, "God save you!"

That night Soviet television again caught me by surprise with *Mother Maria*, a film dramatizing the life of a Russian woman who surely one day will be canonized. Though among the revolutionaries in her youth, she finally had to flee the Bolsheviks, finding refuge in Paris. After the disintegration of her marriage, she became a nun and founded a refuge in Paris for homeless Russians. There was a scene in the film where she is talking to a young exile who wants to fight the Communists. "But you will be fighting your brothers, not Communists," she says to him. During the war, because she hid Russian soldiers who had escaped from the Germans, she was arrested by the Gestapo. She died in Ravensbruck on March 30, 1945, taking the place of another prisoner.

"However hard I try," she said, "I find it impossible to construct anything greater than these three words, 'Love one another' — only to the end, and without exceptions: then all is justified and life is illumined, whereas otherwise it is an abomination and a burden." Her reasons for centering her vocation on hospitality had a profound theological basis: "The bodies of fellow human beings must be treated with greater care than our own. Christian love teaches us to give our brethren not only spiritual gifts, but material gifts as well. Even our last shirt, our last piece of bread must be given to them. Personal almsgiving and the most wide-ranging social work are equally justifiable and necessary. The way to God lies through love of other people and there is no other way. At the Last Judgment I shall not be asked if I was successful in my ascetic exercises or how many prostrations I made in the course of my prayers. I shall be asked, did I feed the hungry, clothe the naked, visit the sick and the prisoners: that is all I shall be asked."[10]

"It is the third time this film has been shown on television," a pastor in Kiev told me. "It is amazing. She was a most cultured person. She knew Berdyaev and Blok — her book on Blok is finally going to be published here, forty years after she wrote it. She loved colors and flowers. She had a gift for breathing life and hope into despairing people. Of course what she did in the war made her a hero, but it is clear that what gave her the courage to do what she did was not political ideology but religious faith. In fact her political ideology was all wrong from the point of view of marxism!"

The Holy Liturgy at Saint Vladimir's the next morning brought out an even larger crowd than had been there for Vespers. A good sound system had been installed outside the church so that those unable to get inside could listen. In fact they had a better chance to hear everything than those packed together within the walls.

Cardinal Willebrands and two other cardinals were present. Willebrands has a round, pink face without a trace of guile. He seemed not to be familiar with the Orthodox Liturgy, which, if so, is remarkable, given the fact that he heads the Vatican's Secretariat for Christian Unity. But at least there was no air of condescension or boredom — rather complete fascination. He watched with the eyes of a child at the circus. At appropriate moments, taking cues from other worshippers, he shyly crossed himself.

There was a long line of people for Communion, and I happened to be standing close by. I was freshly impressed with how the human face shines brightest at moments of deep prayer and love.

"It is not a coincidence," a local priest, Father Boris Udovenko, told me over lunch, "that *perestroika* in our country coincides with

---

[10]A biography of Mother Maria has been written by Sergei Hackel: *Pearl of Great Price: the Life of Mother Maria Skobtsova 1891–1945*, rev. ed. (Crestwood, N.Y.: Saint Vladimir's Seminary Press; London: Darton, Longman & Todd, 1982).

the Millennium. In fact I think it is out of the spiritual life of our country that *perestroika* was born, and that the anticipation of the Millennium gave the country an inspiration to look at everything from the point of view of spiritual values. But we are very far from realizing what we now dare to imagine. There are still thousands of officials who don't want to change and don't want to step down, who like being little czars." He said the man who is curator of the museum at the Monastery of the Caves is one of those who is quite unhappy to see the church receiving back even a minor part of the monastery. "This man claims to be a historian, but he is actually a former restaurant manager. He likes having a famous museum better than having a third-rate restaurant."

"Many powerful civilizations have perished because they lost their moral foundations," said Metropolitan Filaret in a luncheon speech. "Under *perestroika*, the spiritual and moral foundations of society are of tremendous importance. Our guests are seeing with their own eyes what is happening because of *perestroika*. They can see how *perestroika* has touched relations between church and state. It would have been unimaginable ten years ago. Ten years ago we could also not imagine that there would be the destruction of a whole class of nuclear weapons. We can now have the hope that we can meet the year 2000 without weapons of mass slaughter. One or two people cannot do this, but it can happen if we all play our role. If something tragic should happen — God forbid! — we will all be victims, and we will all face the judgment of God where we will each receive according to our deeds. Let us hope for the best. Faith, hope, and love give us the force to overcome evil in the world. Let us raise our glasses to the possibility of the long-awaited peace. May we recognize each human being as a brother or sister."

The evening concert at the Opera House, featuring the choir of Saint Vladimir's Cathedral, was shown live throughout the Ukraine. A number of the hymns had been composed at the Monastery of the Caves when it was still active. The painted backdrop was of a church setting under a huge icon of the Savior's face and an Orthodox cross.

The next morning, June 16, Kiev's gaze was centered on the three hills above the Dnieper River that support the Monastery of the Caves. The highest hill, with the largest complex of churches and buildings, remains a museum, but the two lower hills plus the caves were returned to monastic use June 7. The monks had set up an outdoor chapel in front of one small church.

By nine o'clock clergy shining in gold and green liturgical vestments stood around the altar. Close at hand were foreign guests, the press, and a choir. Beyond them, stretching a half-mile away until heads disappeared over the crest of a hill, were thousands of people from Kiev and beyond. The geography of the hillside and monastery complex was such that lines of participants unfolded in other directions so that, from the air, the crowd took the shape of a tree with budding branches, the altar marking the point where the tree was rooted in the earth.

Among those around the altar was a wiry old man with wispy white beard, one of the monks who had been driven away from the monastery a quarter-century ago. His face constantly attracted my gaze. He has lived long enough not only to return to his home but to see hatred of religion give way to respect. One local woman who managed to get near the altar through a back gate spent most of the Liturgy with her knees on the cobblestones, her thick fingers folded together, and her lips moving in constant but silent prayer. Her attention never wavered from the direction of the altar though all she could see were the backs of priests.

After the distribution of Communion, I wandered toward the back of the crowd exploring faces. Attention was so focused on the Liturgy that I was hardly noticed, though in most cases when I asked to take a photo of a particular person or family assent was given and friendly eyes were turned my way.

"The lamp of the monastery that was extinguished in this sacred place is lit again," Metropolitan Filaret told the crowd. "The monastery was built by faith, and after many trials and tribulations, we have received back part of our holy cloister. We will immediately resume the work of being a monastery where believers can bring their griefs, their joys, their plea for forgiveness, and all their needs." Twenty monks have moved in already.

The Millennium event that will still be talked about a century from now was the commemoration of the baptism of Rus' that occurred late that afternoon at the foot of the monumental Saint Vladimir statue above the Dnieper River. What made this much more than it might have been was bad weather. Half an hour before the ceremony was to begin, rain began to fall, not just rain but a torrent that turned the steep streets of Kiev into spillways. It was a kind of rain I have rarely known in twelve years of living in grey, wet Holland where one should be born wearing a rain coat.

The rain had no impact at all on Russian involvement in the baptismal celebration. People who had been standing on the hillside above the towering statue of the cross-bearing Saint Vladimir since eight in the morning remained rooted to their spots. With or without protection, no one budged except some of the foreign guests. After an hour in the rain I was more than ready to seek shelter in the bus, but hung on because of the example of Father Alexis Voogd, pastor of the Russian Orthodox Church in Amsterdam. It was he who made me notice some of the faces around us: "Look at how they are praying!" They were praying with such absorption that they seemed oblivious to the downpour.

An old monk and three nuns were by our side, kept somewhat dry by a big sheet of transparent plastic they used as a common umbrella. Their black clothing was worn thin, looking as old as themselves. On the other side was a family clustered under one large umbrella. I realized that for most of the people present, the rain wasn't a burden but a blessing. The baptism of Rus' was being renewed. As we hadn't waded into the river, the water had risen to us, and all Kiev was being doused anew: believer and unbeliever, Orthodox and Baptist, atheist and agnostic, journalist and policeman.

Then, perhaps fifteen minutes before the end of a ceremony centering on the blessing of water, just when prayers of thanksgiving were being sung, the grey clouds parted and we were in the spotlight of the sun. It was as if we were on the stage of the Bolshoi Theater in Moscow rather than the steep hillsides above the Dnieper River in Kiev.

Chapter 3

The Orthodox

ACCORDING TO THE PRIMARY CHRONICLE, Saint Nestor's *Tale of Bygone Years* written at Kiev's Monastery of the Caves, Prince Vladimir realized that the time had come to embrace a religious tradition of world standing. Taking great care to make the right choice, he sent emissaries to investigate the religions of neighboring countries. They went to synagogues, mosques, and to both Latin and Greek Christian churches. Receiving Vladimir's representatives in Constantinople, the patriarch brought them to a service in the Hagia Sophia (Holy Wisdom) Cathedral. Incense filled the air, choirs sang, the clergy wore vestments radiant with candlelight, icons gave witness to the link between earth and heaven, time and eternity. The emissaries wrote to Vladimir: "We knew not whether we were in heaven or on earth, for on earth there is no such splendor or such beauty, and we are at a loss how to describe it. We only know that God dwells among these people and that their services are fairer than the ceremonies of other nations. We can never forget that beauty."[1]

On a June day in 988, the people of Kiev, carrying banners and icons, went in procession into the Dnieper River and were baptized. "Joy was seen throughout heaven at the sight of so many souls being saved," the Chronicle records. That same summer the Christian faith spread to the cities of Novgorod, Rostov, Vladimir, and Belgorod.

Before his conversion Vladimir was, says Nestor, "a man insatiable in vice." Afterward he became renowned for his care of the poor, orphans, and the sick. The palace gates were opened to the hungry. He built hospices for the aged. Rejecting the views of his

[1] *Medieval Russia's Epics, Chronicles, and Tales*, Serge Zenkovsky, ed., rev. ed. (New York: E. P. Dutton, 1974), pp. 67–68.

Orthodox mentors from Greece, he prohibited torture and execution of criminals. He was named a saint not only for bringing Christianity to the ancient land of Kievan Rus' — thus given the title Equal of the Apostles — but because of his wholehearted devotion to the teaching of Jesus.

Among the fifteen Orthodox churches, the Russian Church is fifth in rank (after the four ancient patriarchates of Jerusalem, Constantinople, Antioch and Alexandria) and largest in size: 50 million was the estimate given at the Millennium celebration.

Charity in Moscow

On June 20, 1988, Moscow's evening television news program reported that Patriarch Pimen's church, the Epiphany Cathedral, had become linked with a local hospital. An agreement had been signed providing the opportunity for church members to offer volunteer service.

"The Christian religion teaches care of neighbor," said Dr. Anatoly Solovyov, the hospital's director. "This is a concrete way of doing it. Now we have our first contact with a religious group. We think it can help with problems we have offering health care. Some of the patients need constant care, and we don't have the staff to offer that. The feeling you get from believers is compassion. Patients need that. They need the support of faith and love."

The interviewer asked Father Matthew Stadniouk, dean of the patriarchal church, what led the church to help in this way. "Our Orthodox people are part of society," he answered, "and I'm very glad that now the opportunity has come to help people. It is *perestroika* and democratization at work. The time has come for common feeling. It means seeing what you can do today. Tomorrow may be too late. This work is a moral reward for the people. The way people respond already shows that the conscience of our people has not been destroyed. We expect that many in our church will take part. The hospital is our neighbor. We hope to give help every day. After all, to have any success in healing you have to have love."

"If you have a feeling of mercy in your heart," said one of the volunteers at the hospital, "you will do this." A priest was shown making the sign of the cross over a woman too ill even to raise her head. In another room a nurse was standing next to a frail patient. "Do you feel pushed aside by these volunteers coming from the church?" the nurse was asked. "Oh, no," said the nurse, immediately crossing herself, "I am a believer myself!"

"It is the first time," said an astonished Orthodox priest who was watching the news with me, "that anything like this has happened. In the past it has been said that the state provides social services and needs no help in doing it. But it is far from true. At most hospitals the nursing staff is much too small."

Assisted by a Muscovite teacher of English, three days later I visited Clinical Hospital Number Six a few blocks west of the Epiphany Cathedral. We hadn't been able to get through by phone so had come in the hope the director might be there and could find the time for a visitor. Though repair work was under way, the buildings had fallen into appalling condition: broken doors, cracked or missing glass, faded, ancient paint. We searched through several buildings surrounding a small park until we found the appropriate office.

The only decoration in Anatoly Solovyov's dimly lit office were side-by-side pictures of Lenin and Gorbachev. He was a man in his late thirties who six months earlier had been elected by his colleagues.

I asked how many hospitals were involved in the volunteer initiative. "This is the only hospital so far with people coming as volunteers from a local church."

What sort of volunteers are coming? "Ordinary people. There is no pay for it and there are no qualifications needed except the willingness to help."

He laughed when I asked about the history of the hospital's engagement with the local church. "It is so new that it is hard to say there is any history! We began just ten days ago during the celebration of the church's Millennium. There were talks between the staff of the church, Father Matthew and Father Nicholas, and the chief doctors of the hospital. Then it was announced at the cathedral during morning prayer June 8 that we would welcome volunteers. The first one to show up was a man named Sergei Leonidovitch Timofeev. Then came a nun, Mother Marianelle, who brought a group of believers with her. We can say these people are the founders. So far, except Sergei, they are all women. They come when they have time. There's no schedule."

What do they do? "They clean wards, change linens, take care of bed pans, talk to the patients, sit with them, read the newspaper or a book aloud. They make contact with the believers among the patients and, in case the patients ask, they invite a priest to bring the sacraments or to come and pray for them."

How is it going? "We are happy about it. We see how much it

means to the patients, and it is good for the staff also. One of the patients, an old man who has had five heart attacks, asked if he can give his money to the hospital to help others. This is something we never heard from a patient before. You see, you are watching the very beginning. We don't know where it will lead. I have no prognosis. But I have hope. We are in a new period of our history, we are starting a new life. Both the clergy and the doctors have hopes that this will develop. From our side, we are ready to do our best. But we have no experience in it and are learning as we go."

What sort of response are you getting from higher up? "All the responses are positive. I want to believe, in fact I am almost sure, that the church is going to play a big role in health care work in this country. It is time. The Millennium is a good time to start. We have many believing people in our country. It is good that they play the part they deserve to play."

He asked if there were pastors in legislative roles in the United States. I said there were. "I hope," he responded, "to see the day when priests will become people's deputies. They are also Soviet people. They are close to the people. It may seem like a crazy idea but I would like to suggest that Father Matthew should be a people's deputy. He has the life experience. He is honest. He is a helpful man. He is qualified. We need people like that helping to lead our country."

The next day I went to the patriarchal residence near Arbat Street to meet Father Matthew Stadniouk. His desk was covered with papers and books and there were several icons on the wall. He had a short white beard and a shy manner.

"Our Russian word for such acts of care is *miloserdie* — works of a merciful heart," he said. "It means any action done for others out of Christ's love. In her long history the church was always taking care of people. There is nothing new in the task, but the possibility in our situation is new. We are just starting to put seeds in the ground. It is too early to say what will come from them. But the church should do whatever she can, that is the thing, especially for those who are sick and need our help. We hope that the possibilities to do this will improve, especially now that we have a good relationship with the government. As you know, *perestroika* is going on. But this renewal of structures comes from *dukhovnost* — the spiritual life of the people. Our country and every country need *dukhovnost*. In fact I think America needs it even more than we do. *Dukhovnost* is the reason the church survived so many centuries. We should thank God."

How are members of the congregation responding? "One person

asked whether it was more important to go to the church for services or to go to the hospital to volunteer. Well, normally we don't have to choose between one and the other, but I said sometimes it may be more important to go to the hospital. Sometimes the needs there may be the most urgent. We have three hundred thousand people living in our area."

Was he surprised at this new opening in society? "No, not that it happens, only I did not know when it would happen. It is something I expected sooner or later. The government knows that the church has always been with the people. We have lived with them, suffered with them, shared their fate, never abandoned them, and we are always ready to serve in whatever ways we can."

What did he think would happen next? "I can't say. God is giving us such help. All we can do is thank God and pray that this new atmosphere will last for the next thousand years. Now we should try to show our people, not only here but in other countries, that the next jubilee, the second millennium of Christianity, will be in peace and love and mercy and understanding."

In the short time we were together, Father Matthew spoke repeatedly of gratitude: "We are grateful.... We should gives thanks.... Thanks be to God!... We should say thanks to God!" It was his deep gratitude that I felt even more than his words. He is a man with a radiant face. That such a person shares the patriarch's home and serves as pastor of the patriarchal cathedral provides significant clues to the character of Patriarch Pimen himself.

When leaving, I gave him a copy of a biography I had written of Dorothy Day, founder of the Catholic Worker movement, whose houses of hospitality in the United States have been a place of welcome for so many abandoned people. He was amazed. "Dorothy Day! Did you know her?" I said I had worked with her on the Catholic Worker staff in the early sixties and that it was she who first brought me to visit a Russian Orthodox Cathedral, the church on East 97th Street in New York. "I remember you when you were a young man!" said Father Matthew. "I was serving in that church. Dorothy used to visit me, and I once went to the Catholic Worker farm. I remember her bringing you to our church."

"I believe," said Father Matthew, "that there are no accidental meetings. Please come and see me again when you return to Moscow."

Six months later, in January 1989, we met again in an office tucked into the rafters of the Epiphany Cathedral. A Christmas tree stood in the middle of the office, a battered couch to one side, a small wooden desk to the other. While Father Matthew prepared tea, I studied the photos over his desk. One was of the Savior Cathedral, the church near the Kremlin that was dynamited in 1931. After the tea was served in cups of various sizes and colors, I asked how the *miloserdie* was coming.

"More parishes are involved, more volunteers, more patients. Similar work is being done by other churches in Moscow and Leningrad, and we anticipate it will develop quickly throughout the country. We have just established the Federated Society of Charities. Next we will set up the Moscow Society of Charities. So there has been much progress."

What about new churches in Moscow? "One week ago a church building was returned to us and two months ago we received one located in the north of the city near the Sheremetyevo Airport. In the near future we will build a cathedral in southern Moscow dedicated to the Holy Trinity, with a second altar dedicated to the Holy Saints of Russia. The ground was blessed during the Millennium. Little by little, the needs of believers are being met."

Isn't it hard to find people with the skills needed for church construction? "We want the church to be built in a traditional way so of course there will be problems. It will not be easy to find the builders. Yet we notice that in earlier centuries people had no education but they made beautiful churches. In the whole of Russia we hope to find both the people and resources needed."

Can the church afford to put back into service so many buildings in derelict condition? "Money is a big problem. Restoration costs a lot. It is not easy to do so much at the same time. We are now restoring many churches and also two monasteries. But we know our people will give whatever is needed, even everything they have. We find support from many people not belonging to the church. During the jubilee a good atmosphere was created throughout society. Many writers and scientists wrote good articles about church history — what the church has done for the country. They also wrote about the importance of the art and architecture that has been created by believers. There has been much on television and in the press, and this didn't stop with the end of the jubilee year. It is still going on. We feel the respect and affection of our neighbors. It is amazing how things can change so quickly! I thank God."

Is the climate still positive? "God sent us Mr. Gorbachev to give good leadership to our country and now many things are possible. We thank God that we have been given the right man. The atmosphere in society is very good. We pray and the whole country prays that *perestroika* will continue. It helps us and it helps the whole world.

Your country and my country no longer criticize each other so much. Neither country is trying to be the judge of the whole world. This is as it should be for no one gave us such a right. What we have been given is the right to help each other."

Our conversation turned to the subject of forgiveness. "Forgiveness is based on Jesus' saying, 'If you are going to pray and you remember that you have a dispute with your neighbor, leave the gift at the altar, go and make peace with your neighbor, and then return.' The Apostle John says, 'Whoever says he loves God but hates his brother is a liar.' You know in Russia we have the tradition of Forgiveness Sunday just before the beginning of Great Lent. This is a day when all people go to the church and forgive each other. Of course you cannot forgive everyone in one day, but you can make a beginning that goes on throughout Lent. Everyone understands that when you go to the Holy Chalice you must have forgiven everyone from your heart. To live in Christ is to forgive. But this is very hard sometimes. To forgive is not easy. If someone killed your brother it is not easy to forgive the killer. We have to take the example of our Savior who said, 'Father forgive them, they don't know what they are doing.'

"Forgiveness is at the heart of the transformation happening in our country. This rejuvenation is impossible without forgiveness. *Perestroika* cannot happen by itself, without a spiritual life. Just one man can do much evil. We know from our history how much evil one man can do. With one small match you can burn down a big building. But with the light of forgiveness you can do even more. With spiritual fire you can heal.

"I think everywhere in the world people are realizing the need to find some solution to the crisis we are facing and they see the answer isn't some machine. People are asking: Where are we going? Does this direction not lead to destruction? They come more and more to the church to find an inner direction, and also to find the inspiration to forgive. But of course still there are people who think you are crazy if you speak about forgiveness, people who think humility is a very old fashioned word. Yes, there are still many people thinking like that."

Kiev

Sharing our compartment on the night train to Kiev was a *babushka* named Olga on her way home after a Christmas visit with one of her sons and his family in Moscow. "They almost killed me with food," she said, "and then they gave me this big bag of food to take on the train. You have to help eat it, please. All that God gives is blessed." She crossed herself and opened the bag. "So you're welcome!" We ate brown bread, hard-boiled eggs, bologna, and cookies.

Christmas in Moscow didn't please her. "Young people don't know what Christmas is. There used to be a real Christmas. Now it hardly exists. There was no feeling of Christmas in Moscow. In our town, we still have it but not as it used to be. We have two churches in our town, one Orthodox, one Catholic. I am Orthodox."

She talked about her three sons and their families. "My sons are good to me, and their wives. Praise be to God!" She crossed herself.

I was the first American she had ever met. "It's good that it is going better between America and our country. Our children should never know what we had to know." She crossed herself. "I pray for peace and friendship."

While Olga got ready for bed, Sergei and I went out into the corridor. "She is a true *babushka*," said Sergei, "the real thing. She is what we miss so much in our lives. The *babushka* created the soul of Lermontov and Pushkin. She is so plain but she has her special beauty. We have the proverb, 'Of course we are astonished by the beauty of a beautiful woman, but our heart belongs to a nice woman.' Real beauty comes from inner goodness."

Arriving at Metropolitan Filaret's three-story house on Pushkin Street, we found a crowd of people — among them several women who reminded me of Olga — gathered in the back yard, lined up to receive Bibles that were being distributed inside.

Apart from his neatly trimmed snow white beard, Metropolitan Filaret has a child's face — pink, hardly lined, with clear, expectant eyes. Neither while presiding at the Liturgy nor in private conversation does he ever seem in a hurry.

He opened the interview with a general overview of the current situation of the Russian Orthodox Church. "We have got to have changes in the life of the Russian Orthodox Church, changes linked with the general changes in our society, *glasnost* and *perestroika*. When Mikhail Gorbachev received the patriarch and members of the Holy Synod last April 29, he told us that *perestroika* concerns everything, including the church.

"Speaking about how it is manifested for believers, I would point first of all to the Millennium last year. This event was celebrated not only by believers but by everyone. For nonbelievers it was a celebration of national identity and culture. It showed that the wall between church and state is being erased. Churches that were closed are being opened, new churches are under construction. In the past year we registered over 800 new Orthodox communities, 420 of these in the Ukraine. Many new churches serving other religious communities have also opened — Catholic, Baptist, Adventist, Armenian, also Jewish synagogues, Moslem mosques, and Buddhist temples. The weather is good for everyone.

"Part of the Monastery of the Caves has been returned. Please go and visit the monks living there. Now there are eleven monasteries on Ukrainian territory, four for men and seven for women, and we expect the return of the Holy Trinity Monastery at Chernigov. In Russia the Optina Pustyn Monastery and the Tolga Convent are being restored, and we anticipate the return of the Holy Trinity Monastery in Kolomna [forty miles from Moscow] and the Gethsemane Monastery near Zagorsk. We are discussing the return of the Valaam Monastery in Karelia [near the Finnish border] and another monastery in the Ryazan region. We will have the chance to reopen still other monasteries in the near future. The problem is staff, finances, and the extensive restoration work that needs to be done.

"We have three seminaries with approximately twenty-five hundred resident students at Zagorsk, Leningrad, and Odessa. Now we plan to open seminaries in the Ukraine and Byelorussia and another either in Siberia or the Volga River region. Possibly there will be one in Moscow. The Ukrainian one will be in Kiev. We also plan to open theological schools in Minsk, Smolensk, and in Chernigov in the Ukraine to train psalm singers, readers, and other church staff.

"We still have the problem of providing faithful people with Bibles. You saw the line of people waiting for a copy. Many Bibles were given to us by the Scandinavian churches, others from the Bible Society in Great Britain. The Ukrainian Exarchate has also published a Ukrainian edition. A Russian prayer book is being distributed and we plan a Ukrainian edition. The publishing activity of the church is rapidly expanding. We plan to open a church publishing house. The most serious problem we face is the shortage of paper. We are hoping that publishers and churches in other countries will help us with paper. If we had the paper we could issue a short presentation of our faith, for example, a church history and other much needed publications and books.

"Fortunately we now have the opportunity to participate in the mass media. Radio and television programs are broadcast about church life. Orthodox people are being interviewed and also being invited to participate in discussion programs.

"Church workers are active at all levels in many public organizations — the Cultural Fund, the Children's Fund, the Peace Fund, and so forth. Now we have launched a structure for charity work around the country. The church is ready to collaborate with any civic organization. Again there are still problems to be solved, however. We still have old-fashioned laws limiting the activities of the church, but step by step the barriers are being removed. We are expecting a new law for religion in the near future. The separation of church and state will remain as well as the separation of church and school, but we expect that faithful people will be allowed the right to fully participate in social life. We hope the draft of this new law will be openly discussed. By all means the church will present its opinions about the law.

"Society is expecting the church to play her part in the moral and spiritual education of the people, and this is the mission and longing of the church. In the past religious education took place within the family and at church. We would like to address ourselves to the wider character of religious education in the life of this people. We don't want to impose religious instruction at school but we look for other ways to meet this need, perhaps by providing the opportunity for private religious education. We don't yet know how this will work. It is under discussion.

"There is also the church's peacemaking work. This is worldwide and it will continue.

"Another important development is that religious workers have the chance to be elected to Soviet legislative bodies. Religious workers have been nominated by several public organizations. The Holy Synod discussed this opportunity at its recent session and gave its blessing to church workers to participate in the legislature. The patriarch and Holy Synod hope that this will be beneficial to the people, the state and the church.

"Another point: You know about the process of rehabilitation now going on of people killed unjustly in purges in the Stalin period. The Holy Synod, at its meeting December 28, decided to set up a committee to collect material about those who perished, who were repressed, or who suffered in that period."

The interview continued over lunch — fish in jelly, kvass, lemon flavored vodka, caviar, bread and butter — prepared by a sister from the Pokrovsky Convent.

I mentioned the criticism Konstantin Kharchev had made in *Ogonyok* magazine about the resistance of local Councils for Religious Affairs to the new direction taken by the council in Moscow. "He is right. Some local authorities are still resisting the registration of local religious communities. Often the authorities do not want to return old churches that are being destroyed by the weather or being used for secular purposes. When faithful people want to take over a church, it should be given to them. This would be good both for believers and society. The church would be used once again for the purpose for which it was built and at the same time a cultural landmark would be restored."

I asked how money for church restoration is being raised. "We are collecting money to build the new cathedral in Moscow. Partly this money comes from the sale of Bibles. While we give some away free we also sell them in order to raise money for the new church. For example they are on sale at the cathedral here in Kiev. We would welcome any help that churches in the West can offer. We are trying to raise money to rebuild the Assumption Cathedral and to restore the Pokrovsky and Florensky Monasteries here in Kiev. The Dormition Cathedral at the Monastery of the Caves was blown up by the Nazis in the war. We want it to be a place both for divine services and to serve as a cultural landmark for tourists to visit. We will also restore the Holy Intercession Krasnogorsky Convent in Zolotonosha."

What about the church's new opportunities for social service? "Now believing people are able to found charitable societies. This is a welcome development. We see a difference between civil charity and charity in response to the Gospel. Our faith stresses the importance of charity in the heart. In the Gospel story about the woman who gave two kopeks, the reason her small gift was more precious to God was that it came from her heart. Orthodoxy tries to cultivate the heart and this deep feeling of charity."

What about the prospect for improved relations between the Russian Orthodox Church and Ukrainian Catholics? "This problem has been exaggerated. Those campaigning for legalization are a small group driven more by political than religious interests. Their method is not peaceful but aggressive. Under such circumstances how can relations be improved?"

The conversation turned to the approach the Orthodox Church has to confession, repentance, and forgiveness. "Orthodoxy emphasizes careful preparation for Communion — prayer, repentance, forgiveness of others, confession, fasting. We understand repentance to be a rebirth that comes from deep within. The violent person who confesses must end his violence, the drunkard should stop drinking. What you confess you should stop doing. Repentance means a process of renovating your whole life."

I asked what he saw as special characteristics of Orthodoxy. "More than churches in the West, which seem to deal more with civic issues, we concentrate on religious and spiritual issues. We also put special stress on love of enemies. Consider those who suffered under Stalin's purges. You can easily have a feeling for revenge. Many of those who were responsible are still alive, yet in the Orthodox Church you hear no one calling for revenge. Also many suffered terribly from the Germans. We suffered very much in the Ukraine. Yet you do not find longing for revenge. I have been told by German visitors that they feel more welcomed here than in any part of Europe that was occupied by the German army."

He talked about the religious programs on Soviet television. "One of the most important was the film *Church*. Its basic message was that the destruction of places of worship is the destruction of everything that is holy, the loss of a sense of the sacred. You recall the scene where some young people are riding their motorbikes through a graveyard around a church that has been made into a nightclub. There is a lot of noisy dancing inside. This is contrasted in the film with the beauty of church singing. In the Orthodox Church, when you have committed a sin, you must repent before you can improve yourself. The film shows the evil that has been done — the violence against believers and the desecration of places of worship. We can see the film as itself a confession, an act of repentance, a plea for renewal of the soul. The public disclosure of your evil actions is a sign of repentance. It is a way of saying that we don't want to be this way anymore."

For Vespers Sergei and I went to Saint Vladimir's Cathedral. A large church of the Byzantine style built in the last century, it is one of the most ravishing churches in Russia. In a religious goods shop in back, in addition to inexpensive crosses and silk-screened icons, the Bible was on sale for eighty rubles. Hand-painted icons were three hundred rubles.

The dean of the cathedral, Father John Chernienko, was eager to show the iconography covering the cathedral walls, much of it the work of Victor Vasnetsov. "He had a wonderful gift to reveal holiness," said Father John. Just within the main entrance, we looked at a Vasnetsov fresco of Prince Vladimir's baptism. On the facing wall was a painting of the people of Kiev being baptized in the Dnieper River.

"The cathedral is named for Saint Vladimir, whom we call Equal to the Apostles because he led our people to baptism," said Father John. "In an old manuscript it says Prince Vladimir was blinded but in baptism his eyes were reopened. You get this impression in the way Vasnetsov shows Vladimir's face as he comes out of the baptismal water. He has an expression of profound wonder. He is looking at the world with new eyes. But notice that some of the people standing around watching the baptism have very old eyes — some of his warriors are clearly displeased at what their prince is doing."

As Father John talked, a crowd gathered to listen. "Christianity was not new to Kiev but many had opposed it. There had been baptized people in Kiev for generations. There was already the Church of Saint Elijah. Among the prominent people who converted to the new faith was Princess Olga, grandmother of Vladimir. But it was because of the conversion of Vladimir that Christianity became the state religion. In the painting of the baptism of the Kievan people, you can see that while the mass of people are accepting baptism with joy, some are displeased. You can see that our people are only at the beginning of the process of conversion."

Over the entrance doors, between the two baptismal paintings, was a fresco of the Last Judgment, a work in which the crack of doom is almost audible. "If you look at the details, you can sense Vasnetsov's theological depth. He almost graduated from a seminary before taking the path of art." By now the crowd around us was large and pressing hard. "The Last Judgment is a mystical subject — not historical in the sense of the other two but the portrayal of an event we await rather than one we remember. Any sensitive viewer can penetrate the church's theology by looking at it. You see Christ in the center. He is holding the Gospel. This means he will judge us by the law of the Gospel. You see Mary's head almost touching his — the halos are touching. There are tears in her eyes. She is pleading for mercy. You also see John the Baptist making appeals. The condemned are those who failed to maintain the moral level they were called to — people who committed actions against conscience. There is the Archangel. What strict and just beauty! He is holding the scroll with the seven seals described in the Book of Revelation of Saint John. Its text is the history of the world and what each has done or failed to do. There is the scale. You can see among the condemned many who were supposed to be leading others to salvation — notice the priest tearing his clerical garments. And there is a king — you see him grabbing for his crown as it falls from his head. The painting says that salvation cannot be bought by money or authority or ecclesiastical vocation. Your clothes and titles do not excuse you from living a moral life. You also see in the painting the strength of prayer. There is one woman falling toward hell. But you see she is being rescued from damnation by the intercession of someone praying for her. You see in this painting that nothing disappears. The same

God who made you from nothing will reform your body at the end of history even if there is nothing left of your body but ash scattered across a desert. You will be raised from death, body and soul, and be held responsible for how you lived."

Later, away from the crowd, I asked Father John if the cathedral had managed to stay open through the Stalin years. "It was closed from 1931 to 1941, but since that time it has been a working church. It has served not only the needs of believers but people coming to belief. Many visitors come in just to look and begin to discover the treasures of faith. Sometimes we have an entire family to baptize. Through art, architecture, and music, through the witness of our Liturgy, the hearts of many people, especially young people, have been opened. In this church many people have committed themselves to goodness."

Was *perestroika* having a positive effect? "We are feeling it. It gives our people the chance to live in conformity with our conscience. Believers are supporting the process in every way. We only want it to go faster."

Back at the hotel, I gave a Bible I had been presented with that morning to a cleaning woman. She took it in her hands and kissed it.

At the Liturgy the next morning in the lower church at the Pokrovsky (Protection of the Mother of God) Convent, Father Timothy Shaidurov's sermon occasioned a vocal response. "Are you going to consent to a life of materialism?" Several people said, "Nyet!" "Are you going to be careless about prayer?" "Nyet!" Blessing the faithful at the end of the Liturgy, he affectionately tapped some of them on the forehead with the bronze cross in his hand.

Afterward the abbess, Matushka (Mother) Margarita, took us into the upper church, a building consecrated in 1911, now restored except for its missing cupola. "Not so many people were at the Liturgy today," she said. "They are tired after being in church so much during the last two weeks. During the Christmas celebration, there were real crowds. Our four priests and one deacon were kept busy."

She paused in front of an icon of Saint Seraphim of Sarov. "He inspires much devotion. He showed that it was possible to lead a life of constant prayer while loving and serving all those around him. He devoted his life to repentance in such a way that many ascended to God. Such a saint attracts God by the absence of pride in his heart. His eyes are opened and he can see what others fail to see. He can see the thoughts and souls of others. This power is given to him by God. He does not need a car or tram to go somewhere. He can go anywhere without taking a single step. Other people travel a lot but see nothing. To travel is not necessarily to see. The great saints labored hard in the spirit — it is hard to overcome yourself! — and God gave them eyes that were truly open. God gave them a sanctified life. This was God's gift. We come to live in the convent in the hope of obtaining just a spark of such grace. We will not be great saints but perhaps we can have a spark of the fire of sanctity. This is what we seek. Just a spark. We may not be great saints but we want at least not to fall into hell. Our will isn't strong but we rely on Christ." She crossed herself. "He is our hope. He was incarnated into a man's body. He was crucified. He saved us from eternal death. He gave us the spark of longing for eternal life and made us want to pray and to work and to live a tender life."

Over tea in the convent, she told me that fifteen nuns had joined the community since my last visit at Easter in 1987. "One sister dies, another arrives. We have eighty-two in our community now." I wondered if the sisters are all Ukrainian. "No, also Russian, Moldavians, and others. All nations are here."

We talked about the convent's history. Founded in 1889 by Grand Princess Alexandra Petrovna, who was called Sister Anastasia in the convent, the community stressed charity work from the beginning. The nuns opened a school for blind girls, an orphanage, and a hospital with a free outpatient department. The convent was closed by the Soviet government in the late twenties and reopened in 1941 during the German occupation, though a smaller, older church remains closed. Damage to the buildings in the years of persecution included removal of the larger church's cupola, once a landmark of Kiev.

"While the worst things are in the past, still we face obstacles," said Father Timothy. "We have asked permission to rebuild the cupola and to reopen the original church of this community, but so far there is no answer to our letter. Also we hope someday to be able to do more of the charity work that Matushka Anastasia intended when she founded the convent. Of course the sisters have never ceased, no matter what circumstances, to live a life of mercy and charity." He talked about what the nuns had done during the war, opening a scrap book to show a photo of a nun caring for injured soldiers. "Today some of the sisters work in the Kiev hospitals."

I asked if there were other current difficulties. "The sisters would like to reopen a building that was taken away in the twenties and now used as a government office building," Father Timothy responded. "There are several agencies here on the territory of the convent — the Society for Planting Trees, for example. Also the local authorities have constructed some garages on the convent grounds. We feel besieged by inappropriate structures and would like to see them moved to a more suitable location. The idea of monastic life is to maintain some degree of isolation. We see what the authorities have done in the past as an injustice and we would like to put things right. So you see we have faced and still face hardships, a lot of labor and pain. Despite all our difficulties we survived, thanks be to God! But it was a hard life."

"There is a new climate now," said Matushka Margarita. "We are getting more letters than ever from people who want to lead a more faithful life. People write not only to us but to the Council for Religious Affairs saying they want to be monks and nuns. But we still have trouble to get the necessary city residence permits for those we are willing to accept into community. Konstantin Kharchev has publicly spoken about the problem of red tape, all the artificial problems created by bureaucracy. It's true. Our sisters have to spend hundreds of hours to get residence permits. You face all these useless walls! You can smash your head on them. We see that the government is trying to fight the problem and has ordered big cuts in bureaucracy, but the functionaries try to escape the reductions. They move people whose job is only red tape from one section to another and the red tape survives."

I asked about community life. "To be in such a community," said Matushka Margarita, "you need to love prayer and the Liturgy and be willing to get up early. There is morning prayer at five A.M. and Liturgy at seven. On feast days there is a second Liturgy at ten. We often have very large crowds. Orthodox people are praying people! On feast days the Liturgy lasts three or four hours, longer than in a normal parish because we do everything, and take a little more time. Vespers begins at five and lasts until about eight-thirty. At eleven or twelve we go to bed, but not everyone. Some sisters are praying in turn around the clock.

"There is a lot of work to do. We have orchards, gardens, the kitchen. Some take care of sick members of the community. We have twenty sisters in need of care. We have a sewing workshop where we make clothing and liturgical garments. We send some sisters to work in local hospitals. And we have guests, many guests — sometimes five, sometimes a hundred — and so we have sisters doing hospitality work. Some of our sisters are caring for the residence of Metropolitan Filaret. Here at the convent there is cleaning to be done and restoration work. All the art and decoration that you saw in the church is the work of our sisters.

"I think for nonbelievers it seems very odd that we live this way, but for us it is logical. Our life is centered on prayer. We believe that to pray for someone is important. We believe if a person's name is mentioned in prayer, that prayer will ascend to our Lord. If we remember a dead soul, we believe our Lord will hear our prayer and respond. Our Lord teaches us, 'Pray for each other.' And he said, 'You will have what you ask for in prayer.' Our Lord gave us ears. We are sure that he hears what we ask him. He gave us a heart. We are sure that he feels what we pray for."

"At the Liturgy," said Father Timothy, "we pray for many people, living and dead. With each name, we put a small piece of *prosphora* [bread specially made for use at the altar] in the chalice, asking God to forgive the person named. The Holy Liturgy is at the very center of life. Our Lord said, 'Eat my body, drink my blood, and you will have eternal life.' During the great feasts, thousands of people receive Communion here. We hear thousands of confessions. People come to us with their tortured consciences, seeking forgiveness. To forgive and be forgiven is part of Communion. Before we receive the body and blood of our Lord, we purify ourselves with confession and fasting."

Father Timothy told the story of a certain person who walked to the Pochayev Monastery in the western Ukraine to bring back some water from a healing spring for a Jewish friend who had an eye disease.

"The Mother of God once appeared at this place and caused a spring to flow from the stone where she was standing. Its water is associated with many miracles. But it was a hot day. On the way back the woman became so thirsty she drank the water she was carrying and then put water from the tap into the bottle when she got home. She gave this water to her sick neighbor. The neighbor believed it came from the special spring and her eyes were healed! Faith is what is important. All water is holy water if you have faith. But faith is not just what you think. It is what you do. Faith is linked with deeds. Read the Scripture. Follow the regulations of Christian life. Faith is encouraged by good deeds."

"It isn't enough to believe in God," said Matushka Margarita. "The devil knows God exists. You have to live according to the commandments of God. You should believe and act with goodness, and also without pride. If we have pride in our good deeds, they are useless. The effect disappears. You must know that good deeds come to us from God. Our hands are used by God. There is a story from the early years of Christianity about Saint Anthony of the Desert. A devil came to him and said, 'You fast often but I fast always. You sleep little but I never sleep. Still you are victorious over me. How do you do it?' 'Because I am meek,' Saint Anthony said. We need meekness. With meekness, any ordinary person can be accepted into the Kingdom of God. A Christian never abandons respect for science or loses interest in reading, but heaven is not only for the clever. Anthony of the Desert was asked by some philosophers, 'You are illiterate and we read a lot but your name is on every tongue. Why?' 'Which came first,' the saint asked, 'science or mind?' The philosophers said, 'Mind.' Anthony said, 'If I have mind, what need have I for science?'

"This is not to criticize science," said Father Timothy, "but it is clear that science without faith brings destruction. Perhaps it is because of all the destruction caused by science that today many scientists are turning back toward faith. They begin to see that there is a divine force ruling creation."

Before my departure I was able to talk with three nuns in the community, Sisters Anne, Nina, and Tatiana.

I asked Sister Anne Rudenko, the oldest, what had brought her to the convent. "Faith! Faith in God! Love toward God!"

How long have you been here? "Thirty years."

How did you choose this community. "My father brought me to visit when I was a child. I liked the services. I always wanted to live here."

What are you doing in your work? "I help clean the church but I am glad to do anything that is needed."

Sister Nina, a young woman with a round face and large dark eyes, was still a novice. She told me she also came from a family of believers. "My mother sang in the choir so I was in church a lot. I fell in love with singing! I am Ukrainian. We Ukrainians have a deep, ancient tradition of singing. When I grew up I became interested in monasticism. I began visiting different convents, studying details. First I went to the Pochayev Monastery. This was where my interest in monasticism started. Then I went to the Krasnagorsky Convent. When I met the sisters of that community I felt love in my heart. But this one was my favorite. I loved everything about this convent — the way ritual was done, the choir singing. I was accepted here and then I was sent to Leningrad to learn choral direction at the Choral School at the Theological Academy. Now my main work is our choir."

The youngest was Sister Tatiana, twenty-five. "My parents were deeply believing people interested in Christian spirituality and tradition. Because of them I also came to love the church. My being here is really thanks to them. Since childhood I had a feeling in my heart of wanting to devote my life to God. Coming here was a response to my soul's longing."

In an old building near the city center, we stopped to talk with Boris Ilyich Oleinik, a much loved Ukrainian poet who is now chairman of the Ukrainian Culture Foundation. "Personally, I am Orthodox. As I see it, the Orthodox Church always tried to cultivate enlightenment," he said. "In all these years, the church was one of the few forces in society never to waver. It has passed through many adversities still bearing the soul of our culture."

The Foundation was set up in 1987 to protect architecture, art, music, and literature and is, he said, "not only very democratic but is among those groups working to revive the nation's spirituality.

"The highest sensibility is in the spirit," he continued. "Both the artist and the church are preoccupied with the soul. Look at the writing of Dostoyevsky and his attention to the interior man. His goal was beauty, the spiritual perfection of the human being. The road of religion and literature converges in his writing. You see this also in our Ukrainian author, Gogol. He was a devout Orthodox believer. It was Gogol who caused a thaw in Russian literature. The Russian language was bookish while Ukrainian speech was rooted in folk language. I don't want to insult the Russian language but it was a little cold and heavy. Gogol helped to warm it up. After Gogol, the Gulf Stream flowed into the Russian language."

Arriving at the Monastery of the Caves the next day, I was impressed with how much had been transformed since my first visit two years earlier. In 1987 many of the buildings on the "far hill," the part since returned to the church, were almost derelict. The renewal of monastic life on these hilltops above the Dnieper seemed a distant dream. Now they were either fully restored or the restoration was well under way.

We were met by the vicar of the monastery. Archimandrite Jonathan Eletskih was tall, young, energetic, and very dashing in his flowing black robes. I recalled the vast crowd that had been at the monastery for its first Liturgy the previous June. "We had many outdoor Liturgies after that and want to have more," said Father Jonathan, "to make it a tradition. Anyway for major feasts it is impossible to fit all those who come within the church. We also like it because it means good contact between clergy and people." He regretted that I hadn't been at the monastery for Christmas. "There was a nativity play in the courtyard. It was the first time. Formerly religious plays were forbidden. Next Christmas we hope to perform the play all around the city."

He was proud of the repairs so far accomplished. "You saw how these buildings were last year. Everything was falling down. Look how it is now! We have still a lot to do but already you can see the difference. Come back next Easter and see what it's like then!"

The change was impressive. Despite scaffolding, the area returned to the monks had a new-born quality. What had been dull or rotting when I first saw it was now shining. "If you tried to do something like this under a state plan," he said, "it would take at least three years, but we have religious enthusiasm on our side and that's a big factor."

He showed us a newly restored church. "It is dedicated to the Mother of God. It was a museum for more than a quarter century. The restorers were the same ones who restored the czar's palace at Pushkin near Leningrad. The icons have been given to us by faithful people who were saving them until the monastery was brought back to life. They are real treasures. We consider some of them miracle-working icons — they are linked with specific miraculous events. In hard times they had to be hidden. There are other icons that should be returned still in museums, but we believe that just as God has returned part of this monastery, in time icons will be returned to their rightful places."

I asked about the condition of the caves. "We have much work to do there as well, but the chapels are now used for services and the bodies of the saints are no longer tourist curiosities but places of prayer. Also we have even experienced what we consider a miraculous sign. There are several skulls that were formerly dry bone and are now continuously exuding a myrrh-like oil. You will see it yourself. To protect the monastery from the charge of falsification, I had the oil tested. Scientists found a high percentage of protein, 72 percent. They have no explanation for how this can happen. We accept it as a miracle. A lifeless skull is giving birth to a living substance. It is a holy event, an action of the Lord, a blessing for a monastic community that has been restored to life."

Father Jonathan led us up a staircase. "Before you go into the caves, I want you to see our pilgrim church." He pointed to bedding piled up along the walls. "Not only is this a place for worship but a place for pilgrims to sleep, although in fact many of them pray more than sleep at night. But it is too small. When the restoration gets further and other churches are restored, we plan for this room to be a refectory."

He pointed to an icon of a bishop. "This is the image of Metropolitan Vladimir of Kiev who was killed by a member of the Anarchist party in 1918. We are permitted to venerate his memory in this church. He is one of the New Martyrs [martyrs of the Soviet period] already regarded as a saint by Orthodox of the Synodal Church [Russian Orthodox believers outside the Soviet Union who have no bond with the patriarch in Moscow]. Please let them know that we have this icon here. The proposal that he should be canonized is under consideration, as is true for others who gave witness to their faith with their lives. This is a manifestation of the deep change going on in our country."

I asked if he expected the rest of the monastery to be returned. "We are optimists! We are waiting for the second *perestroika* when the rest of the monastery will be returned. But until then we have a lot to keep us busy."

With the arrival of another guest, Father Jonathan put us in the care of a younger monk who led us into the caves, the final resting place for the bodies of 116 canonized saints plus thousands of others who took monastic vows.

The last time I entered those narrow, damp passages deep within the hill above the Dnieper River, they were lit by electric lights installed after the monks were evicted. The light fixtures remain but have been switched off. One hand holding a candle, the other the thin railing, I made my cautious way downward step by step.

In 1987 a museum guide passed by the bodies of saints like someone avoiding beggars on a city street. Her bored voice reverberated in the caves. Today we were engulfed in silence.

The bodies of the saints lay in glass-topped coffins. Their mummified hands are all that was visible of these remarkable ascetics of Kiev who did so much to shape the spirit of Slavic Orthodoxy. The monk leading the way quietly named them and then gently kissed the glass above their silk-covered faces.

"Some pilgrims are overcome by tears," the monk said. "They start crying and they can't stop. They fall down on their knees."

Carved into the rock was the Church of Saint Theodosius, named after the monastery's founder. "This is a living church again," the monk said. "We have the Holy Liturgy here at 7 A.M. every Thursday. Also we have the ceremony here for tonsuring new monks. Before the Revolution there were more than forty Liturgies a day in the caves. Only one other place in the world had so many, Mount Athos. Before 1922 there were still twelve a day."

I entered Saint Theodosius's narrow, low-ceilinged cell. Touching the rock shelf that had been his bed, I tried to imagine what it would be like to pray day after day deep in the earth, truly buried with Christ. "The relics of Saint Theodosius aren't here," the monk said. "We hope to find them when we excavate the Dormition Cathedral."

In a cabinet in a small alcove nearby there were a number of cylindrical glass jars holding skulls. "These are remains of saints whose names we do not know," he said. Several were dark and glistening, partially submerged in an amber oil — a wonder and blessing to Orthodox believers, a puzzle to scientists, and a source of revulsion to those for whom the spiritual life ought to be rational, well ordered, and disembodied.

We venerated the body of Saint Nestor the Illiterate whose teaching is summed up very simply: "You will not find the truth in books, only in your heart."

Kiev's caves also hold one of Orthodoxy's most literate figures, the biographer of Theodosius and author of *The Tale of Bygone Years*, Saint Nestor the Chronicler who died in 1113. His body was in the part of the caves that remains a museum.

When we stepped back into the world above the caves, it was a kind of resurrection from the dead. Perhaps it was to better celebrate Easter that the Kievan monks spent so much of their lives hidden in the earth.

As we left Father Jonathan was receiving yet another guest.[2]

Siberia

Our approach to Irkutsk was by air, a flight from Tashkent that began with a vista of the Tien Shan range, China's border. A thread-thin road disappeared under the snow. The land was quickly stripped of all trace of a human presence. We were flying over an eternally frozen ghost world that seemed to have been done in finger paints by a cosmic child working in dark purple and lavender white. Darkness fell and with it came a blackness below that more than equalled the night sky. Occasionally there was a sprinkling of light: a town on the edge of a lake or river. More provocative were the rare pricks of orange light in a sea of blackness. What would it be like to live in that kind of vast, fierce solitude? Are there still hermit monks in the Siberian wilderness? Finally there was the urban neon glow of Irkutsk and we were on the ground.

The word Irkutsk means "fast-flowing," referring to the Angara River, the one body of water flowing out of Lake Baikal. A wintering camp for fur traders set up in 1652 became a town in 1686. The Irkutsk shield granted that year displays the basis of its frontier pros-

---

[2]A few weeks later he received Raisa Gorbachev who, *Izvestia* reported, "showed great interest in the spiritual sources of Slavic culture." Father Jonathan and she discussed the Russian Primary Chronicle.

perity: a sable in the jaws of a Siberian tiger. In the mid-nineteenth century, gold was found, bringing a new wave of wealth to Irkutsk, but great suffering too. Many political prisoners spent long years — often their last years — in the mines. The wealth was so immense that Irkutsk's governor plated his carriage wheels with silver and shod his horses with gold. For "unheard of theft," he was hanged in 1771 at the order of Peter the Great. The first school in East Siberia, at the Resurrection Monastery, was just outside the city. In 1898 the city became linked to Moscow by the Trans-Siberian Railroad.

Though Irkutsk has become the industrial, administrative, and educational center for eastern Siberia, much of the old city remains unspoiled. Log buildings have not only survived but proved better suited to the Siberian environment than concrete.

In the heart of the city, on the shore, is the Church of the Savior, now a museum. Built in 1706, it was Siberia's first stone structure. Three other museum churches stand nearby. Two were Orthodox: the Church of the Apparition of the Lord and the Church of the Exaltation of the Cross. A third was Catholic, built by some of the 18,600 Poles exiled to Siberia after the 1863 Polish uprising. The Tikhvin Cathedral is gone, dynamited in the thirties.

There are only three working Orthodox churches left in Irkutsk and nineteen in the Irkutsk diocese — an area bigger than Texas, encompassing three hundred thousand square miles and 2.5 million people.

The bishop of the diocese, Archbishop Chrysostom, has his residence next to the gleaming white cathedral of the Holy Sign, originally part of the Znamensky Convent. Two old nuns still live there though the convent was closed half a century ago.

The Epiphany Liturgy was in progress when Sergei and I arrived at the cathedral. With several other late arrivals, we stood shivering on the church porch. When the Liturgy ended we were invited into the watchman's room in the corner of an adjacent building, a dingy space with a bed in the back that doubled as a couch, a table in front covered with magazines and newspapers, a hot plate and radio on a small cabinet near the door, a small icon on the upper back corner. Our host, the watchman, turned out to be a scholar. Items of reading on the table included recent issues of *Novi Mir* [New World], the prestigious Soviet literary journal. I noticed a Russian-Chinese dictionary. He was interested in herbal medicine and so was learning Chinese. "Being a watchman is a good job for scholars," he said, serving us tea.

Word came that the archbishop was waiting.

A 1974 report by the Council for Religious Affairs identified three categories of bishops in the Russian Orthodox Church. In the first category were those who "in words and deeds" demonstrated "not only loyalty but patriotism toward the socialist state, strictly observing the law on cults and educating the parish clergy and believers in the same spirit, [and who] realistically understand that our state is not interested in proclaiming the role of religion...and...do not display any particular activeness in extending the influence of Orthodoxy among the population." In the second category were those who, while having "a correct attitude to the laws on cults," in "their everyday administrative and ideological activity strive toward activating servants of the cult and active members of the church [and] stand for the heightening of the role of the church in personal, family, and public life...and select for priestly office young people who are zealous adherents of Orthodox piety." Finally there were those who "have made attempts to evade the laws on cults" and who are "capable of falsifying the position in their dioceses and the attitude which the organs of authority have formed toward them" and might even attempt to bribe officials in order to gain concessions for the church.

In this third category the report's author placed Archbishop Chrysostom, at the time Bishop of Kursk. Shortly after arriving in Kursk, the CRA report said, he had undertaken "zealous activities to revitalize religious life," ignoring "the recommendations of commissioners of the council and the local authorities." He was bold enough to say to his interrogator, "I am a bishop, I am forty years old. I don't intend to leave the church. I've heard a good many insulting and offensive things from atheists, but these are the times we live in, there's nothing to be done about it."[3]

The archbishop's office was impressive for its austerity. A small icon of Mary and Jesus hung over the door behind his desk. Archbishop Chrysostom was as plain as his office: a thin man with a long beard and black rosary around his wrist. His beard is just beginning to grey. The lack of an autocratic quality was striking. An old ink stand was on the desk, the crystal ink pots empty, a brass woman's head shining between them. A jar of pencils and a telephone stood to one side. Resting against his desk calendar was a postcard icon of the baptism of Jesus.

Hearing that I had come into the Russian Orthodox Church from Catholicism, he expressed surprise. "I was part of a Russian

---

[3] Jane Ellis, *The Russian Orthodox Church: A Contemporary History* (London: Croom Helm, 1986), pp. 215–22.

Orthodox delegation that visited Jerusalem in 1966," he recalled. "Jerusalem is the center of all Christian churches, and we visited many of them not only in Jerusalem but also in Nazareth and Bethlehem. I have to say I was shocked by the attitude of the Greek Orthodox toward other churches. We saw negligence and a lack of purity in the Greek churchmen — greed and carelessness. Many of them were highly educated yet they were proud and inaccessible. They showed superiority. This wasn't pleasant to observe. Yet when we visited churches in the care of Catholics, we were pleased. The clergy were also well educated but they weren't snobs. The churches were neat and beautifully maintained. I left full of gratitude for the care Catholics took of these places of pilgrimage. Since then I am imbued with a deep respect for the Catholic Church. I have now had much contact with Catholics, all sorts of people of various ranks including members of the hierarchy. The Catholic archbishop in Athens was the one who impressed me most of all — he has a face shining with love, deeply sensitive, generous to everyone, the kind of pastor that attracts all kinds of people, old and young.

"In 1974 I met Pope Paul VI — a small man, very thin, modest, but a man of character, not only someone of great intellect but with the strength of holiness. Also in Rome I was impressed by the human diversity of those receiving Communion — so many people and with every color of skin, yellow, black, and white. I also liked the masses for young people. They were playing guitars and singing. The climate was impressive. I felt the Holy Spirit was present. I was educated in a different way, but I have come to understand that both churches have spiritual treasures."

We moved on in our discussion to Russian Orthodoxy. "The Russian Orthodox Church has a deep tradition of iconography. Our Holy Trinity icon by Rublev is now known throughout the world. And we have a special tradition of church architecture. When you see our icons and church buildings, you cannot help but feel proud of artisans who were capable of such masterpieces. We descend from such people. Yet our pride in them can be dangerous.

"When we celebrated the Millennium of our baptism last June, of course we felt this pride. Our church council occurred in such a good climate. There was the canonization of the new saints, who remind us of what has been achieved. But even in such a moment we shouldn't close our eyes to ourselves. We have to ask ourselves what have *we* contributed to this treasure trove? What will *we* leave to coming generations? At a certain moment I looked around the council hall and was stunned. I saw so many empty faces, empty eyes. I thought, 'Selfish fools!' Their gazes were selfish and senseless. If this is our condition, how can we take care of the faithful?"

I mentioned a translator I had talked with just after the council who had been disappointed with the faces of many bishops. She asked me, "How many of them do you think are really believers?" Her guess was about half while I said one can't judge such a thing so easily and that, in any event, many of them would be quite different if they weren't surrounded by other bishops.

"I understand well what she felt," said Archbishop Chrysostom. "I felt so strongly the same thing that I took the floor at the council and spoke out against many present, and against myself as well. It was a criticism of the clergy, especially the higher clergy. It wasn't well received!" He laughed. "In fact many in the hall showed their irritation. There were some evil eyes focused on me, I can tell you. This anger mainly came from those who have no pastoral responsibilities — rather the ones close to the Council for Religious Affairs, that so-called 'linking body' that is really a chaining body. Some of our clergy are willingly in conformity with the demands of these atheists.

"The years of stagnation [the Brezhnev years] were very hard — more deadly for us than the years under Stalin. In the Stalin years we had martyrs and confessors. Some died. Others gave witness in their suffering. But the years of stagnation drove us down. These were years of real degradation of mind and morality, degradation of personality. It was a time especially hard on the bishops of the Russian Orthodox Church. It was hard also for the Catholics and Protestants but they resisted more successfully. The Baptists had their 'grassroot groups.' The most slavish people were Russian Orthodox bishops. True, we had some great personalities like Metropolitan Nikodim of Leningrad, a great ecumenical figure. But these were exceptions. In the years of stagnation, at a lower level, there were many priests doing their job — a hard job! — to resist those deadly trends. They helped to prepare the way for the fresh winds now blowing — *perestroika, glasnost*, democratization."

I asked him about his former assignment. "I was bishop of a diocese in the Kursk region. We had 108 churches to serve a population of five million people. But it was even worse than it sounds because 45 percent of our parishes were without a parish priest. There were forty-five churches that hadn't had divine services for two to five years. There were 159 priests. Among them the average age was seventy. I had the challenge to rebuild the local church. I don't want to be a modest liar. In five years I managed to fill the gap. We didn't have a single parish without a priest. I left 182 priests serving 108 working churches. The average age of a priest when I left was thirty years old. More than twenty of them had a higher education. But in order to ordain them, one had to have a serpent's wisdom! All the administrative authorities and party bosses were absolutely against what I was trying to do. Somehow it happened anyway. [laughter] Also I was able to deprive of their posts those occasional rotten people who had penetrated the church and who were discrediting it by their faithless attitude and their immoral behavior. This was my second task. Such people had to be kicked out. The passage of the Helsinki Final Act helped me in doing this. When it was signed, the climate was more favorable. I was able to succeed in this cleansing work. I deprived two scoundrels wearing clerical garments. They were stripped of their ranks and the right to serve as priests. But this proved to be the last straw. In 1984, after ten years as bishop in that diocese, I was sent, as you see, to Siberia, to Irkutsk. I wasn't able to last in the Kursk region until the first years of *perestroika*. Now of course, the climate has changed in a way that no one could have imagined a few years ago. Last year, seven hundred Orthodox churches were opened. In the former time, the officials wanted to send to Moscow statistics every year showing that there were fewer churches than the year before. So you can imagine how the officials felt about me! I was a blank spot, or worse."

How is the situation now? "Our church is facing the most difficult and complex period in her history. Atheism has greatly deteriorated. It used to be atheists could do whatever they wanted — discharge clergy, publish articles. Of course people didn't take very seriously what they said. Their ideas weren't respected. But they had power. They were able to keep the Orthodox Church under strict surveillance. They were able to make sure that only politically reliable people entered the seminaries, and also to make sure that only the most slavish people were promoted. True, there were capable people among those promoted, but these were exceptions and morally they didn't fit. Or they were nice people but useless, without courage. But we found ways around all this vigilance. Sometimes people can be ordained without entering the theological schools. And one must add that, after so many years in power, the atheists were sometimes complacent. They were lax in their vigilance. In various ways it was possible to ordain good people to service in the church. But our problem is that, at this moment, we don't have unity. The higher ranks of the clergy are very far from the lower clergy, and from the rank and file people in the church."

Have you particular people in mind? "I wouldn't like to single out anyone. In any event, all of us are compromised, all of us are sinners, none of us is adequate. Although all of us were anointed with the same chrism [holy oil], we became obedient slaves, doing what was 'recommended' by the civil powers — bowing down, bending our backs. Nor were we prepared by our theological schools to answer the hard questions that people increasingly bring to those with pastoral responsibility. There is very little purposeful preaching. There are few pastors who can evangelize those who are educated. The one seminary rector who tried to prepare clergy for evangelical work was Archbishop Kyrill. For ten years he was the rector in Leningrad. He was preparing people not only to be capable of doing the rituals correctly but to be pastors. You know what happened. He was sent away from the seminary to head the Smolensk diocese! The civil authorities were disturbed at his success in preparing thinking pastors. He and I were like the Decembrists[4] sentenced to hard labor in Siberia. We were removed and sent to remote places."

Aren't you painting too dark a picture? "It is true that despite our problems we have many people of deep faith and real intellect, priests and monks with an appropriate inspiration. Still there are barriers on the way to their promotion. We also have many faithful people among the Soviet intelligentsia. Though it is widely thought that Soviet intellectuals are all atheists, this is far from true. Many are believers. But few of them have contact with the Orthodox Church. In fact many of them don't trust the clergy. Some had built up unofficial contact in the past and then got into trouble — it seems the clergy informed on them. The intellectuals were betrayed. So there is a residue of distrust. Nor do we have any publications within the church that can serve as a point of encounter. *The Journal of the Moscow Patriarchate* is published every month but it is mainly church news, ecumenical news, news about peacemaking activities. You find nothing about the problems within the church or the society we are part of. If you want to find writing about spirituality or the real history of this century, you had better look in the secular publications — the literary journals or certain magazines and newspapers. There you will find classic essays by Florensky or Solovyov, pieces that are thrilling to read. Or look on the television screen. Recently there have been many good films and documentaries on television in which religious life is presented in a thoughtful and positive way. The problem is that these films may raise up expectations in those who see them that will not be met by

---

[4]The Decembrists were officers who attempted to force a constitutional government on the czar in December 1825. Five of its leaders were executed and many others sent in chains to work the mines in Siberia.

our clergy. A passionate interest has taken hold of many people about their history, their lost culture, their religious roots. This is now a focus of national attention. Society is prepared to offer its repentance. But all they find in the Russian Orthodox Church is complacency! We are suddenly on the stage, face to face with the people. But we have a blank face! We are not ready for the dialogue that is offered to us, a dialogue between believer and nonbeliever, a dialogue not to convert but to make contact, to illuminate, to help each other."

What is the situation of the church in Irkutsk? "For three years I knew only our *babushkas*. Many were frail and sick. Yet we grew very close. I think they found in me an open window into the sky, into life. It was very nice. The year 1988 was a strong year, a productive year. We built up contacts with local institutions, with the local branch of the Academy of Sciences, with all kinds of informal organizations. There were some meetings where we had an audience of a thousand people talking about all sorts of issues. We still have far to go. In the immense territory of this diocese we have only nineteen parishes. Although there are seven hundred churches newly opened in the last year throughout the Soviet Union, none are in this diocese. There are three Orthodox churches serving this large city. We badly need a fourth, but where would we get the funds to restore a church?"

What about the condition of the Russian Orthodox Church following the council? "We have a much better church law now. The priest is the head of the parish once again, not someone pushed on the church by those who have no love for us. At the same time there are also some disturbing signs. There was one bishop appointed recently, Gavriel, who now heads half of my former diocese, the eastern part. He was father superior of the Monastery of the Caves near Pskov where he was criticized for his rough manner. There were many complaints about him and his disgraceful behavior. Yet now he is made a bishop! If in this period of *perestroika* and *glasnost* the Russian Orthodox Church nominates disgraced people to high pastoral responsibilities, it is likely that we will have a schism. In fact we can see indications of such a trend. Here we are, in a society returning to Lenin's period. Remember that in Lenin's time there were many splits within the church. The Russian Orthodox Church was under great pressure then, and it is under pressure now. But the times have changed. Now the people can express themselves freely and can act freely. If the civic leadership controls the activities of the church in such a time, those who cooperate with them will cause a schism. But let us hope that we'll not have it and that instead the *perestroika* process will start in the Russian Orthodox Church."

Doesn't the consecration of bishops like yourself indicate that there are people of integrity and courage leading the Russian Orthodox Church? "Yes, there are good people in the Holy Synod. They work hard. They are faithful people, believing people. The only major failure is a lack of courage and will. I don't condemn them. I wouldn't disgrace them. But I cannot understand how they can appoint someone unsuitable to head a diocese."

What brought you to serve the church? "I was born in 1934 into a believing family. My parents were passionate in their faith. My father was director of the church choir. I started going to church early in life. Then I cooled down because of the severity of church regulations — the strict fasts, the ban on going to the movies — but that period in my life lasted only two years. I returned to church and began working as an assistant icon painter. From 1948 to 1961, I almost lived in churches, helping to gild and doing ornamental work. We were restoring churches in many parts of Russia. In 1961 I entered the Moscow Theological Seminary. I was twenty-seven. That was a very hard year for the church, a year many churches were closed. Until that time I had little education. I hadn't completed high school. My meager education actually helped me get into the seminary — the less promising you were, the more willing the civil authorities were for you to take a place in the seminary! They would have been happy if we were all insane and illiterate. People like me. In 1972 I was consecrated a bishop. At the time few realized my thinking was on the wrong path, though Metropolitan Nikodim placed high hopes in me. It was he who wanted me to be a bishop. But I never wanted it. I wanted to be a parish priest. In fact that is what I still want. I am ready today to stop being a bishop and just to be a local pastor."

Serving at the cathedral with Archbishop Chrysostom was Father Evgeni Kasatkin, who took time to show us around. After the tour we sat on a bench in a chilly corner where restoration work was under way.

I asked what had brought him to religious belief. "While visiting the church I was more and more filled with a feeling of veneration. The will to serve the church penetrated to the depth of my soul."

Did your parents sympathize? "My mother died in the siege of Leningrad so didn't live to see it happen. My father was against it."

What brought you to the priesthood? "I wanted to be a priest since I was a boy. Before entering the seminary I had studied rigorously by myself. I had a diploma from the University of Leningrad and so had the right to use the Leningrad Public Library where all the books printed since Peter the Great are in the stacks. I was accepted by the Moscow Theological Seminary during the time Metropolitan Filaret [head of the church's External Affairs Department at the time of the interview] was rector. He was much loved by all the students. He knew us all."

Has *perestroika* had any impact on the church in Irkutsk? "After the church council at the Holy Trinity Monastery last summer we had a public concert of church music. This had never been possible in the past. Any interested person could come. It was a charity benefit."

Is the local church undertaking charity work? "It is beginning. We founded a charity society just a few days ago. It is too early to say what we will be able to do, but I think believers can play a role in the local hospitals."

Are there new churches opening in this diocese? "Throughout the country many have opened though so far there are no new ones in this diocese. But the process of change is started and is moving in one direction, even if very slowly."

Do you sense more people moving from disbelief to belief? "Yes! Of course! Many. We have many adult baptisms here."

The next day we drove to Listvianka, a village of log houses on the shore of Baikal. The lake draws one's attention from the village. Here is one-fifth of the world's supply of fresh water, nearly as much water as flows out of all the world's rivers in one year. We broke the ice and drank a glassful.

Baikal is fed by 336 streams but has only one outlet, the Angara River, a tributary of the Yenisei River. The legend is that the tyrant Baikal had 336 sons and one daughter. The sons did as they were told, giving all the wealth they collected to Father Baikal, but the daughter, Angara, was strong-willed and independent — in other words a true Siberian. She fell in love with Yenisei. As Baikal opposed their wedding, they eloped, thus creating Baikal's one exit point.

While the pure water of Baikal is one of the wonders of the world, a less noticed miracle is the fact that the village of Listvianka has its own church, Saint Nicholas's. There are whole cities without churches in Siberia. The pastor, Father Sergei Kozlov, was thirty-five years old. "Orthodoxy is not just a faith," he said. "It is a unified way of life. But in modern society there is no unified life. The ordinary believer today is likely to have two lives running side by side — a civic, 'Soviet' way of life and a private life that includes a religious area. At work you are one person, at home and in church another. But, as the Gospel says, you cannot serve two masters. Yet how can you do otherwise? This is the tragic tension we are experiencing today."

What can be done about it? "Russia needs to become Russia again. This doesn't mean that all Russians will be believers. There will continue to be atheists because there will continue to be freedom of will. But atheism would no longer be the dominant religion. It would no longer be imposed."

Are *perestroika* and *glasnost* moving society in this direction? "Yes, yes! Increasingly people are moving toward belief and toward the church. But still we have many serious problems. Too many people are thinking primarily about the economic problems and neglecting spiritual ones. Our main attention — even the attention of political leaders — should be focused on religious problems. There is an urgent need to remove all the impediments that stand in the way of religious education and religious formation. Before we can recover our economic health we must recover our spiritual health."

Did you grow up a believer? "I was an atheist until I was twenty-seven. Neither was Irina, my wife, a believer. We moved to belief together."

What led you toward the church? "There were so many things, so many personal religious experiences. A crucial event was my first reading of the Gospel. It stirred me deeply."

How did you prepare for the priesthood? "In the monasteries. I didn't go to a theological school. I was what is called an 'obedient' [a guest sharing in the monastic life without taking monastic vows] at several monasteries including the Danilov Monastery in Moscow. Then two years ago Archbishop Chrysostom ordained me in Irkutsk."

Standing silently at Father Sergei's side while we talked was Ivan Ilyich, the church warden. He had a sober face and white beard and wore a traditional embroidered Russian shirt under his jacket. I expressed my hope to him that the day would soon come when no Russian town or village would be without a church. "Let's hope!" he said. "But it is God's will that decides."

The Far East

Although I went to Ulan Ude to meet the Buddhists who live beyond Lake Baikal, on the Sunday I was in the city I went to the Holy Liturgy at the Church of the Ascension. The church was crowded, the congregation singing with the choir in the more familiar places, while in the side chapel baptisms were going on.

The twenty-one who were baptized ranged in age from Anastasia, age four, to Georgi, about thirty. A girl of fourteen was Buryat;

the rest were of European descent. About half were teenagers or adults, the rest children. Among them was a mother and her two grown daughters. Together they renounced Satan, spat on him, and expressed their will to be united in Christ. Father Andrei, the young priest, after explaining how to cross oneself, made the sign of cross with oil on the brow, on the breast, between the shoulders, and on the hands and feet of everyone being received. A bit of hair was cut off, an ancient symbol of dedication to God. Each person was then baptized by the pouring of water on the head, a real dowsing that was as close as one could get to total submersion without going into a river, and then given a white ribbon — symbolic remnant of a baptismal garment — and a small cross to wear. Each of the godparents was blessed as well.

Father Andrei spoke about the meaning of baptism and the responsibilities that come with membership in Christ's church. "This is your second birth. First you were born from your mother's body. Now you are born into Christ's body, a spiritual rebirth. You have started a new life. Live it worthily. Love God with your whole heart and soul and love your neighbor, even your enemy, as yourself. By ourselves we are powerless to love. How can we love an enemy? This is the major challenge. Many fail. We are blind. But God can open our eyes and show us how to love." The service ended in reception of Communion.

The pastor, Father Martiri Torchevski, asked about my impression of his church. I told him I had never seen so many baptized at once or seen such an assembly-line method. Neither had I expected such a large portion to be students or adults. "This is normal," he said. "We get at least twenty every Sunday. I wish it could be done more slowly, but we haven't enough priests and everything is done in too much of a rush."

I asked about the history of this church. "This used to be a graveyard church. It was dedicated in 1786 and was brought back to life in 1945. Our main church in Ulan Ude, the Church of the Mother of God, Consolation of the Sorrowful, is used as a storage building for the museum. It was taken away many years ago. We have hopes of its being returned but even if we had it, I don't know how we could restore it. Just a few years ago we put a great deal of money and time into restoring this building."

I asked about his background. "My parents were believers. I grew up in the far east beyond the Amur River. After serving in the army I worked with a local publisher. In that province there was no church. Perhaps that is why I was a little slow in realizing I wanted to serve in the church. I went to the theological school in Odessa and was ordained in 1970 when I was thirty-two."

How did you go to church if there was none in your province? "There was one in the next province. I could get there by bus. Every four or five weeks I went for confession and Communion."

As we left, Father Andrei was presiding at a wedding in the main part of the church. The young couple were wearing the crowns that are the most remarkable symbol in the Orthodox marriage service.

Archangel

I had visited the Baikal region in January. Back in the USSR in late April, I went to the Arctic north to celebrate Easter.

Six months of the year, Archangel's harbor on the White Sea is frozen in ice, but — at a time when Russia had no access to the Baltic — Peter the Great saw in the remaining half year a maritime opening to western Europe. A statue of Peter, the first beardless czar, stands on the Archangel embankment. Peter seems to be peering out not only toward London and Amsterdam but also toward the Dutchified Russia he was determined to build no matter how many Orthodox whiskers he had to shave in the process. Despite Peter's later conquests on the Baltic and the establishment of Saint Petersburg (now Leningrad), Archangel remains a busy working port, though the modern city is mainly a timber center.

At Saint Elijah's Church, the celebration of the Resurrection began an hour before midnight and lasted until dawn.[5] The church was filled to capacity with many standing outside. For the first time local television covered it — with a crew that was more engaged in the Liturgy than I expected. I noticed the sound man holding a microphone in one hand and a burning candle in the other.

After the all-night service Sergei and I were invited to join in Easter breakfast — a feast of eggs, meat, and vodka — at the nearby apartment of one of the parish priests, Father Alexander Kozaruk, and his wife, Maria. I asked them what *perestroika* had meant for them. "More freedom!," said Father Alexander. "Bell ringing! More publishing!"

The day after Easter was May Day, a national holiday. In Archangel the observance seemed routine at first — crowds parading

---

[5]In 1989 Russian Easter was on April 30, more than a month after Easter had been celebrated in Western churches. On average the date for Easter coincides in East and West every four years.

into the city's central square, kids riding on fathers' shoulders, mothers pushing baby carriages, balloons in the air, clusters of teenage girls laughing. There were the standard red-and-white banners with texts praising the Communist party and its goals. But there was much that was without precedent. Many carried home-made green-and-white banners bearing environmental messages: "Save Life," "Save the Fish," "Save the Ecology of the North," "Protect the Dvina River," "Preserve Nature for Our Children," "Full Glasnost in Ecology," "The Fate of Our River Is Our Fate," "Open the Way for Alternatives to Nuclear Power," and "We Call for a Referendum on Nuclear Power." A Polish flag was held aloft at the edge of the crowd. I smelled the scent of Solidarity. "I never saw anything like this," Sergei said.

One of the speakers was Vladimir Kasakov, an actor who chairs the regional environmental group founded last November. "For nature there are no borders," he said. "Whether we are atheists or believers, rich or poor, Russian or Georgian, we have one common home. We share the same fate as the environment. The issue is how to live together, and this means how to end the violence against nature. Nature will not accept this violence against her. The main victims of ecological devastation are our children. It is in our power to save nature — to purify the water, the air, and the soil. To save nature means to save our children and our grandchildren. We claim to be reasonable. Let us prove it by our actions." His speech drew lively and sustained applause.

After the assembly in the square dispersed, there were informal gatherings in the city center where people set up signs and exhibitions on topics ranging from housing problems to the forthcoming meeting of deputies to the Supreme Soviet. A display about state cruelties in the past included a quotation from a letter written by a prisoner to his wife: "What I am leaving to you is very modest. My wealth is my love for you. I have never done anything wrong. I am guilty of nothing. For no reason at all they made me a criminal. I know that you do not doubt this. Be proud and never, never, not even for one moment think that I could possibly cast a shadow of disgrace on you. Hold your head high." It was the last letter from a prisoner in the Davidov Camp near Ertsevo, Barrack Three, in the Archangel district.

Sergei spoke of the awful way Maxim Gorky had allowed himself to be used for deception by Stalin. "For example Stalin sent Gorky to visit a prison on Solovetsky Island, a former monastery in the White Sea to the north of Archangel. Everything was made clean and humane for his arrival. They even set up a reading room. When Gorky entered the room, there were prisoners on display reading newspapers. One of them had the courage to hold his newspaper upside down. Gorky put it right. He must have understood what such a gesture meant. But he wrote what Stalin wanted about the 'humanitarian treatment' of prisoners on the island. This was because Stalin wanted an answer to a book about the island that had been published in the West by an escaped prisoner."

The environmentalists gathered in front of the cultural center, former site of Archangel's cathedral, destroyed in the thirties. Amid signs protesting nuclear power, Vladimir Kasakov was selling tickets to a meeting to be held a few days later. "We have ecology groups in various plants, offices, and schools. A lot of people are preoccupied with environmental problems, especially the negative impact of nuclear plants on the environment. There are ecology groups all over the country, and we have ties with similar groups in West Germany and Norway. We realize that we can't solve environmental problems alone — it requires international solidarity."

I asked how he got engaged in this. "The writer Vladimir Rasputin and his campaign to save Lake Baikal was a big impetus for me. I came to know him in 1977."

I commented on the reference he had made in his speech to cooperation in the movement between believers and atheists. "You find many believers active in the environmental movement," he said. "This is because there is a deep connection between ecology of the soul and ecology of nature."

We had lunch with the pastor of Saint Elijah's Church, Father Vladimir Kuzov. Father Vladimir, a Ukrainian, was born in 1947. He has a long face, fine features, and a closely trimmed beard. He gestures constantly with his hands, Italian-style. Outside the church he wears a dark suit with a small gold cross on his lapel. He studied at the Leningrad Theological Seminary, was ordained in 1977, served for a time in Petrozavodsk and Leningrad, then came to Archangel in 1981.

"At present I am both pastor and chairman of the church council. The council is a small group that makes decisions about everyday matters. If there is an important matter, then we have an assembly which any regular church-goer can attend. If we want, we can elect someone else in the congregation as chairman. It doesn't have to be the pastor. But no one is imposed from the outside."

Did he miss the Ukraine? "No, I feel at home here. The north has been good for believers. There were many monasteries in the northern wilderness. In the old times monks would go to the forests because they were the Russian desert. They found the forests were a creative place to pray. The singing of the birds was good for the soul. Most monasteries were built in the forests. You might be walking through the forest and suddenly discover a beautiful scene — churches with golden domes, white bell towers. Seraphim of Sarov went to a *staretz* [holy elder] for advice and was directed not to an existing monastery but to the forest."

He was nostalgic about village life — real Russian stoves, *babushkas*, mushroom picking, an unhurried way of life with a religious core. "But now the villagers are mainly old people. They are the ones carrying on the traditional way of life."

Is the church attracting young people? "It's common to hear a young person say, 'I don't pray very much but I am a believer.' You saw yourself how many in church Easter night were young. With *perestroika*, many more are coming. The number of young people being baptized is growing fast. There have been documentaries about church life on television, especially during the Millennium. These stirred interest. It isn't as easy for young people to get involved in church — they have their studies or their jobs — but they come on weekends. When you ask how they came to belief, many of them say it was their grandmother who taught them to pray and to be aware of God and the fundamentals of religion. We see a number of teachers and doctors coming to church, being married in church, and bringing their children to be baptized. There is a big demand for literature about church life — calendars, Bibles, prayer books."

And what about older people? "You could say the same. A few days ago a man of about forty came to ask me about sacraments, the Eucharist, God. He said, 'I wouldn't yet say I am a faithful person but I feel interest. I want to learn.' Some people ask about parts of the Bible — what does a certain story and commandment mean. The picture is encouraging. It is a big change. The only problem is that it is very hard to meet all the needs."

Can you manage? "Yes, but it is a huge job. We have three priests in our church and this isn't enough when you think of all the services to conduct, the confessions, baptisms, marriages, and funerals, the people who are sick, all those who need to talk to you, those who are preparing to enter the church. You need to call on the help of others. Otherwise it would be impossible. You have to keep time for your wife and children."

Are there study groups for those who want to know more? "It isn't ideal but now we can educate people in the back of the church. We teach basic prayer, the meaning of baptism and marriage, how to prepare for confession, information about fasting, the meaning of certain symbols. It's very basic instruction. Also there are occasional opportunities in places where we were never invited. Last summer I was able to speak about the meaning of Christianity and the Orthodox Church before students in a local school. There is now another invitation — somehow I have to find the time. I was interviewed twice in the local newspaper. My picture was in the paper! My hope is that the new legislation on freedom of conscience will increase the possibilities for religious education."

Is your church involved in charitable work? "Not yet on a regular basis, but we have made some gestures. We went to a local orphanage and presented a television set. Now we are preparing ourselves for regular engagement."

What about the local Council for Religious Affairs? "We find it easy working with Mikhail Feodorovich [the head of the local Council for Religious Affairs].[6] We like him. He has a warm heart. He responds quickly to any requests. If we have any troubles involving civic organizations, we turn to him for help."

While in Archangel, I twice happened to catch religious programs on Soviet television. On the afternoon before Easter, the documentary *Church*, first aired during the Millennium the previous June, was rebroadcast. On the evening news two days later there was a feature about Saint Xenia of Petersburg, a member of that peculiar tribe of saints especially beloved in Russia, the *iurodivii* — fools for Christ's sake. Age twenty-six when her husband died, Xenia felt as if it were she who had died. Afterward she gave away everything she possessed, saying, "The Lord feeds the birds of the air. I am no worse than a bird." Relatives attempted to prevent the distribution of her husband's estate on the ground that she was insane, but the physician who examined her declared that she was of sound mind. For eight years she disappeared from the city. When she returned she was wearing her husband's old uniform, now reduced to rags, and would only answer to his name, Andrei Theodorovich. She was often seen on the streets of the poorest districts. The copper kopeks she was given — she never accepted more than a kopek — she in turn distributed to others. She became a source of solace and guidance to many people. Workers building a church at the Smolensky Cemetery noticed that someone was carrying many bricks to the top of the scaffolding at night — it was discovered she was responsible. She refused all offers for indoor lodging yet managed to live her wandering life for forty-five years. Throughout

---

[6]See profile, pp. 193–94.

that time she always radiated a deep happiness, meekness, humility, and kindness. When she died at the age of seventy-one, she was buried in the Smolensky Cemetery where her grave became a place of pilgrimage. Eventually a chapel was erected over her body.

In recent years the Smolensky Cemetery was designated by city planners as a site for apartment buildings. The people of Leningrad, wanting to protect the grave of Xenia, protested. Finally the city council agreed to erect the buildings elsewhere.

The reporter interviewed various people who had come to pray at her grave — old and young, men and women. "I come for consolation," said one woman. "Does she help you?" "Yes! Of course!"

Karelia

Karelia — the Karelian Autonomous Soviet Socialist Republic — is part of the Russian north. Most of the land is forested. The Karelian economy is centered on wood products and paper manufacture. The eastern region has been part of Russia since the fourteenth century but the border with Finland was not established until 1947. The capital, Petrozavodsk (Peter's Foundry), was founded on the western shore of Lake Onega by Peter the Great in 1703 to provide armaments. The foundry has since become a huge tractor factory. There are hundreds of lakes. In January, when I was there, ice on Lake Onega blocked access to Kizhi Island, location of the most famous wooden church in Russia, the many-tiered Church of the Transfiguration with its ascending ranks of twenty-one silvery grey cupolas. In the summer, connections between lakes and rivers make it possible to go by boat not only from Petrozavodsk to nearby Kizhi but all the way to southern Europe.

In Stalin's time the statue of Peter the Great that used to stand in the center of the main square was replaced by a bronze Lenin. "Now there is a desire to put the statue of Peter the Great back where it was," said a city guide. "That would mean moving Lenin's statue. The city council has put this off on the grounds of expense. The statue of Peter has been moved twice so far — from the central square to an inconspicuous courtyard and then, ten years ago, down to the lake front."

Archimandrite Manuil Pavlov, vicar of the diocese of Karelia, is a large man with sympathetic eyes and wispy black beard streaked with grey. On the walls of the living room, apart from the icon corner, were pictures of old churches. A small model of Kizhi's Transfiguration Church stood on the upright piano.

His grandfather, Pavel, now eighty-five, shares the house with him. He laid stones for the first churches built in the north after the last world war. Thirty years ago he helped restore the Holy Trinity Cathedral in Leningrad.

"Easter is the *real* time," said Father Manuil after we exchanged the traditional Easter greeting. "Truly these are bright days. Whether people believe or not, heaven and earth are celebrating the Resurrection. During the Easter days, we experience a natural closeness."

What effect has *perestroika* had on Karelia? "If you drop into a shop, you don't see changes. On the other hand *we* have changed. The most important thing is that we have lost the feeling of fear. It used to be that I didn't care what newspapers were saying. Now I do care. I want to read them. Of course I am especially happy about what is happening for believers. The government no longer thinks of the church as a foreign land within the country. We are now recognized as an important part of our country, people able to do something for the improvement of society. It used to be that the role of the church was limited by the law of 1929. In fact it is still the law. But life advances before decrees. The activity of the church is beyond the 1929 limits. We await the new law on freedom of conscience that is being considered right now."

What sort of changes are occurring in Karelia? "Valaam Monastery is in this region, in Ladoga Lake. It hasn't yet been officially returned but we anticipate having it back. Its restoration is under way. A lot must be done. People with the skills for the indoor repairs and fresco restoration are rare. At least we have managed to prevent further decay of the structures. I was amazed by the sense of sacred space when I visited Valaam last year. Even after these many years without a living monastic community, it is still a blessed place. There is a halo around it. I long for the day when Valaam is a living monastery again.

"We now have a charity fund in Karelia. I am on the committee that decides how to use the funds. Members of my parish are now helping in local hospitals and our priests are able to visit patients. I participated in the opening of a new home for elderly people.

"Another change involves education. A year ago I would never have imagined that I would be invited to give lectures on the history of the Russian Orthodox Church before history students at the Petrozavodsk University. It used to be that some students would come one by one for private conversation, just to communicate on matters of faith. Others wanted to come but were afraid. To a large extent the clergy were kept separate from the people, even from believers. I could give a sermon but otherwise I had no contact with my own flock. Konstantin Kharchev commented that by cutting off the priest in this way, we were unable to do much to raise the level of public morality, and thus it was a stupid policy on the state's part."

I asked about rumors that Kharchev would not continue in his post. "Now he is in the hospital but next he will be appointed an ambassador. He did a good job. The two interviews with him in *Ogonyok* were excellent. They expanded the horizon. But I don't think his departure means a setback for religious developments. The Council for Religious Affairs is going in a new direction. It used to block the way. Now it actively helps in protecting religious rights. Their staff in Karelia are active reformers. They say yes even before they are asked."

What is the role of the Orthodox Church in the new situation? "We have accumulated traditions and values important not only to believers but to all human beings. The time has come to open these treasures to everyone. Not that everyone will become believers. But they can use our store of knowledge and moral values to improve themselves and society as a whole and move closer to a life in peace. This will be a benefit to all."

How can the church prepare more people to respond to the possibilities that now exist? "Archbishop Kyrill has just opened a school for readers in Smolensk. He is a good man. He was much loved when he headed the seminary in Leningrad. He has done a lot to prepare people to bring the message of belief to others. There will be another similar school in Minsk next year."

I commented that there seemed to be more attention in Orthodox churches to the importance of sermons. "When I am giving a sermon, I look and see what sort of people are there. If they are young, I try to explain things that may be strange to them. The church shouldn't be foreign."

On Bright Thursday — all the days of the first week after Easter are prefixed "bright" — we drove together to Olonets, a small city near Lake Ladoga.

On the way out of Petrozavodsk we stopped to visit the Church of Saint Catherine the Martyr, a cemetery church in an old part of the town where the old wooden houses survive. With tears in her eyes, an old woman praying in the church, Lidiya, told me that she "listens every day to God's Word on the Voice of America." She instructed me to kiss my wife.

"There used to be thirty-eight Orthodox churches in this city," said Father Manuil as we drove away. "Three are still in use. One had its domes removed. The main periods of destruction were 1930–32 and 1934–38. After the war some churches could reopen but then there was another big wave of church closing in the sixties, the Khrushchev time. Now we are in a period where not only city churches are being reopened but churches in towns and villages. There are many places where new churches are under construction or are planned. Under the new legislation we expect that local authorities will have no right to retain a church building that is empty or used only for storage purposes. This will make it easier to start new parishes. But there is often the problem that a confiscated church is used for another purpose — a club or office. Then it can be quite difficult to get it back. And there is the problem of all those churches that were destroyed. New ones must be built and even if the local authorities are willing for this to happen, it isn't easy to get the money and materials needed. Even though we expect many positive changes in the new law, at the moment all we have is the old law that denies religious communities the right to get loans. Even the diocese is not supposed to loan money! On the other hand life is going beyond the limits of the old law. Our diocese is helping local churches. In such matters you depend on the good will of local authorities and their willingness to consider the old law dead. But not all local authorities are like that. We are among the lucky ones."

What are the statistics for the diocese as a whole? "Besides the three in Petrozavodsk, we have three other working churches — the fourth opened five years ago in Segisha and the fifth opened last year in Olonets. Another church is near the Finnish border at Sartavala. In addition to the six, now we have permission to use a number of local chapels for services. These aren't full-time churches and so under the present law can't be registered. They are in a new category altogether. We haven't enough priests, and the villages near the chapels are very small, but we can have occasional services at these places — liturgies, weddings, baptisms, funerals. In the former times such chapels couldn't be used. It was impossible. They just stood there rotting. Now priests can come on certain dates — perhaps once a month — so faithful people won't have to travel to the city. Local believers have been given keys to the chapels. They are cleaning and repairing them and bringing back the icons they were keeping in their homes. There are now nine chapels like this in the territory. We hope to have use of another six but there are still problems to be solved in a few places. Not everything goes smoothly, but we have no problems with the Council for Religious Affairs." Passing through the village at Novinka, we stopped to see a chapel dedicated to the Archangel Michael, now used for occasional services.

Bells were ringing in welcome as we arrived at the Church of the Dormition, in a wooded area outside Olonets. The pastor was a tall young man, Father Alexander Varlamov. He led us into church to sing Easter prayers before the iconostasis. "We celebrated the two-hundredth anniversary of our church this year," said Father Alexander. "It's a graveyard church with many icons of the old style of the Northern Russian School from the seventeenth and eighteenth centuries."

He introduced an old woman who, for fifty-two years, took care of the church, helping to safeguard it through the years, first from the early thirties until after the war, then again in the sixties until last year.

"In the years the church was closed we lost some of the festal icons and also the royal doors of the iconostasis. The new doors were carved by a local with love in his heart. The Dormition icon has a text at the bottom recording the visit by Catherine the Great for the church's consecration on May 28, 1788. Local people have brought us many ancient icons that were handed on within their families for generations. Collectors would pay a lot for them, but believers want them to be in the church. Many people are coming here. We know each other. It is like a family. We are well disposed to each other. There is a climate of sympathy, a feeling of the presence of the Holy Spirit. Not every church is so blessed. One problem faced in many places is that the church is too small for the many people who come — it's hard to develop a spirit of community in such circumstances. In former times people would say, 'We are going to our church.' They didn't say *the* church. They felt at home there."

Back in Petrozavodsk that night, I talked with Nikolai Stepanov, Father Manuil's assistant, recently graduated from the Leningrad Theological Seminary but not yet ordained. He mentioned that there is already a small monastic community at Preoversk, near Valaam, "a seed of the revived Valaam."

I mentioned to him how impressed I had been in 1987 to notice the large number of people receiving Communion at the seminary church in Leningrad. "This is the merit of Archbishop Kyrill from the time that he was rector. He often explained what the Eucharist is and encouraged more frequent Communion. He also did much to restore a closer relationship between the priest and the people. For many years the priest was cut off from his flock, allowed no role except to stand at the altar. He could explain things in a deeper way only with a trusted inner circle. Now every Sunday we meet the church-goers, and seminary students explain the meaning of Orthodox faith and many other things. This is not only for believers but for anyone who wants to come. Many people in Leningrad show their interest. The seminary hall holds about a hundred, and that really isn't big enough. People come from all walks of life — workers, people with desk jobs, intellectuals. Every week there is a special topic decided after consultation with the participants and students — sacraments, history of the church, how Orthodoxy differs from other confessions, the place of faith in the life of writers like Gogol and Dostoyevsky. One week we discussed the Optina Pustyn Monastery and the writers who visited there. Whatever the topic, first we present a report that can be accompanied with slides or a film, and then there is a general discussion. The seminary choir performs. Sessions last about two hours, until Vespers."

What happens if there is no longer a hall big enough? "Maybe eventually it will become a television show."

The next day, with two local priests, I had lunch with a local Orthodox family living in a large log house. "In our house you find many old traditions of Karelia," said my host, an old man with a white beard. "Here my wife and I have been living for forty years. Here our children have grown to adulthood. Here we have prayed. Here we have known death. Today we are remembering Anastasia's death. Many have been guests at this table, and not only those who share our Orthodox faith. We welcome you! Today we have eternal joy. All of us know that if Jesus hadn't risen from the dead, our hope would be in vain. Christ is risen! May God protect you and your family and send you his bliss."

One of his daughters, a teacher, told about recent events at the music school where she works. "We have started a choir that is singing classical religious music. More and more people want to hear this and even to sing it. Right now we are singing many works by Saint John of Damascus and Easter music."

One of the priests, Father Vladimir, whose greying beard had enough room inside to give shelter to a hibernating bear, told the story of a Russian who, late in the nineteenth century, went to the West for his education, entered business, married a German woman, and built up a fortune. "Late in his life he became deeply restless. His wife understood that his unhappiness had to do with his homeland and convinced him to return to Russia for a visit. He finally agreed. When he had crossed the border his carriage had a minor accident —

the driver had to stop for repairs. The man went for a walk. It happened the path he followed brought him to a church. There was no service going on but the door was open. Inside an aged woman was praying in front of a respected icon. She cried. She groaned. Her prayer took the plank away from his eyes. He understood the emptiness in his life. It was crystal clear. He lost his blindness and fell in love with Orthodoxy. He brought his family to Russia and lived a faithful life, not seeking wealth but serving God and his neighbor. Finally he passed away in peace."

Late that afternoon, at the Church of the Exaltation of the Holy Cross, Father Vladimir blessed a small icon that Sergei had just purchased, a photo mounted on wood made by a local cooperative and sold for ten rubles in the city's main department store. Father Vladimir gave the icon the maximum benediction rather than the quick blessing I had anticipated. In his hearty voice, he sang and prayed for a quarter hour, finally splashing both the icon and ourselves with blessed water. Boris Feodorovich Detshiev of the Council for Religious Affairs, who witnessed the blessing, says Father Vladimir is deeply loved by local believers. I could well believe it.

It happened that a group of teachers was in the church at the same time, the Friday group I had heard about who come after school to better understand the Orthodox Church. Father Georgi, a young Ukrainian, was leading the informal discussion. "Christianity teaches tolerance and forgiveness," he said. "Impatience even about little things can do harm. If someone steps on your foot by accident and you get angry about it, soon everyone around you is snapping. The whole atmosphere is poisoned."

As we left the church, Boris Feodorovich made the comment that the headache he had had earlier in the day disappeared the moment he entered the sanctuary. "You can believe in God or not believe, but when your headache goes, you know it."

He recalled a story told in the magazine *Science and Religion*. The author asked an old woman in front of the church, "Why do you stand here so long? What does being here give you?" She said, "It gives me a sense of godliness."

"You know," he said, "*babushkas* don't waste words!"

Vilnius

The center of Orthodoxy in Vilnius — mainly a Catholic city — is the Holy Trinity Orthodox Cathedral in the heart of the old town.

The present church was built in the seventeenth century but stands where a church was first built in the fourteenth century. Two monastic communities, one for men, the other for women, have buildings on the same grounds: the Monastery of the Holy Spirit and the Convent of Saint Mary.

I had lunch with Bishop Antony Tcheremissov and Father Vasili Novinsky. Until Bishop Antony's consecration, he was at the Danilov Monastery in Moscow. "Vilnius is my native city," he said, "but I never expected to be its Orthodox bishop. This is my second week as bishop and you are my second foreign visitor. The last one was Cardinal [Jean-Marie] Lustiger from Paris who visited our monastery and took part in our Easter celebration. The next day I was his guest when he visited the seminary and other Catholic centers in Kaunas."

I asked Bishop Antony what were the local church's plans for the immediate future. "We are hoping to build a new church — but probably we will close another church, not because of pressure from the authorities but because the church in question isn't self-financing. There are too few Orthodox believers in that town."

Is it hard for Russians being a minority in Lithuania? "We are trying to do things to promote Russian culture, just as Lithuanians are promoting theirs. Within the Lithuanian Culture Union a Russian Cultural Center has been started — also a Polish Center. We are planning a Russian folk festival in connection with the Feast of the Holy Trinity. There will be the traditional decoration of birch trees. We will have Russian artists and circus performers. A choir is going to sing. It's a beginning."

He spoke at length about the church's responsibility to initiate charitable work. "Be merciful! This is a command of God. It is essential for all believers. The tradition of Christian charitable service is as old as the church but was prohibited by the Soviet government sixty years ago. A year ago it became possible to begin the revival of this tradition of mercy here in Lithuania. Following the example of the Russian Orthodox Church in Moscow, I want to encourage our local flock to take responsibility for works of mercy. There is a tremendous need. We have many people who are disabled, sick, lonely — people in need of love and help, who have no one close. There is a shortage of nurses in some places, but even where this is not the case, there are sick people who have no family nearby who are longing to hear a word of goodness. There is an urgent need for merciful actions. The need is not only material but spiritual, the need to illuminate souls. Believers should be in every hospital at least a few times a week and priests whenever they are needed. We don't

need a list of people to visit. It needn't be costly. We don't need to
bring luxurious food. It is enough to bring an apple or an orange.
The thing is to show our care, to open our soul to whomever we are
visiting. If we do that, those we visit will do it to us.

"The Danilov Monastery is a center for such activity in Moscow.
We formed a relationship with a hospital for the mentally ill. We sent
volunteers to visit patients there three or four times a week. Vladimir
Nicholaivich, the director of the hospital, told me, 'We have enough
hands but not enough good words.' He knows that not even the best
medicine can heal the sick. Many patients are in such a hospital
because their trust in human goodness was destroyed. If they are
ever to leave the hospital, it is essential that their trust in the power
of goodness is restored. Our volunteers were allowed to read from
the Bible or other holy books. In former times, something like this
couldn't be imagined. We couldn't dream of it! In such a hospital,
talk about religion was regarded as simply one more indication of
mental disorders. Now such talk is welcome. The director said that
our work there is a miracle.

"This is not only something good for patients in a hospital. I recall
two older women in Moscow, both very lonely, without any relations.
All they had was their small pension, just enough to maintain life.
They were losing interest in life. They felt abandoned. No one had
any need for them. When the chance came to visit the hospital, they
responded. Now they go to that hospital every day for seven or eight
hours. They are needed. They are doing something important in the
lives of these sick men and women. Patients meet them with tears in
their eyes. Life is converted into a new form for both the visitors and
those they visit. This is the kind of activity by Orthodox believers I
hope to encourage here in Lithuania."

"Last year," Father Vasili added, "we laid the foundation for relations with a residential school for children who for some reason can't
be with their parents — they were abandoned or their parents are
alcoholics unable to care for children. A number of Orthodox people came to the school at Christmas to bring presents. The children
put on a performance for us — it was lovely! Part of it was shown
on television. We had a lively discussion with the children, and the
teachers were pleased as well. It was of enormous importance for the
children. We have agreed that next the children will come for a visit
to the monastery so they can see how monks live."

"Now we have many invitations from schools, institutes interested
in arranging discussions about religion," Bishop Antony continued.
"In the past only atheists were permitted to teach religion. We are

asked to talk about the situation of the church, to give some historical information, to explain fundamentals of religious life. The invitations are still put in a rather ambiguous way with an eye on the law of 1929 and its restrictions. But what used to be impossible is now going on. We are on the way, even though it isn't clear what is going to be allowed under the new law. The hope we cherish is that the new law will not veto initiatives like this."

Do you expect the new law on religion to permit religious education in public schools? "No, but I hope it will be possible to invite religious people to speak in school. I assume regular religious education will be permitted only on church premises. I think we will have the right to set up schools for religious education."

"I hope we can have Sunday schools," said Father Vasili.

"But eventually," said Bishop Antony, "we should have the possibility of religious education in public schools — not compulsory but for students who want it."

Our conversation turned to the Bolshevik revolution and its consequences. "My impression is that the czarist government lost the wheel of power long before the Revolution," said Bishop Antony. "Many actions that should have been taken on behalf of the well-being of the people were not taken. The need for democracy was ignored. These things made the idea of revolution very sweet. Many followed with no idea what the actual results would be. At the beginning the Revolution seemed to live up to its promises. The first Decree of Lenin, the Decree of Peace, made people very enthusiastic. Then the notorious events followed. Now we have experienced the consequences and have to ask: What is the remedy?"

"While Stalin was alive," Father Vasili said, "there were still many people who didn't regret the Revolution. People believed in Stalin so much. Many prisoners wrote him letters, sure he wasn't to blame for what had happened to them. They believed that if he would read their letter, he would understand and correct the injustice. I know of people facing the firing squad whose last words were, 'Glory to Stalin.' Anyone could be blamed but not Stalin. And Stalin knew this. He encouraged the idea. Therefore the people accepted him. When he died, the whole nation was in grief. It is only little by little that we have come to understand what happened, and still there are those who cannot stand criticism of him."

"I was in the fourth grade at school," Sergei remembered. "The teacher was called out and then came back and we could see something was wrong. We were given the news. The teacher cried. We all cried. For days afterward we all wore black mourning bands."

"There is a story that the patriarch of the Georgian Church came to Moscow and was summoned by Stalin to come to his home, " said Bishop Antony. "When he arrived, Stalin asked, 'Who do you fear more, Stalin or God?' The patriarch said, 'God.' And Stalin said, 'No, it is me you fear, otherwise you would not have worn a civil suit when you came to see me.'"

I saw Bishop Antony again in the early evening at an annual Easter *panikhida* (requiem service) conducted in the cemetery. He greeted many people as he arrived, then spoke briefly from the front of the small cemetery chapel, the Church of Saint Efrosinya, to say how happy he was to be home again and to have become Bishop of Vilnius.

"Jesus taught us to live by the Gospel," he said, "to cherish goodness, peace, humility, and forgiveness. This is the way of life we should follow. He has given us the hope of being raised from the dead. Despite all of us being sinful, we can live in the hope of the Resurrection. As believing people, praying people, let us pray for those who have gone before us that they will enjoy eternal life. Let our Easter joy reach the dead."

Baku

From Catholic Lithuania, I flew 1500 miles southeast to Moslem Azerbaijan. Arriving in Baku at 3 A.M. on a warm May morning, I found myself in the middle of curfew. My passport and visa had to be shown at five military checkpoints between the airport and my hotel on the shore of the Caspian Sea. A fleet of tanks was parked next to the government building. Half a year before — November 1988 — the tanks had taken up positions blocking Baku's central plaza following a rally at which four hundred thousand Azeri demonstrators waved the purple and red national flag and applauded speeches denouncing the Armenian desire to separate the territory of Nagorno-Karabakh from Azerbaijani rule.

The Armenian church, Saint George the Enlightener, stands by a large plaza in central Baku. The pastor, Father Vartan Dilouyan, was the only Armenian priest still remaining in Baku. The stress of local ethnic tension was clearly visible in his face. I asked him about the tension between Armenians and Azeris.

"Until the tension in Nagorno-Karabakh, the climate was very favorable. If you had come here last year, you would have found a crowded church with a good choir. On holy days the church was completely filled. Now most of the young people have left. Mainly it is the old people still in the city. Now some people have returned from Armenia. They say they cannot imagine life without Baku. But there are others still leaving the city — they don't trust the future here. In my sermons I try to persuade people to stay. I express my hope that the situation will be normalized and friendly relations restored. Baku was always a place of welcome and safety for every sort of person. Azeris are by nature hospitable. Everyone was treated with respect."

Is there reason to be hopeful? "Having lived in Baku fifteen years, I know the Azeris very well and I am confident in the long run, but right now the prospects are gloomy. While the situation has eased, Armenians still living in Azerbaijan are terrified. The problem will remain this way until the issue of Nagorno-Karabakh is resolved. When the situation gets worse there, it immediately gets worse here. The government has taken measures to prevent attacks but there is no way that they can guarantee security."

What has happened to members of this church? "In December our church wasn't attacked, but many flats where Armenians lived were attacked by gangs of young people. The windows of my flat were smashed. Thanks to a neighbor, I was able to escape. Then soldiers came and drove the gang away."

What about the other clergy? "None were injured but they have now left the city. It is almost a miracle that none of them were killed. They are married and have families. I am a monk and so I have stayed."

What is happening with other Armenian churches in Azerbaijan? "In Kirovabad the church is now closed. The priest escaped, and no other priest is prepared to take his place. I know his feeling. I am living in my apartment again but I feel frightened."

Who are in these gangs and why do they attack Armenians? "They are just young people — fifteen, eighteen years old. I don't think it was their idea. Armenians never hurt them. Someone guided them. But who? We don't know. All we know is that young people are always used by older people to do their dirty work."

But what is provoking the older people behind the gangs? "There are fanatics on both sides. In Azerbaijan you find the idea that Armenians are trying to take what doesn't belong to us. There are Armenians who only use Nagorno-Karabakh. They don't really care about it. They have other plans. Their interest is only to stir up trouble between the two nations. When we had our terrible earthquake in Armenia last year, Gorbachev came and walked through the ruins. There he was among grieving people who had lost their dear ones and their homes. Yet in this moment when we should be putting all our energy into rebuilding, there were some shouting at Gorbachev about Nagorno-Karabakh. I was ashamed. It is a fragile situation in which even a small event can have tragic consequences when this idea exists. When Gorbachev visited the United States, some rich Armenians living there gave a present to Raisa Gorbachev. Here in Azerbaijan some people said, 'Look, those Armenians are bribing Gorbachev!' It is ridiculous, but there are those ready to believe it."

How can fanatical forms of nationalism be overcome? "The national issue is very delicate. In this instance, it means finding some solution for Nagorno-Karabakh acceptable to both peoples. When that happens, Armenians will be able to live in safety among Armenians again. The Armenians are not vengeful. At the forthcoming meeting in Moscow on the nationalities issue, perhaps they will make decisions that help us. If the central authorities aren't able to solve the problem, the problem will continue."

What solution do you hope for? "It makes no difference to me whether the territory of Nagorno-Karabakh is considered part of Azerbaijan or Armenia. The major point for me is simply that we should live in peace."

Assuming a solution is found, how long will it take to bring relations between Armenians and Azeris back to their former level? "If there are no more tragedies, fifty or sixty years. Not sooner. The younger generation is poisoned with enmity."

Orthodox Journalism

Metropolitan Pitirim directs the publishing department of the Moscow patriarchate and was one of the three Orthodox bishops elected to the Supreme Soviet. He also heads the diocese of Volokolamsk to the south of Moscow, teaches New Testament at the Moscow Theological Seminary, and is pastor of the Resurrection Church near the Kremlin. He is a friend of Raisa Gorbachev. Both are active in the Fund for Culture. With his massive snow-white beard, he is also one of the most photogenic Russian prelates.

On May 19, 1989, he launched his latest project, the *Church Messenger*, at a press conference in Moscow. A weekly newspaper operated by the Russian Orthodox Church, it is the first church-run newspaper for public sale (thirty kopeks a copy) rather than restricted distribution since the Revolution. A staff of ten had been hired.

The first issue included a report of the baptism of forty-eight children in a Moscow children's home where parishioners from Our Lady of Tikhvin Church are doing voluntary service. There was news of successful work in religious education being carried out by monks of the Danilov Monastery. While reporting that seventeen hundred churches and eighteen monasteries had been returned to the Russian Orthodox Church in the past eighteen months, the paper noted continuing resistance by officials in specific cases, such as the refusal of the Council for Religious Affairs to authorize the return of a cathedral in Saratov. Perhaps most surprising was an item about the picketing of Patriarch Pimen's office in Moscow by a group protesting the transfer of Bishop Vladimir from the diocese of Krasnodar to the diocese of Pskov. The picketers, all from Krasnodar, wanted him back.

The newspaper's print run — fifty thousand copies of the first issue done on the *Izvestia* press — is minuscule by Soviet standards. "Once the paper supply problems are solved," said Metropolitan Pitirim, "the *Messenger* will be printed in much larger numbers."

"I expect that the paper will be read not only by believers but by those indifferent to religion or interested but not committed," he said. "While the main focus of the *Church Messenger* will be religious news, we will also be considering important issues of cultural and social life such as environmental issues. We are concerned about care of natural resources. How can the destructive process be brought to a halt? This is a spiritual as well as a technical question. A healthy ecology depends on healthy *dukhovnost*. The spiritual person understands his responsibility for life."

Asked about future development of the publishing department, he responded, "We have big plans. We are reorganizing to increase our publishing capacity. This requires overcoming the paper shortage and solving problems regarding hard currency. We depend on help from our ecumenical partners. One project we have in mind is a multi-volume Bible ornamented with the old Slavonic script. We also plan books on the saints and works by Russian theologians like Pavel Florensky. Regarding the enlargement of our printing shop and bindery, we want to set up a collective. We are organizing a network of correspondents for the newspaper."

Metropolitan Pitirim announced that the Orthodox Church has requested return of the monastery at Volokolamsk, his own diocese south of Moscow, and awaits with optimism the response of the USSR Council of Ministers. "My hope is to celebrate the feast of Saint Joseph of Volokolamsk on the monastery territory September 22 [1989]. In time the monastery will provide the place for an International Orthodox Cultural Center where we can receive people who want to learn about Orthodox monasticism."

Meeting privately with Metropolitan Pitirim later in the day, I reminded him of Dickens's opening sentence in *A Tale of Two Cities*, "It was the best of times, it was the worst of times." I wondered in what ways this applied to the present situation in the USSR?

"It is the best of times in the sense that there is an awakening of the will of people to work for *perestroika*," he responded. "It is the awakening of a sense of initiative and responsibility, a sense of hope about what can be done. It is the best of times in the sense that the spiritual life of the people is much more in the open. But it is the worst of times in the sense that many people still don't have a clear idea of what to do and how to do it."

I asked about the consequences of *perestroika* for the church. "Formerly the separation of church and state was interpreted as the separation of the church from social life. But traditionally the church was deeply engaged in social life and charitable activities. Now you see the church becoming engaged in responding to many social needs. *Perestroika* has reawakened the life of the community. You see artists, writers, and scientists boldly discussing the history and role of the church. More and more you hear discussion about *dukhovnost*. You see what is happening with religious publishing. Religious concerts are becoming commonplace. There is a different social climate. There is also widespread public attention to the victims of purges. The church has established a commission to gather information about believers who perished in confinement. Everyone who died for their religious beliefs was a martyr. So for us it is not only a question of the rehabilitation of these victims but liturgical commemoration." He showed me the April issue of *Moscow Church Herald*, a colorful eight-page monthly publication of the Moscow patriarchate issued in Russian plus four other languages. On the first page there was an article on religious services at a ravine in the Kalitnikovskoye Cemetery in eastern Moscow where victims of Stalin's reprisals were secretly buried in the thirties.

I asked about the problem of anti-Semitism. Did the church have a responsibility to help combat hatred of the Jews? "The church has never taught or condoned anti-Semitism. The Jews are one of the nationalities. In the church itself we have many Jews and also Jewish priests. Outbreaks of anti-Semitism have resulted from domestic rather than religious factors, especially economic and social inequality. There are many instances of believers rising to protect Jews."

Was it not difficult to combine his many church responsibilities with being a member of the Supreme Soviet? "I am used to much work! I do not sleep more than five hours a night. Still, yes, it is difficult to find all the time."

My last question concerned his life story. "I was the eleventh child of my parents. It was a believing and praying family. My father was a priest as were several grandfathers and great-grandfathers. In the thirties my father was arrested. After three years he was released but he was very sick and soon died. I was fourteen years old when he was taken away. It was at the moment of his arrest that I remember deciding that, while I wanted to be a priest like my father, I would be a monk and have no children, and you see this is what happened. My secular schooling was at a technical institute. I think I can say that I was a lively young man and an active worker. I never joined the Young Pioneers or Komsomol, but I always was very involved with people. I had many friends. My fellow students used to say that it was hard to prepare for exams when I was around because I had a tendency to tell funny stories. But somehow we passed our exams and even got good marks. The conditions of life were very difficult. I know what poverty is. I am familiar with grief. These eyes have seen terrible things. Therefore it is my duty as both as a priest and deputy to do what I can to help people."

One of those questioning Metropolitan Pitirim at the press conference was Father Mark Smirnoff, an Orthodox priest. Since 1988 Father Mark has been on the editorial staff of *Moscow News*, a weekly newspaper that in the pre-Gorbachev years ran page after page of official fiction about Soviet well-being, never reporting human rights violations or official corruption and never noting religious events. Now it is one of the most outspoken voices of *glasnost*, respected for its coverage of human rights and controversial events. It regularly carries religious news including reports of the violation of the rights of religious communities. There are often profiles of believers.

Father Mark was also co-editor of *On the Road to Freedom of Conscience*, to be issued in Moscow in the fall of 1989 by Progress Publishers. "The book is news," he said. "There was a press conference announcing its publication yesterday. We have never had a book like this before. It is a kind of stage, a place for a public meeting on conscience and religion where you can hear all sorts of speakers, some with familiar names, some never before officially published. The authors come from a wide ecumenical spectrum — Orthodox, Old Believers, Catholic, and Protestant. Among them is Father Gleb Yakunin [the Russian Orthodox priest and former prisoner]."

I asked about the book's content. "One author, Father Alexander Men, provided an essay about the theological problem posed by the cult of personality. This is not just the cult of Stalin but the cult of the divinized ruler, a problem that goes back at least to the emperor cult in Roman times and that still remains with us in this country. Another author focuses on the problem of the Russian Orthodox Church normally being subservient to political rulers. A priest writes about the problems faced by believers outside the cities where the local authorities can be much more oppressive."

Has mass media attention to the church been reduced since the Millennium? "The amount of information was much bigger during the Millennium weeks, but that is understandable as many things were tied to the event. So it's true there is less in the mass media today than a year ago, but it is far from the nothing we used to have. It is clear that a social process is now under way that is laying the foundation for a new attitude regarding religion and the church. You see indications of this every day. At the same time you can see the left and right in high relief. The left wing of the mass media comes back to the topic of church and religious life again and again. You see examples of this in magazines like *Ogonyok* and *Novi Mir* and in television programs like 'Outlook' and 'Before and After Midnight.' Right-wing publications either ignore religious life or provide a platform for the rear guard to attack changes going on in regard to the church. One publication recently had an article on the 'ugly symbiosis' of the mass media cooperating with religious associations. Part of the right wing tries to combine patriotism and nostalgia for totalitarianism. They miss Stalin's purges. They like that kind of strict order."

Do you face obstacles in working as a journalist? "I am a stumbling block for both believers and atheists. Not only some atheists but also some believers object to a priest having such a job. I serve part-time at the Church of the Archangel Gabriel [near the Krasniye Vorota — Red Gates — Metro stop] but their view is that I should be doing pastoral work full time. They forget that Saint Paul supported himself making tents. There are Protestants who object to me reporting Protestant news and Orthodox who wish I would only give attention to Orthodox events. In addition there are problems for any journalist in this country who tries to cover religious news. I can tell you stories about priests and monks who would rather be interviewed by a reporter from *Time* magazine or any foreign publication than someone from the Soviet press. You can say whatever you like to a foreign journalist. No one here will read it. But what you say in the Soviet press is read here. The reader will compare your words with reality and know what is true and what isn't true. You have to be careful about what you say.

"I am an example of the kind of change occurring in the mass media because I am not only writing for *Moscow News* and doing reports on religion for Novosti [the state press agency], but I am appearing on television. Two years ago, I could have been charged with anti-Soviet propaganda and been sent to prison for saying privately what I can now say on television. It is amazing! Also I was the first cleric to be called by my religious title on television. It used to be that even bishops were addressed only by first name and patronymic. The 'program director asked me how I should be addressed. I told him, 'When you have a general, you call him General So-and-so. When you have a professor, you call him Professor So-and-so. Well, when you have a priest, you should call him Father.' He agreed. Now this practice is generally followed on Soviet television despite criticism from the old guard in the Communist party. What they really censure is people like me being on television at all. There was an article in the April issue of the publication of the Union of Journalists saying it was tolerable in these times to have a priest on television, but why call him *Father* Mark?"

How did you get into journalism? "By accident — a car accident. I was badly injured in 1978. For a long time I could work only while sitting. I couldn't stand at the altar. I became an archivist. For years I worked in Leningrad on the papers of Vladimir Solovyov. Now some of the material I discovered is being published — for example a Solovyov letter to Czar Nicholas II was published in *Novi Mir* earlier this year. When *perestroika* started in 1986–87, I was doing archival work at the Danilov Monastery here in Moscow. The chance came to do some writing about religious events for *Moscow News*, and that was my real starting point as a journalist."

Did you grow up as a Christian? "My parents were not believers, but they were sympathetic to my religious development. I was baptized soon after my birth in 1951 but had no religious education. I didn't take any interest in religion until I was a young man working at a factory, studying in evening school. The Komsomol [Young Communist] environment didn't satisfy me. It opened no doors of real knowledge. Everyday life aroused a protest in my soul. There was a vacuum, and it's not in the nature of life to accept a vacuum. One thing has to take the place of another. Those were long nights! I read the Russian classics in prerevolutionary editions — Tolstoy, Dostoyevsky, Gogol. I became aware of Solovyov.[7] Also I began to

---

[7]Vladimir Solovyov (1853–1900), friend and disciple of Dostoyevsky, worked to overcome division between the Catholic and Orthodox churches. One of his essays,

take an interest in religious art. I began to see myself as a believer. I was about twenty. I can't give an exact date that I realized I was a believer, but I had a feeling of providence, a surge of inspiration. Tolstoy had a deep impact. In time Dostoyevsky became more important to me. Finally I understood it is neither Tolstoy nor Dostoyevsky who provide the fundamentals of faith but the Gospels."

Was it a foregone conclusion that you would be Orthodox? "For some time it was not clear what kind of Christian I would become. I found attractive features not only in Orthodoxy but Catholicism and in Protestant churches too. The Catholic Church struck me as having a more modern outlook, and I still see it as offering a pattern for renewal in Orthodoxy and want to do my utmost to bring the two churches closer together, to help find a common language. I have many Catholic friends and knew the Catholic cardinal in Lithuania when he was still a bishop living in exile in a village on the frontier. Visiting Protestant churches in Leningrad, I was impressed by their way of preaching and praying. Preaching in the Orthodox Church is often very poor. On the other hand the climate of Protestantism seemed to me too severe, too bitter. The Orthodox Church was more familiar, the natural environment for a Russian intellectual. The Orthodox Church is in possession of basic cultural values. It is linked with our literature, our music, our art, our philosophy. It is a rich tradition, and wide. It has produced such saints as Sergei of Radonezh and Seraphim of Sarov. Orthodoxy is the source of Russian culture. The final choice of Orthodoxy was quite conscious. From that choice came the decision to apply for a place in the Leningrad seminary. For a time while studying I was secretary to Metropolitan Nikodim, who also had a profound ecumenical spirit. He had been the Russian Orthodox observer at the Second Vatican Council and knew both Pope John XXIII and Paul VI."

And then? "I went from the seminary into the Theological Academy where I wrote a study of Solovyov's ethics. After ordination I served in a parish on the outskirts of Leningrad, then came to the Holy Trinity Cathedral at the Alexander Nevsky Monastery, and from there went to a parish near the Finnish border. Then came my accident...."

I asked about the situation of the Eastern-rite Catholics in the Ukraine. "There is no structural change so far. The Uniate Church is still not legally recognized. There is progress in the sense that the

"Beauty, Sexuality, and Love," is included in *Ultimate Questions: An Anthology of Modern Russian Orthodox Thought*, ed. Alexander Schmemann (Crestwood, N.Y.: Saint Vladimir's Seminary Press, 1977), pp. 71–136.

Ukrainian Catholics are no longer pursued by the police — in other words the 'progress' of a husband who hasn't beaten his wife in recent days. It is an issue still in the control of the Ukrainian government, not Moscow. My guess is that significant change in the Ukraine will only occur when the present Ukrainian leadership is replaced."

He is deeply engaged in helping raise money for church charity work, an area of life from which believers used to be banned and which he also sees as the natural environment for ecumenism. "On May 16 we had a concert — 'Charity, Ecology, and Beauty' — at the Bolshoi Theater. Orthodox, Baptist, and Adventist choirs were the main attractions. Imagine such a thing in the Bolshoi! The concert will be repeated in several other cities."

The next day he took me to a Baptist concert to raise money for a school for deaf children. The recital was in the auditorium of the Moscow Institute for Civil Aviation in the Sokol district of northwest Moscow, the neighborhood of the school. Every seat was filled. In the lobby, people were lined up to buy a paperback edition of the New Testament at ten rubles a copy.

"Thanks be to God," said a Baptist pastor from the stage, "we live in a time when we can not only speak about charity but act on charity." He described the happiness of some handicapped children to whom wheelchairs had just been given. Various hymns were sung, including "If You Want to Know the Reason, It's Jesus," and "Were You There When They Crucified My Lord?" When the choir sang the Lord's Prayer, everyone in the audience stood up. An official from the Children's Fund thanked the musicians, a church orchestra from Finland, for their role in the concert. "You are helping to open a stream of charity and mercy that will flow into a river of goodness on behalf of children needing help."

Walking back to the Metro after the concert, I mentioned to Father Mark my impressions of a *Pamyat* member whom I had seen haranguing a crowd on Moscow's Arbat Street, a pedestrian boulevard in central Moscow where spontaneous debates occur in the spirit of Speakers' Corner at London's Hyde Park. Founded in 1980, *Pamyat* (remembrance) originally was a movement with the goal of saving monuments of Russian culture, but the last few years it has taken an anti-Semitic turn. The speaker on Arbat Street charged Jews with the creation of the police state, the annihilation of national identity, the subversion of culture, even the high rate of alcoholism and the Chernobyl disaster. Religious persecution in the thirties was blamed on the one Jew (the word means a nationality rather than a religion in the USSR) in Stalin's Politburo, Yamelyan Yaroslavsky, who headed the League of Militant Godless. In a television interview one *Pamyat* activist denied he was anti-Semitic: "I like the Jews, at least the ones who leave the country. Let them study Hebrew and go to Israel. It is only the ones who stay here that I don't like."

The anti-Semites are often Christians, said Father Mark. He recounted an exchange between a woman on the editorial staff of *Science and Religion* magazine, a boy of ten, and the boy's father, an Orthodox priest. It was clear to the editor from comments the boy made that he was anti-Semitic. She said to him, "Did you know that Jesus was a Jew?" The boy, shocked, turned to his father and said, "Is it true?" The father responded, "Jesus Christ is the second person of the Holy Trinity. You cannot speak of him belonging to any race." The editor then said to the boy, "Did you know that Mary, the mother of Jesus, was also a Jew?" Again the boy asked his father, "Is it true?" This time his father looked sad and answered only with reluctance. "Yes, unfortunately it is true."

I asked how anti-Jewish prejudice can be overcome. "In 1905, a year of pogroms in Kiev, many honest priests went out with the cross in hand, blocking the way of thugs and calling on the people not to participate. Sometimes the priests succeeded, sometimes they were victims themselves. All this was an indication of strong will and belief in goodness. If such things happened today in Moscow or Kiev, I don't think we would find many priests blocking the way. It isn't only that there are fewer priests or that the few priests we have are without conscience. But in 1905 the church had authority in society. Now it doesn't have such influence. Fewer people would stop and listen. Fewer would respect a priest. Even so, of course, the church has to take a lead and speak with authority on such matters."

To what extent is nationalism a factor among Russian Orthodox Christians? "You find two trends. There are those who prefer the church to remain independent and there are those with strong nationalistic views who would like the Russian Orthodox Church to become the official state church as it used to be. But the situation of the Orthodox Church before the Revolution was not one that benefited either church or society — in some ways it was even worse than after the Revolution when believers were treated like criminals. Before the abdication of the czar, the church was deprived of an independent role in influencing the life of the people. It was really a department of the government. One has to say that the church herself doesn't like to be separated from the state. Even in the time of Stalin there were bishops eager to glorify the tyrant, to describe him as a man sent by God. In an old issue of the *Journal of the Moscow*

Patriarchate you will find it said, 'Stalin is an ideal man, a pattern to be followed by everyone.' Even under those conditions, the church tried not to be separated from the state. This tendency has existed throughout Christian history and it exists now. When Khrushchev criticized Stalin, the church was silent. The reason — totalitarianism is imbued into the cells of our lives. We have had it for so long it is hard to imagine anything else."

Are there any indications of change? "Public criticism of Stalin by bishops occurs but is still exceptional. There was a two-hour film produced last year by the publishing department of the Moscow patriarchate that, in a section on church history, shows the destruction of churches, the burning of icons and the faces of some of the bishops and theologians, like Pavel Florensky, who were killed or died in prison camps. We begin to name the victims but are still hesitant to name the executioners. It is the patriarch that needs to do this, not Gleb Yakunin or Mark Smirnoff."

Attending the Sunday Liturgy at Moscow's Church of the Archangel Gabriel, I happened to meet Yuri Alexandrovich Aksyonov, an artist. He brought me to a nearby Indian restaurant, the Djaltarang, where some of the congregation gather for a late breakfast together every Sunday after the service. Over Easter cake, fried Indian bread, cherries, and coffee, they talked about restoration work they had been involved in at the Optina Pustyn, a monastery recently returned to the Orthodox Church. Vera Sidorenko, a young architect in the group, was searching for high-quality bricks to be used in the reconstruction of the monastery bell tower.

Two nights later I met some of them again at Yuri Alexandrovich's studio, a large basement room with an icon corner and many paintings and photographs revealing a passionate love of Orthodoxy. One painting was of Moscow's Savior Cathedral, blown up in 1931. Another was of a *staretz* at the Holy Trinity Monastery to whom many go for confession and spiritual direction.

Vera's husband, Yuri Leonidovich, turned out to be a conscientious objector. Luckily, his refusal of military service resulted in his becoming an outpatient at a Moscow psychiatric clinic rather than a prisoner, the fate of many others who have taken a similar stand.

"There is a stamp in my identity papers that I am under psychiatric care," he said. "This makes it hard to get a job and that causes financial problems. On the other hand I have more time for the things I really like to do."

One of those present at Yuri's studio was Irina Fedonova, a young woman directing the first children's church choir in Moscow. Formerly children were not allowed to sing in choirs, still less to have one of their own. Her choir had made its debut three weeks before, on Easter.

I had a long talk with Sergei Markus, an editor of a recently founded "informal" magazine, *Slovo* (Word). In 1984 Markus had been sentenced to a three-year term for "willingly spreading false-hoods" against the Soviet state and system. At the time he was a department head at Moscow's Kolomenskoye Museum where he organized a youth club that discussed ancient Russian culture. His early release from prison in 1986 was due to his issuing a public statement of regret for the contact he had maintained with Western journalists.

I asked if articles in *Slovo* touch on abuse of believers' rights. "One of our projects is to publish an article by Father Dimitri Dudko about his years in labor camps and prison."[8]

Markus spoke about the profound interest the marxist philosopher Ivan Timofeyevich Frolov takes in religion. "Frolov is one of the people whose ideas have most influenced Gorbachev. He was the other person with Gorbachev and Kharchev when Orthodox leaders were received in the Kremlin last year. He heads the Soviet Philosophical Society and does a monthly television program broadcast from Gorky House called 'Philosophically Speaking.' Metropolitan Pitirim is among those who have participated in this program. I think it is the first time a church leader has had such an opportunity to teach millions about the Christian vision. It's remarkable. I started reading Frolov while I was in prison. If you want to understand the connection between *perestroika* and religion, study Frolov. Read his book, *Perspectives of Man*. He is really the philosopher of *perestroika*. Kharchev may be replaced but Frolov will remain and

---

[8]Dimitri Dudko served more than eight years in labor camps for the possession of religious poetry. Ordained to the priesthood in 1960 and assigned to a church in Moscow, his sermons — often touching on taboo subjects — drew many into the church. He later began a series of Saturday evening catechetical dialogues (*besedy*) with those wishing to deepen their understanding of Christianity. No doubt bowing to government pressure, the Orthodox Church reassigned him to a parish fifty miles from Moscow. Nonetheless many Muscovites managed to go there for services. One of his controversial actions was to openly support the canonization of believers martyred by Communists, including Czar Nicholas II and members of his family. He was arrested in January 1980 by twelve KGB officers, all the religious literature in his home was confiscated, and he was taken to the infamous Lefortovo prison in Moscow where presumably he was subjected to intense pressures. He was released six months later after making a public statement regretting his "anti-Soviet slanders" and declaring that he had learned that "God's work is done meekly and quietly, patiently and humbly, not in the way I imagined." A collection of his dialogue sermons, *Our Hope*, has been published in the West (Crestwood, N.Y.: Saint Vladimir's Seminary Press, 1977).

he is far more important, someone very close to Gorbachev.[9] One of Frolov's main points is that marxism must be an open rather than a closed system. A dogmatic marxism can't know the real situation in the world. Marxists have to be constantly ready to revise their view in the light of reality. They must take seriously, for example, the work of Christian authors like Solovyov and Teilhard de Chardin."

I asked him his opinion of Kharchev. "Kharchev gave two good interviews to *Ogonyok* — brilliant. But at other times he says whatever comes into his mind without serious reflection. Though he was an ambassador before, a diplomat, at times he seems to lack diplomatic qualities. It was nonsense for the government to appoint him to head such a crucial ministry. He is someone new to religion and doesn't understand it. He is sometimes like Boris Yeltsin — popular but not deep. He has a tendency to make promises but then ignore them. An Orthodox bishop from the Ukraine asked him to help arrange the return of a cathedral. No problem, Kharchev said, it will be taken care of. But it wasn't taken care of. The local Council for Religious Affairs told the bishop once again, 'No problem — you can't have it.' You get the impression that Kharchev says what you want to hear but then forgets about it."

What about Orthodox response? "Metropolitan Pitirim criticized *Pamyat*. He supported the patriotic and cultural aspect but disagreed with their ideas on national struggle and their attitude toward Jews. He said that to believers there is neither Greek nor Jew but all are one in Jesus Christ."

What is the role of *Slovo?* "We see ourselves inside the church. We aren't dissidents. In *Slovo*, we don't want to criticize but to publish material we hope will be helpful to intellectuals who think the faithful are only *babushkas*. We are publishing writings from the church Fathers and articles introducing Orthodoxy. Father Vladimir Tumkoff wrote an article on the history of the church. Father Yuri Florovsky provided an essay on Holy Wisdom. We have published liturgical material about Father Amvrosi of the Optina Pustyn who was canonized last year. We published an article by Metropolitan Filaret of Minsk on religion and television. One author wrote about Rachmaninoff. Our general aim is to show that Orthodoxy isn't just something from the past but that our God is an eternal God. Believers are not people looking into the past but into the future. The future depends on our spiritual vitality. Without *dukhovnost* there can be no *perestroika*."

---

[9] On October 19, 1989, Frolov was appointed editor of *Pravda*.

Chapter 4

Old Believers

IN 1914, A GUIDE LED A SCHOLAR through the forests and swamps of northern Russia to the shore of a small lake. In log houses at the water's edge he found a community of Old Believers retaining ancient customs and traditions and still speaking the Russian language of the seventeenth century.[1] Nor were such remnants of old Russia entirely swept away by the Revolution. In the 1950s two Old Believer monasteries and four convents were discovered in the Siberian forest.[2] Other Old Believer communities disguised themselves as collective farms. Now, under the new conditions of Soviet life, Old Believer churches are being registered, but how many Old Believers there are, no one knows. Estimates start at two million. Some think there are five times that number.

Despite different theological convictions, the Old Believers have much in common with America's Amish. Both are witnesses to life as it was in an earlier time and to a faith refusing compromise with secularism. In their respective countries both are often admired, even envied, though few imagine taking the giant step away from modern life that joining them would require.

Old Believer origins go back to a reform movement during the reign of Patriarch Joseph (1642–52). Among those working to restore the purity of church service books were Nikon (then Metropolitan of Novgorod) and a married priest serving in Moscow, Avvakum. As a result of their work, new service books were printed in the 1640s.

---

[1]Francis House, "Non-Conformists in Pre-Revolutionary Russia," in *The Russian Phoenix* (London: SPCK, 1988), p. 45.

[2]John Lawrence, *A History of Russia*, 7th rev. ed. (New York: New American Library, 1978, seventh revised edition), pp. 133–34.

In 1652, following the wish of Czar Alexis, Nikon was elected patriarch of Moscow. In 1653 he ordered Russians to emulate Greek usage in all cases where Greek ritual differed from their own. Among the changes ordered, one in particular provoked a storm of protest and resistance: Nikon demanded that henceforth members of the Russian Orthodox Church must cross themselves with three fingers rather than two. To a people profoundly sensitive to symbols and gestures, this was a betrayal of a tradition handed down to them from the apostles. In 1666, the dispute became a schism.

"It was common in the past," Nicolas Zernov writes, "to see in this schism a proof of the ... backwardness of the Muscovites before their Westernization in the eighteenth century. The cause was said to be an obscure dispute about details of ritual, and the patriarch's opponents were stigmatized as narrow-minded fanatics who preferred to split the church rather than to consent to minor alterations. In reality there were serious political considerations which prompted the patriarch to start his campaign for the unification of the Muscovite and Greek and Ukrainian rituals and no less weighty reasons for repudiation of his reform.

"[At the time] Russians were the only independent nation among the Orthodox and they received urgent appeals for help both from the Christians suffering under the Turks and their kinsfolk oppressed by the Poles in the Ukraine.... The Russian government, now planning a campaign for the liberation of Eastern Christians, ... required unity and concord among all Orthodox.... For the sake of this mission they were ready to sacrifice the beloved customs of Moscow Orthodoxy.... [The patriarch's opponents] were convinced that the Greeks and Ukrainians, deprived of political freedom and obliged to train their clergy in Roman Catholic and Protestant seminaries, no longer preserved the authentic tradition. Recent research has preserved the Old Believers' assertion."[3]

Among those who sought to convince the patriarch that the Greeks had been less careful than the Russians in preserving tradition was Archpriest Avvakum. Unfortunately opposition only hardened Nikon's resolve. He successfully called upon the czar to enforce his rulings. Avvakum responded by declaring Patriarch Nikon and his followers, including the czar, apostates. Those who clung to the old ways were ruthlessly persecuted. Many were tortured and martyred.

"What can be done about it?" Avvakum wrote. "Let them all

---

[3]Nicolas Zernov, *Eastern Orthodoxy* (London: Weidenfeld and Nicolson, 1961), pp. 145–46.

suffer bitterly for Christ's sake. So be it, with God's help. It is fitting
to suffer for the Christian faith. This archpriest formerly enjoyed
discourse with the great, and now, poor wretch, let him delight in
suffering to the end. For it has been written: Blessed is not he who
begins but he who perseveres to the end."[4] After many years of exile
in the Siberian wilderness and fifteen years in a subterranean prison,
Avvakum was burned.

Old Believers sought refuge in remote places — the Arctic north
and the Siberian forests — or outside Russia. Today Old Believers
are found in Lithuania, Latvia, Poland, Germany, Argentina, Brazil,
New Zealand, Canada, and the United States.

In Russia the initial persecution of Old Believers gradually eased,
and many of them became prosperous. In 1791, Old Believers were
permitted to build a church near Moscow. After the Revolution in
1917, persecution resumed.

Lithuania

In Vilnius I met Ivan Isayevich Egorov, chairman of the Supreme
Council of Christian Old Believers in Lithuania. He looked remarkably like Leo Tolstoy. I asked him how Old Believers had come to the
Baltic region. "In the first years of persecution those who could not
withstand torture either sought refuge in the wilderness or escaped
the country. You find Old Believers here, in Latvia, in Poland, in
Germany and other European countries — even in Turkey and across
the ocean. The Lithuanians accepted us warmly. Our first Lithuanian
parish was founded in 1710. It is still alive. We came to Vilnius in
1830. At present we have fifty communities in this territory."

What sort of government does the church have? "We are very
democratic. Democracy is nothing new for us. We have a council
so that when a decision has to be made, we can hear all voices. The
council serves our material needs. Council members include pastors
and delegates from all parishes. The council publishes church literature and our calendar, makes arrangements for candles and prayer
and music books."

Will the schism ever end? "I believe it will. We have friendly relations with the Orthodox Church. A big step toward reconciliation
was taken by the Russian Orthodox Church at its council in 1971

---

[4] The full text of Avvakum's engaging autobiography is included in *Medieval Russia's
Epics, Chronicles and Tales* (New York: E. P. Dutton, 1974), pp. 399–448.

when anathemas proclaimed against Old Believers in 1666 were with-drawn. It was recognized that Old Believers are going on the right way and that traditions we have preserved are correct. There have been articles on this subject in the *Journal of the Moscow Patriarchate*. Metropolitan Pitirim has published books for us and these have had the blessing of Patriarch Pimen. Several Old Believers were guests at the council last June at the Holy Trinity Monastery. The council called for collaboration between our churches. Our council the fol-lowing month sent a positive response. A dialogue is coming and we look forward to it. We see the Russian Orthodox Church changing for the better. We are moving toward each other. Old Believers have preserved the rules, tradition and faith unchanged and this is now valued. There is more friendship and understanding."

Does this mean Old Believers are changing? "We will stick to our ways. We are obstinate still."

Is *perestroika* having any impact on life for Old Believers? "We are not being persecuted. We feel more at ease. We can register our churches without difficulty. Recently we were received by the Lithuanian Council of Ministers where we put forward our requests. We have opened two churches. In Dukstas we received an abandoned Orthodox Church. In Utena we were allowed to build a new church. We will have another church in Silute — the local authorities have promised us a building. To better train our pastors, we hope to open a seminary in Riga. We have large communities there — about twenty-five thousand believers. At present all our education takes place little by little within the church, which means it is only old people who fully know the rites, the traditions, the music. But there are more and more young believers with a higher education. Some are ready to attend a seminary. Also we plan to start a magazine that we will call *The City of Kitezh*. This comes from our legend of a holy city, Kitezh, miraculously preserved under the waters of the Svetloyar Lake [two hundred kilometers northeast of Gorky]. In Kitezh the old way of life and worship has continued without pause. Occasionally the city rises from the water and appears to the devout."

Are young people attracted to become Old Believers? "In my parish we have three hundred young people. This speaks for itself."

What happened to Old Believers in Stalin's time? "It was the same for us as for others. Many thousands of Lithuanians were sent to Siberia. About ten Lithuanian Old Believer pastors were exiled. Several of them perished, some managed to come back. It was a difficult time."

He urged me to visit the Old Believers in Moscow. "They have a similar tradition, only more monastic. Now we have a Metropolitan, Alimpy, whose office is there. And you will see a beautiful church and belfry. In the thirties the authorities wanted to destroy it. The bishop said they must shoot him first. Stalin received him personally and asked him what he wanted. The bishop said, 'Don't destroy our church; it is a historic structure.' Stalin said, 'I know your church. When I look from the Kremlin, I see it has the tallest belfry. Let it remain.'"

Moscow

The Old Believers' Pokrovsky (Protection of the Mother of God) Cathedral, built in 1791, is next to the Rogozhski Cemetery in the east of Moscow. Only one Russian church is larger, the Cathedral of the Holy Trinity in Leningrad. The church is often filled to capacity — up to ten thousand — but my visit was on a weekday morning when the worshippers were few and elderly.

Inside the air smelled of linseed oil. On the far side of the church, scaffolding supported artisans restoring the dark ceiling. The church's amber floor was covered with wide wooden boards like a ship's deck. The absence of gold and silver gave the church a gentle and yet austere character. The cathedral walls were lined with icons — twenty-five hundred, I later discovered, some dating from the thirteenth century. The dominant colors were cream, golden yellow, dark red, and many shades of brown and green.

Stepping outside the church, I was welcomed by Romil Khrustalev, chairman of the church council and assistant to Metropolitan Alimpy of Moscow and All Russia, Primate of the Russian Old Rite Orthodox Church. He had a long thick beard just beginning to grey.

We had hardly introduced ourselves when an official from the Council for Religious Affairs happened to arrive by car, delivering some freshly printed posters showing Moscow's Church of the Savior as it looked before its destruction in 1931. A campaign for its reconstruction was under way in Moscow. As the official approached, Romil gave him the Easter greeting, "Christ is risen." "Truly he is risen," the visitor responded.

Not waiting for me to ask questions, Khrustalev had questions for me: "Are you a believer? What church? Do you come from a family of believers?" And then a question that I have thought about often since it was asked: "Are you sensitive to symbols?" I said I was or I wouldn't be Orthodox, but I pressed him to explain why he had asked.

"Our faith is tied to sacred symbols," he said. "We don't make a dramatic Protestant difference between 'important' and 'non-important.' Everything that was sanctified by apostolic tradition is preserved by the Old Believers. This is why we Old Believers cross ourselves in the same way that it was done at the time of the baptism of Rus' a thousand years ago, a tradition we are confident goes back to the Apostolic times.

"To many people this seems a trivial detail. What does it matter whether you join two fingers or three when you cross yourself? But if you are sensitive to symbols, then the older way is significant because these two fingers represent the dual nature of Christ, God and Man. It means Christ suffered as a human being but as God he didn't suffer. As Holy Father Kyrill of Jerusalem said, 'Don't be embarrassed to identify yourself with Christ.' When we cross ourselves, we identify ourselves with the crucified Christ. Every gesture has profound meaning. As we make the sign of the cross [touching his forehead], we recall that the Second Person of the Holy Trinity, Christ the Logos, incarnated in the body of Mary [touching the upper belly], who sits at the right hand of the Father [touching the right shoulder], saving us from those on the left side [touching the left shoulder] — the heretics and sinners. And then you bow.

"These actions symbolize the essence of Christian faith. Even an illiterate Russian who made this sign was worshipping in the Orthodox way. Orthodoxy means the right way to pray. But in the time of Patriarch Nikon, the symbol was changed. The three fingers are said to represent the Holy Trinity. It is as if the Trinity was crucified. The change was theological nonsense. Patriarch Nikon rejected the old way. It was the major point in the controversy. It was only in 1971 that the patriarchal church withdrew the anathemas against us that were proclaimed three hundred years earlier. At the same time the ban of the two-finger sign of the cross was withdrawn. They recognized its equal significance."

I asked if there were other differences. "We believe that only full immersion is valid in baptism. We preserve the old style in icon painting — we don't accept the westernized school. We preserve the monophonic method of church chant and also we still use hooked musical notation — we are the only ones to preserve these customs."

What about splits among Old Believers? "There are three main branches. The largest, centered here, is the Russian Old Rite Orthodox Church, the name adopted at our 1988 council. Before that we were called the Church of Old Believers of the Belo-Krinitsa Hierarchy. We unite most of the Old Believers who recognize the priesthood. We have about 150 registered parishes throughout the country. [At least as many nonregistered churches exist.] In 1963, before Khrushchev's purges, there were 250 parishes. [He made an axe stroke motion with his hand.] In Moscow alone, before the October Revolution, there were forty churches of Old Believers. Today there are six. Now the process of the revival of our parishes is under way. In the last three years, about ten parishes have opened. We expect another thirty or forty in the next few years.

"Then there is the Christian Old Believers of the Pomorye Communion, sometimes called the *Bezpopovtsy* Church [the Church Without Priests]. This came about a generation after the Great Schism when the priests of the early years died out. There was no bishop to ordain new ones. The believers accepted it as God's will that they had no priests. Their one sacrament is baptism. They are mainly in the Baltic region but also in Siberia and the far east.

"A third branch, the *Beglopopovtsy* [fugitive priests], also recognizes priests and has a normal sacramental life. It has an independent hierarchy organized in 1923."

What about relations with the Russian Orthodox Church? "The reformed [Russian Orthodox] Church does not recognize our hierarchy as valid, but part of the clergy respects us — for example, Metropolitan Pitirim. He knows that to revive what was lost it is necessary to have a spiritual environment. He is a great lover of the traditions of the early Russian Orthodox Church, traditions either ignored or forgotten, and so he has a deep respect for Old Believers. He is doing a lot to revive the old way of singing. Our publishing departments cooperate."

What sort of publishing? "Before the change we could publish very little. Now we can do a lot — in fact we are unable to fully meet the opportunity because we haven't a large enough staff or facilities. We are publishing service books and starting a journal called *The Church*. We are preparing our theological history. We have issued a record of our music."

We had lunch — black bread, pickled mushrooms, and herring — in a plain room. The decoration included a painting of one of the most prominent opponents of Patriarch Nikon, the Boyarynia Morozova. While being dragged away in chains, she defiantly raises her chained hand in a gesture of adherence to tradition: the index and middle finger raised in the manner of Old Believers. Some of the bystanders regard her with derision. Others see her as a saint. Another painting shows an earlier moment when she was visiting the imprisoned Archpriest Avvakum.

"Since the time of Nikon, we had a hard time," said Romil. "In the early years many were tortured, maimed, and executed. Finally we were tolerated but we knew much suffering right into the time of Soviet power — strange when you think that we were persecuted by the czars! You would think we might have been regarded more kindly by those who pulled down the czarist system."

What is behind such persecution? "Many people think Russian totalitarianism began with Stalin, but I believe it has its roots in Patriarch Nikon's reforms. The portion of the people who preferred to go on the road to democracy joined the Old Believers. You know the parable of the Grand Inquisitor in Dostoyevsky's *Brothers Karamazov*, the dialogue about freedom. Old Believers preferred freedom to prestige and security. In terms of this parable, we took Christ's side, not the Inquisitor's. The civil service had to take the government's side. [He gestured a salute.] They had to follow orders. These were the nobility — today's *apparat* — the administrative apparatus that does what it is told and says what it is supposed to say and believes what it is required to believe. The old faith survived mainly among those not directly dependent on the government — merchants, farmers, cossacks. These sections of the population were mercilessly persecuted — imprisoned, tortured, burned. It happened again in the years of Soviet power. During the worst years the fact of being an Old Believer was enough to lead to imprisonment. If you were a priest, it was a death sentence.

"This notorious tradition of ruthless repression goes back to Patriarch Nikon. However much our Peter the Great, Alexander I, Nicholas II, and Stalin differ from each other, they were all totalitarians. But it isn't only the state rulers we should consider. The Orthodox priests like to say that the purges began under Stalin. They don't like to remember that the Orthodox Church persecuted the Old Believers. The very fact that the government now desperately seeks to inspire the creative soul of the people has a mysterious connection with the faith of Old Believers. Old Believers have never followed the official line. An Old Believer has always been independent and therefore someone disliked by officialdom. On the other hand the official church has always served the rulers."

But the Orthodox were also ruthlessly persecuted under Stalin. "Yes, they have their martyrs and their history of suffering. But when Stalin made his peace with them, their bishops praised Stalin and they rode in sedans with white tires. We did not praise him and we got no sedans. The Church of Old Believers has a history of true Russian freedom. This refusal to bend to state power was the major reason for the elimination of whole segments of the population — the very portion of the population we are now called upon to restore! As a result of repression the Old Believers' Church today has lost its foundation within the population."

Do you find many converts? "Many people who are now finding their way into the Orthodox Church don't see the difference between the two churches except they know it is easier to be in the patriarchal church. To know and understand the difference between the two churches requires a major effort of mind and intellect. It requires study. But even if you are willing to study, what do you read? There is nothing in the library, nothing in the book store. This is the context of the present crisis for Old Believers. Nonetheless there are those who are drawn to us, but it isn't easy for them to enter because there are many strict rules in our church."

For example? "Beards. God has given beards to men — we should not cut them off. Some object. Perhaps his wife disapproves. Perhaps he thinks he will look older or that people will make fun of him. But until he is willing to let his beard grow we do not accept him for communion. Also he can be refused the burial service. These strict rules are the canonical traditions we have received from the ancient church and which we maintain and live by. There are many whose way of life makes it difficult. There are those who come to our church who cannot be completely accepted because their civil life is so at odds with the church. So, apart from the factor of repression, you can understand why our church isn't large. On the other hand, it is a miracle that it survived at all! The church you visited today was built just after a period of severe repression. But since that time it was not closed even one day. Nor was it damaged by the Moscow fire that drove Napoleon back to France. In that time this was a settlement outside of Moscow, Rogozhskoye."

And what about the Soviet period? "Neither was the church closed in the time of Stalin. Once in the thirties they tried to turn it into a youth club, but the believers stayed inside and refused to leave. They remained day and night, praying to God, until the authorities changed their mind. In that period we had only one priest serving here. This church has been here three hard centuries, and it has been a place of prayer every day and everything inside has survived. In the Stalin time they damaged the bell tower and the Church of the Dormition in its base [the tower stands near church], but even here there is a kind of miracle because it was their intention to destroy the tower. They put dynamite charges around the base and these were exploded, but the tower, although cracked, withstood the blast. It was built in 1913, and built with care, not the kind of building that is done today. So they made the church into a storeroom and painted over the icons. But much survived under the paint. We are in the last stages of restoring the icons. At that time they also closed our Cathedral of the Nativity of Christ. It was a place with the most wonderful acoustics. Now the state has taken responsibility and has started restoration work. We anticipate its return."

If Old Believers were so persecuted, how was it possible for the cathedral to be built in 1791? "Despite the persecution, large numbers wouldn't submit. Also a large part of Russian capital was controlled by Old Believers. They were a major force in society. It was recognized that toleration was better than persecution. In the last century, it is estimated that 40 percent of Russian capital was in the hands of Old Believers."

Is there appreciation of Old Believers in the wider society? "The poet Alexander Blok and some other writers have shown an interest. But I think the writer who best understands the truth about Old Believers is Alexander Solzhenitsyn. In his 'Letter from America' written in 1975, he wrote, 'It may seem strange that, in order to prepare for the twenty-first century, we must first repent for our great sin committed in the seventeenth century. But the greatness or smallness of our sin is not due to its antiquity or the number of surviving victims but because of the extent and meaning of the crime committed. No one can deny that a crime was committed. Isn't it up to Christians to prove that without repentance, life is not possible? Without repentance there can be no movement toward the light. But the mystical meaning of repentance for a three-hundred-year-old sin is difficult to predict. It extends beyond church politics and practice. It may even open another direction in the history of our country....'[5]

---

[5]Romil quoted Solzhenitsyn from memory but when I checked my notes against the text, I found he had it nearly verbatim. In Solzhenitsyn's essay "Repentance and Self-Limitation," there is a related passage: "But with the soulless reforms of Nikon and Peter the Great began the extirpation and suppression of the Russian national spirit, and our capacity for repentance began to dry up. The monstrous punishment of the Old Believers — the burnings at the stake, the red-hot pincers, the impalements on meat hooks, the dungeons — followed for two and a half centuries by the senseless repression of twelve million meek and defenseless fellow-countrymen, and their dispersal to the most uninhabitable regions of the country or even expulsion from the country — all this is a sin for which the established church has never proclaimed its repentance. This is bound to weigh heavily on the whole future of Russia" (*From under the Rubble*, trans. Michael Scammell [Boston: Little, Brown & Co., 1975.])

"What Solzhenitsyn insists is that, if the people remain blind to Old Believers and what was done against us, then the shadow of that great sin will continue to enlarge. It was the starting point for the death of Russia."

Chapter 5

The Catholic Church

Eastern-Rite Ukrainian Catholics

The ecumenical movement in the USSR has mainly occurred either at the very top or in prisons and labor camps where believers from different confessions found themselves suffering side by side. In general each community of believers has done its best to ignore the others, always remembering the sins committed against its ancestors by the ancestors of those in other churches and religions. Moslems still remember the slaughter done by Crusaders when they captured Jerusalem in 1099. Orthodox recall with bitterness the sacking of Constantinople in 1203 by Catholic Crusaders and the plundering of churches that followed. Nor is it forgotten that, with the fall of Kiev at Tatar hands, Catholic warriors attacked the Orthodox in the name of the pope. Poland's King Kasimir regarded his campaign to take Orthodox Galicia, once part of Kievan Rus', as a holy crusade. In the fourteenth century much of the area now composing the Ukraine came under Polish rule. A long and often bitter struggle ensued to bring the Orthodox into the Catholic Church.

In 1596, at the Union of Brest Litovsk, a number of Orthodox bishops, including the Metropolitan of Kiev, linked themselves with Rome rather than Moscow. Rome permitted the Uniates, as they were called, to retain the Eastern-rite Liturgy, use of the Slavonic language in church, and the married clergy.

Beginning in the seventeenth century a process of Russian-Ukrainian union began that led to the return of the Metropolitan of Kiev to the Russian Orthodox Church. But in the western territory, still under Polish rule, the Uniates became deeply rooted.

108

The western Ukraine, with its Uniate Catholic population, was annexed by the Soviet Union in September 1939. Large numbers of believers suffered in the first brief period of Soviet rule, experienced new cruelties under the German occupation that began in the spring of 1941, and endured additional waves of persecution when the Red Army regained the territory in 1944.

In 1946 the Ukrainian Catholic Church was merged with the Russian Orthodox Church at the Council of Lvov. In the view of the Russian Orthodox Church it was an action fulfilling Jesus' teaching that "all may be one."[1]

From the Ukrainian Catholic point of view, the Council of Lvov was no council and there was no reconciliation. Shortly before it met, all their bishops had been imprisoned, charged with collaborating with the Germans despite numerous actions of resistance to the Nazis and the hiding of many Jews. Many priests and believers refused to accept the merger. They were regarded by the state authorities as members of an illegal church, and a period of intense repression followed that resulted in the closing of hundreds of churches, mass arrests, and the creation of a Catacomb Church. Not all priests and believers openly resisted. Many superficially conformed, seeing it as the only way to survive.

During the two periods of Communist rule, Uniates report, ten bishops, fourteen hundred priests, eight hundred nuns and thousands of lay people perished, and many thousands more endured a nightmarish life in labor camps. The most prominent prisoner was Archbishop Joseph Slipyj, head of the Lvov diocese, the only bishop sent to the camps who came out alive. "I had to suffer imprisonment by night, secret court rooms, endless interrogations and spying upon me, moral and physical mistreatment and humiliation, torture and enforced starvation," he later wrote. "As a prisoner for the sake of Christ I found strength throughout my own Way of the Cross in the realization that my spiritual flock, my own native Ukrainian people, all the bishops, priests, and faithful were walking beside me on the same path. I was not alone." Witnesses recall him wearing rags and his feet in bandages while at a camp at Inta, near the Arctic Circle. "Made to march in deep snow at dead of night," recalls a fellow prisoner, "he collapsed. A guard forced him up with his rifle butt. Again he fell and could not rise even under the guard's brutality."

In the time of Pope John XXIII, he was allowed to leave the So-

---

[1] *The Lvov Church Council: Documents and Materials, 1946–1981* (Moscow: Publishing Department of the Moscow Patriarchate, 1983), p. 9.

viet Union. In 1963 he arrived in Rome, limping from frostbite. Consecrated a cardinal by Pope Paul VI in 1965, he died in Rome in 1984. During his years in Rome he founded the Ukrainian Catholic University and built the Cathedral of Saint Sophia on the Via Bocca.

During the Millennium celebration in Kiev in 1988, I spoke with an Orthodox priest who shares his apartment with an underground Catholic priest. He said that four or five million Ukrainians are Eastern-rite Catholics. There are eight Uniate bishops and more than two thousand priests. He estimated that 5 percent of the clergy have a "double obedience" — when the Orthodox bishop tells one of these priests to move, he cannot do it until he gets permission from the Catholic bishop, and vice versa.

I asked how the Uniate and Orthodox Liturgy differed. Only in details, he said. Uniates use the Orthodox ritual but pray for Pope John Paul II rather than Patriarch Pimen. "The big difference is not liturgical but political and cultural. Part of the glue is strong Ukrainian nationalism."

The priest praised Metropolitan Filaret for moving slowly at the parish level. When an old priest of Uniate loyalties dies, he said, the Metropolitan replaces him with an Orthodox pastor. The new pastor introduces changes slowly and carefully, explaining them one by one so that the congregation can move together.

A Catholic Ukrainian, however, strongly disagreed. "Uniate sentiment is strong," he said, "and our resolve is growing. There is irritation with Metropolitan Filaret for not accepting the Ukrainian Catholic Church and regarding it only as a political and nationalistic movement, though it's true we won't make the kinds of compromises the Russian Orthodox Church has made with the government. The result is that we are the largest illegal religious body within the Soviet Union. While there are no more deportations, we are still paying the price of following our conscience."[2]

In the months following the Millennium, Uniate priests began

---

[2] Also to be noted is the independent Ukrainian Autocephalous Orthodox Church. Nearly destroyed by repression, it began to emerge from the underground in 1989. On August 14 the Church of Saints Peter and Paul in Lvov broke away from the Russian Orthodox Church, calling on Patriarch Demetrios in Istanbul to take the parish under his protection. The Lvov Council for Religious Affairs rejected the application by the church for registration and warned that the church building would be closed if the congregation did not return to the Russian Orthodox Church. The priests were warned that they were breaking the law if they officiated at a Liturgy in the church. The CRA tried to seize the church but was stopped by a picket line surrounding the building organized by the Ukrainian Popular Front and the Ukrainian Helsinki Union. In September two congregations in villages of the western Ukraine declared their adherence to the Ukrainian Autocephalous Orthodox Church (Keston News Service, nos. 333 and 335).

emerging from the underground, and in 1989 the Ukrainian Catholic Church began a vigorous campaign for legal recognition.

In May 1989 Metropolitan Volodymyr Sterniuk, the Catholic archbishop of Lvov, received Father Mykhailo Nyzkohuz, formerly a priest of the Russian Orthodox Church, into the Ukrainian Catholic Church. The following day his parishioners in the village of Stara Syl took the same step. A week later government representatives, accompanied by eighteen Orthodox priests, came to the village in an effort to obtain the church keys and expel Father Nyzkohuz. An estimated fifteen hundred faithful blocked their way and retained the church.

On May 16 several Catholic bishops began a hunger strike in Moscow after failing to meet with a member of the Presidium of the Supreme Soviet. Three days after the hunger strike began, they were received by Yuri Khrystoradnov, head of the Council of the Supreme Soviet, who told them that the problem had to be "resolved with the authorities in the Ukraine and that the Russian Orthodox Church was a roadblock in the legalization of the Ukrainian Catholic Church."

On May 24 other Ukrainians began a rotating fast in front of the offices of the Council for Religious Affairs and on Moscow's Arbat Street. Four days later, at the Dynamo Stadium in the Ukraine, 8000 people participated in a rally for the church's legalization. On June 18 an estimated 150,000 Ukrainian Catholics participated in public services in many towns and villages of the western Ukraine. Bishop Pavlo Vasylyk and four priests who were to have presided in Ivano-Frankivsk were detained by militia but a fifth priest, Father Mykola Simkailo, managed to be present and led the service, which an estimated 100,000 people attended. Father Simkailo was later charged with disturbing public order. On the same day uniformed and plainclothes police attacked and beat several participants who were attending a service on Vladimir Hill in Kiev.

In a statement addressed to the Congress of Peoples' Deputies in Moscow, Ukrainian Catholics said that so far they had been left untouched by changes going on in the USSR: "The years of *perestroika* and the accompanying liberalization in Soviet society have not affected the Ukrainian Catholic Church and its believers. With the emergence of a section of the clergy from the underground, the repression has increased, especially in the last year." Clergy had been subjected to arrests and fines as well as "slanderous attacks" from both state officials and clergy of the Russian Orthodox Church. "When the tens of thousands of believers turned to the USSR Supreme Soviet" to demand recognition of their church "the authorities began to transfer Ukrainian Catholic churches to the Russian Orthodox Church."

"Dear Deputies, freedom of worship in one's chosen religion is a fundamental human right recognized in all basic international acts and by Article 52 of the USSR constitution. But believers of the Ukrainian Catholic Church are deprived of this right." They called on the deputies to rehabilitate both the Ukrainian Catholic Church and the Autocephalous Orthodox Church, recognizing them as victims of Stalin, to return churches and church property to their rightful owners, to recognize as a criminal act the persecution of believers, and to appoint a commission "to formulate new laws on religion in accordance with international legal norms."

Unable to ignore sign-carrying demonstrators on the streets, the party first secretary from Ivano-Frankivsk spoke at the July meeting of the Central Committee of the Communist party about the "reactionary essence of the Uniate movement," which he said was nothing more than "a cover for nationalism." (In late September, Vladimir Scherbitsky, the first secretary of the Ukrainian Communist party, a strong opponent of *perestroika* and no friend of the Ukrainian Catholic Church, was forced out of the Central Committee.)

From late July, twenty-eight Ukrainian Catholics stood with signs outside the Moscow hotel where the World Council of Churches' Central Committee was meeting. When not in conversation with participants in the WCC meeting, the Ukrainians sang hymns and prayed the rosary.

On September 17, 150,000 people participated in a two-hour outdoor Mass in Lvov before marching to the square in front of the Cathedral of Saint George, a church turned over to the Russian Orthodox Church in 1946. The text of a telegram to Gorbachev was read aloud calling on him to legalize the Ukrainian Catholic Church. Similar public services were announced for October by Ivan Hel, head of the Committee for the Defense of the Ukrainian Catholic Church. After darkness fell, city residents turned off their lights and put candles in the windows to commemorate the millions of victims of Stalinism and Soviet rule.

One of the members of the Russian Orthodox Church who joined in the campaign for recognition of the Ukrainian Catholic Church was Alexander Ogorodnikov.[3] He had been at a labor camp in the

─────────────────

[3]Ogorodnikov founded the Christian Seminar in Moscow in 1974. The seminar brought together young intellectuals recently converted to Orthodoxy who wanted to discuss their newfound faith, build up a Christian fellowship, and carry out missionary work. Expelled from academic institutions, they were forced to take menial jobs. Ogorodnikov was arrested in 1978, charged with "parasitism" (not being gainfully employed) and was sentenced to a year in a labor camp. Just before his release a

Perm region with Stepan Khmara, a Ukrainian Catholic arrested for publishing an underground newspaper. "It was really a death camp," said Ogorodnikov. "There were prisoners who starved to death. We were shut in punishment cells without heat, warm clothes, light, or space to move." Stepan Khmara, he said, was frequently sent to such a cell for praying on his knees. Ogorodnikov was similarly punished for his efforts to obtain a Bible.

"I believe," he said, "that the fate of the Ukrainian Catholic Church depends on how boldly the Russian Orthodox hierarchy asserts itself and its readiness to repent of its past sins against this community of fellow believers."

While in Rome December 1, Gorbachev met for more than an hour with Pope John Paul II. Gorbachev assured the pontiff that the forthcoming passage of the new law on freedom of conscience would assure Catholics the "right to satisfy their spiritual needs." The two leaders agreed to establish diplomatic ties between the Vatican and Moscow, and the pope expressed his readiness to visit the USSR if "developments in the Soviet Union would enable him to accept" Gorbachev's invitation. In Kiev, Nokolai Kolesnik, the head of the republic's Council for Religious Affairs, told reporters that Ukrainian Catholic congregations were now allowed to register and gather legally "like other religious groups."[4]

Catholic Lithuania

The change under way in the Soviet Republic of Lithuania is visible on every flagpole. In May 1989 the yellow, green, and red standard was flying over government buildings in Vilnius, worn on lapels and for sale at every newsstand and department store. The Soviet flag was nowhere to be seen.

"We have a modern interpretation of the colors," said my host, Jonas Stepanavichus, an editor. "Yellow stands for an independent economy. Green represents care for ecology. The red symbolizes international solidarity. A year ago you could be sent to prison for

---

new charge was filed against him, anti-Soviet agitation and propaganda, and he was sentenced to six years in a strict-regime labor camp to be followed by five years of internal exile. In April 1986 he was given a further three-year sentence for "malicious disobedience to the requirements of the administration of a corrective labor camp." In February 1987, along with Father Gleb Yakunin and 138 others, he was released. It was an action, *Izvestia* reported, responding "to the spirit of *perestroika*." Once freed, Ogorodnikov founded a new publication, *The Bulletin of Christian Community*.

[4]*International Herald Tribune*, December 2–3, 1989, pp. 1, 4.

several years if you displayed that flag. Last July there was a public gathering where many people raised the banned flag. The first secretary of the Communist party told the crowd that he wouldn't speak if people didn't put down these flags. They wouldn't, and he didn't speak. Now he is no longer first secretary. He was replaced last October by a real reformer, Algirdas Brauzauskas. The second secretary is also without his old job. Since the elections there have been many more changes."

What happened? "We have a joke. The old-style elections — what were they like? It was like God saying to Adam, Here is Eve, take her or leave her! The Eve that God gave Adam was nice to look at, but the Eve we got was never that pretty. The Lithuanian Adam finally decided he wanted another Eve."

The old Eve was the Communist party and she lost? "I wouldn't say the party lost but it didn't win. None of the party secretaries were elected. Most of those nominated were people who had been in power for many years. They lost. A parliamentary group from West Germany was amazed. They said that they couldn't do such a thing in the Federal Republic! Here we have the chance to *non*-elect people even if we don't elect anyone. To be chosen you have to get a minimum of votes. In many districts there had to be a second election, in some places a third. It's a good idea. This way eventually you get leaders who respect the people. That's why relations between church and state are getting so much better now."

Who is in the government? "Communists won but not those the party put up. The supporters of *perestroika* announced their own slate. Almost all of these people won, thirty-six out of forty-two seats. These are all people in *Sajudis* [Movement]. *Sajudis* was formed last year by people who reject the old ways and want change for the better. At the beginning *Sajudis* had a lot of troubles, but now it has its own press and is on television for an hour or more every two weeks."

Is religion a significant political factor? "A major one. About 75 percent of Lithuanians are Catholic — not less. And then there are Orthodox, Old Believers, Lutherans. At least 90 percent of the people are religious believers of one kind or another. One of the first actions by Algirdas Brauzauskas when he became party secretary was to announce the return of the Catholic cathedral."

How many churches are there in Vilnius? "Thirteen Catholic churches now, two more under restoration, plus a new one to be built in a suburb. There are eight Orthodox churches in the city plus two under restoration that will open later this year. We have one Lutheran church, one Baptist church, and one synagogue. A former mosque will soon reopen for use as a Tatar cultural center but, if they wish, it will become a functioning mosque again. Throughout Lithuania churches are being returned — 189 churches were registered by the Lithuanian Council for Religious Affairs in the past year."

Reaching the Dawn Gate, an entrance point to ancient Vilnius, we climbed the steep stone stairs leading to the small Mater Misericordia Chapel that houses the nation's most revered icon, the Ostrobramskaya. Mary is shown as the Queen of Heaven, a crowned woman with crossed hands "standing on the moon, clothed with the sun." The twelve stars of Saint John the Divine's vision surround her. The large icon is overlaid in silver and gold. "It is a place dear to both Catholics and Orthodox," said Jonas. The chapel was crowded with pilgrims. There was a quiet, intense murmur of people praying the rosary.

A few yards down the street was the gateway to the Orthodox Cathedral. It was Sunday, the Liturgy had just ended, and a crowd of the faithful were streaming out. Adjacent to it was another Catholic church, Saint Theresa's, filled to capacity, where Mass was being celebrated in a combination of Latin and Polish. "Vilnius was under Polish rule from 1919 to 1939," said Jonas, "and there are still Poles who think of it as a Polish city. In any event, Poles feel at home here — we get a lot of Polish visitors."

We came to the Church of Saint Kasimir, named for a fifteenth-century prince who refused to take up arms in a war he regarded as unjust. Kasimir renounced wealth, declined marriage, died as a young man, and became one of Lithuania's most beloved saints. The church bearing his name, having been expropriated from believers after World War II, was turned into the city's Museum of Atheism. A museum guide book still on sale in Vilnius included the following text: "The museum exhibits reveal the reactionary essence of religion and its servants, proving on the basis of facts how religion dealt with dissenters, persecuted science, culture, and free-thinking.... Religion always loyally served the interests of the exploiters and enslavers." The Museum of Atheism was recently closed. When restoration work now under way is completed this summer, Saint Kasimir's will be a living church again. There are no plans to find new quarters for the Museum of Atheism.

I asked Jonas how atheists view these developments. "Practically no one takes atheism seriously. The professors of atheism at the university — perhaps they take it seriously. But no one takes them seriously. I know some of those teaching atheism. They are told by their colleagues and rectors, 'Your subject is no science! It has no place in this school. You should leave.' Even people in high posts of the Communist party have such views. Their own children and grandchildren are baptized."

We reached the Catholic cathedral in Vilnius, restored to church use on February 5. "It was taken away forty years ago and eventually was used as an art gallery. You should have seen the crowds in Vilnius the day of the first Mass! You could hardly move. It was a very joyful day throughout the country. The Mass was broadcast on national television." Outside the front doors of the cathedral lots of religious goods were on sale: rosaries, prayer books, holy pictures, crucifixes, statues of Mary, and photos of Pope John Paul II. Trade was brisk. Inside the church was still crowded though Mass had ended.

"The interior restoration is finished, but some outside work is still needed. There used to be a cross on top of the cathedral and two big statues of saints, but these were removed one night in the early fifties. Now the state has agreed to have duplicates made to replace those that were taken down. The old ones can't be returned as they were destroyed."

The national flag was hung in a chapel inside the cathedral. It hung as well from a trailer parked next to the cathedral where a week-long hunger strike was in progress organized by the Lithuanian League for Liberation, advocates of the total separation of Lithuania from the Soviet Union. "The League's basic argument," Jonas explained, "is 'We never joined the Soviet Union. It was forced on us. Hitler and Stalin carved up eastern Europe like a cake and we were put on Stalin's side of the plate.' They want a referendum to choose between the USSR or the EEC. Their slogans are: 'Red Army Go Home, Russians Go Home.'"

A sign on the side of the van expressed "solidarity with all nationalities repressed by Soviet power: Latvians, Estonians, Poles, Byelorussians, Ukrainians, Georgians, Armenians, and Moldavians. The same concerns Russians, who can't be free because they oppress other nations." Another placard was in remembrance of Lithuanian partisans killed by the Soviets after World War II when an attempt was made to set up an independent Lithuania. Among the fasters' demands posted on the trailer were the rehabilitation of all those condemned for their political views, recompense for those who suffered repression, and publication of the names of those responsible for punishing such people. Most surprising was the final demand: repentance on the part of those who took part in purges. One of the fasters, a gifted musician, played a slow, heart-breaking sonata by Bach on the violin, his solemn eyes pausing on the faces of those listening.

The newsstand in the main post office nearby was selling not only the usual assortment of Communist publications but such Western newspapers as the *Herald Tribune, Le Monde* and the *Manchester Guardian*. It was the first time I had seen them in the Soviet Union in a location accessible to the general public.

As we walked along Lenin Prospekt, Jonas pointed out a big statue of Lenin in the center of Lenin Square. Lenin has an outstretched hand — a rhetorical gesture. "It so happens that his hand is directed toward the local KGB office. What is he saying? According to the local joke it is: 'Either you come with me — or you go with them!' "

"The next time you are here," said Jonas, "at least part of this street is likely to have its old name back, Gediminas Prospekt. Gediminas was the founder of Vilnius." Many other streets that had Soviet names have already been changed. Jonas pointed out a spot on the wall at one corner where the old street sign had been removed leaving a bare patch. "In the Vilnius Executive Committee," said Jonas, "there is a special commission responsible for renaming streets and squares. We had one street named after a man whose claim to fame was his role in suppressing the Lithuanian language! The commission renamed the street after Dowkantas, a professor at Vilnius University who did much for the Lithuanian language and culture."

We talked about Lithuania's past. "It has been a hard history," said Jonas. "In the eighteenth century Lithuania was annexed by Russia. In 1830 and again in 1863, Lithuanians rebelled. In the period of repression that followed, it was forbidden to publish in the Lithuanian language. Russian was the only language permitted. Sentences of those convicted for violating the ban were severe. Two thousand people were sent to Siberia between 1864 and 1904. The policy of Russification lasted until 1905.

"Most of Lithuania was occupied by Germany during the First World War. In 1920, the Soviet government signed peace treaties granting independence to Lithuania as well as to Latvia and Estonia, though a large part of Lithuania, including Vilnius, was under Polish occupation from 1919. In 1939, a secret protocol of the Hitler-Stalin pact recognized the Baltic states as being within the Soviet sphere. The Soviet government demanded that the Baltic states sign a mutual assistance treaty permitting the USSR to set up military bases on their territory. The Baltic governments acceded. What else could they do?

"On June 14, 1940, the Red Army entered Lithuanian territory. In elections the following month, only Soviet-sponsored candidates were allowed to stand. The Baltic Parliaments, once elected, voted for the incorporation of their countries into the USSR, proposals accepted by the Supreme Soviet in August. Many fled to the West, knowing what to expect from Stalin if they stayed. An estimated forty-five thousand Lithuanians were arrested and executed within the first ten months of Soviet rule. Then came the attack by Nazi Germany and the incorporation of the Baltic Republics into the Third Reich. Several hundred thousand more died in those years, mainly the Jews.

"With the return of Soviet rule in the fall of 1944, there was a new wave of repression. By 1949, half a million people from the Baltic states had been deported — only about a quarter returned after Stalin's death in 1953."

Does this mean that most Lithuanians want to get out of the Soviet Union? "For most people," said Jonas, "that is some kind of fantasy land. But within the Soviet federation we want real autonomy for our republic instead of the fiction of autonomy."

What happened to Catholics after the war? "Bishop Stepanavicius was forced to live in exile in an isolated border village for twenty-seven years. At the beginning of this year he received permission to return to Vilnius. He hasn't yet taken up residence here but the building he will live in is being repaired. He will be in it before long and Vilnius will again be the center of the Lithuanian archdiocese. He is seventy-seven. He was consecrated thirty-three years ago. He steadily refused to carry out any of the 'recommendations.' The authorities wanted him to forbid religious instruction of children or anyone under eighteen assisting at the altar. He refused. 'It is your instruction,' he said. 'I have my own.' That is why he was forced out of Vilnius. He wrote many letters to the prime minister and the first secretary of the Communist party. Their response was basically: If you won't live by our rules, you get nothing. The people were deeply offended by such policies. The more courageous were sent into exile, mainly Siberia. But now things have changed dramatically."

Jonas introduced me to his director, Juozas Nekrosius, chairman of the Lithuanian State Committee for Publishing, whose office is across the street from the cathedral. On his desk was a newspaper with a front-page story on families adopting children, an activity in which Juozas Nekrosius is involved as chairman of the Children's Fund of Lithuania.

"This happened yesterday," he said, "and it was wonderful — many guests holding candles standing in a circle around the children and their foster families. If each of us lit a candle there would be no more darkness in Lithuania. It was an important event. It grew out of our decision that not one Lithuanian orphan will be sent out of Lithuania. A collective farm purchased a building and found a young family that has two daughters of their own. They are taking another six children into their family. In this case the children lost their parents in a traffic accident. This is the beginning. We want to make it possible for more families to take children."

The Children's Fund is, he said, "helping raise the level of compassion. We hope eventually that handicapped Lithuanian children will be able to participate in the Special Olympics for the handicapped."

He showed me some of the most recently published Lithuanian books. "These come from a new imprint called Conscript Archives from Vyturys Publishers in Vilnius. Its symbol is a candle with a barbed-wire halo around the flame.[5] The titles in the series so far are *Cattle Trains*, *The 'America'* [in the sense of New World] *behind the North Pole*, *Graves on the Shore of the Pechora River* [in Russia's far north], *The Second Day of Easter*, *We Were 'Politicals'* [Political Prisoners], *Teachers and Students*, and *Three Notebooks* [of a Latvian prisoner]. The latest title is *In the Land of Eternal Frost*, an account of what happened to one group of Lithuanians sent to a remote place in Siberia. The text on the back cover speaks about 'this school of poverty far from Lithuania, camps of hell set up in the Stalin years, a school not yet described in sculpture or film and about which we still know very little.'"

"It was an awful life, beyond description," said Jonas. "They were brought to a place where no one had ever lived. They had nothing. They had to work twenty hours a day — disease, hunger, cold, hard labor. It was like the Nazi camps. The book's main concern is to tell how they managed to survive. The answer is God and religious belief. They often were singing religious songs. They prayed every day. The military men guarding them couldn't understand. 'Why are you singing?' they asked. 'The only alpha and omega you have is the *taiga* [Siberia's sub-arctic forest]. This is where you die. The only question is when you will die.' Sixty thousand copies were printed. They sold out in one day even though the price is rather high — two rubles fifty kopeks. Of this, one ruble forty kopeks goes to the Lithuanian Fund for Culture. The money will be used to build a monument to the victims of Stalin."

"As a consequence a lot of people face deep emotional problems that have to do with traumatic events in the past," said Juozas Nekrosius. "Every family has within it terrible events that cannot be forgotten."

---

[5] Apart from the halo, the symbol is strikingly similar to the Amnesty International logo.

He showed me some old photos taken from an envelop on his desk. "This boy, Antanas Cibylskis, was a student in his early teens when this was taken. He wanted to become a journalist. His dream was to travel in western Europe. A romantic soul. When he was fifteen he was arrested and sent to the far east, sentenced to fifteen years in labor camps. Later he got another ten-year sentence. Second sentences on completion of the first term were common. Finally he was able to return to Lithuania, but two years ago he drowned. Now we have been given a collection of his poems. We plan to publish them.

"This poet's life is one story. In the Stalin years 10 percent of the Lithuanian population was sent east in cattle cars — about two hundred thousand people. We talk about there being two Lithuanias — the one here, the other in Siberia. The Siberian Lithuania was better educated than this one — those sent included many intellectuals, teachers, priests. But the one in Siberia had a much higher death rate. Many thousands of Lithuanians are buried in Siberia. Many were sent to an island in the Laptev Sea, far above the Arctic Circle. It was just a piece of ice. It is incredible that anyone survived."

He hoped that Lithuanian culture and history would become better known. "Few people know we exist. Many nations and troops have marched back and forth across us, but they didn't find out who we were. It is forgotten that Lithuania played a crucial role in European history. We Lithuanians shielded the West from the Tatars."

I asked about religious publishing in Lithuania. "We have been giving assistance to publication of *Kataliku Pasaulis* (Catholic World). There have been three issues so far. Also in our World Literature series we plan to publish ninety thousand copies of the Bible. It will be the first time for a publisher in the USSR. All other editions have been from the churches."

How do you explain the recent political developments in Lithuania? "Despite the presence in the republic of many people from other nationalities, 80 percent of the population is Lithuanian. Also Lithuania is one of the oldest nations within the territory of the USSR. Therefore our political situation is a bit different. There are some republics where the nationality is now a minority in its own borders. We have favorable preconditions for a fresh start. We want to expand our ties West as well as East. At the same time we want to recover our sovereignty. That is something that cannot be given to anyone. The most valuable quality of our new party secretary, Algirdas Brauzauskas, is his ability to see things as they are. This is a big gift for us. Sometimes two men can do more than two states.

Look at Gorbachev. Or think about what Erasmus did five hundred years ago. One of his principal disciples, Mikolec Letuvis, was a Lithuanian."

At his office next to the Saint Nicholas Church, we met Father Joseph Tunaitis, Catholic priest and chancellor of the Vilnius diocese. "This is one of the oldest Catholic churches in Lithuania," he said, "built by the famous knight, Gediminas, who died in 1341. Lithuania wasn't yet baptized. It is the only Catholic church in Lithuania named after Nicholas and is one of the churches that wasn't closed in the post-war time. In 1948 many churches were taken away but this was one of the exceptions. Now we are restoring the Gothic elements. Special bricks have been made. All the bricks that aren't good will be replaced.

"Thanks be to God, the situation is normalizing," he said. "Not long ago we had 630 parishes. In the past year seven have been added, including the Cathedral in Vilnius. Saint Kasimir's will re-open and also Saint Stephen's is promised. A number of churches are under construction. One will be in Pashilaichiai, a modern district of Vilnius without a church. The Council for Religious Affairs has been quite responsive to requests to build churches in areas where there are none. All in all, it is much better than it was, though there are still problems — some churches and church premises that have not yet been vacated. But the return of such buildings is promised. We wait the return of a building being used as a residence for pilots. We will add it to the Kaunas Seminary. It can house 150 students. Eventually we will have all the priests we need."

What about publications? "In general we have the right to publish but still not everything we would like. We are preparing a Missal. We printed 10,000 New Testaments and plan to print another 20,000. It would be more, but there are problems getting paper. The Austrian church is sending us 150,000 New Testaments. Canadians are sending the Old Testament. We issued a catechism in two editions, both for youth and prayer books. We have launched a magazine, *Catholic World*. There are three issues so far. Our plan is to bring it out every two weeks. Unfortunately we are still not able to publish religious fiction, philosophical books, and works of history. We also face the problem of a shortage of creative workers. We need to increase the number of those engaged in Christian publishing."

What about religious education for the larger public? "In a religious sense, people are very poorly educated. There is still very little we can do to change this, but we are thinking of what we can do to catechize children. I don't expect we will have the chance to do it in school, but perhaps the situation can develop in a way that is similar to Poland."

Does atheist education have much effect? "I don't think so. Rather few would consider themselves atheists. But the effort to discourage young people from going to church has had its impact."

Can the church help those who have suffered in the period of persecution and may have serious mental or physical problems as a result? "We now have organizations like Caritas that try to find those who were sent to prison or to camps. Many of these people have started special clubs and try to help each other."

When I mentioned my impression that the church in Lithuania was pre-Vatican II, Father Tunaitis smiled. "All that the council decided is reflected in our church. We didn't go quickly with everything but did it step by step. I think the results are good. My impression is that in the Western countries the process was too rapid. Before the war, we used to think of the Dutch church as exemplary. Holland seemed to be the most Catholic country! Then there was the Dutch catechism. We weren't very happy with that. Now there is a Lithuanian bishop in Holland. We hope he can help."

How are relations between clergy and people? The clergy seems rather remote. "It could be better. Perhaps more closeness, more warmth."

How many Lithuanians are Catholic? "It is impossible to say. It is said that 75 percent are Catholic but certainly we don't have 75 percent coming to Mass. In Vilnius I would guess about 10 percent are deeply engaged. In Kaunas it would be more. In villages it can be less. You find rather empty churches with mainly old people in the pews."

Why the decline? "Secularization is going on here as in many countries. Young people are following Western fashions and share their fascination with loud, oppressive music. On the other hand, it is clear that some of the young people are thinking more positively about religion, especially those who are twenty to twenty-five years old. They are thinking in a new way. It doesn't mean that they are necessarily becoming Catholic. Perhaps it shows itself through interest in Eastern philosophy. Some young Lutherans visited here from Sweden and made quite an impression on young people here. A lot depends on the talent of speakers, their gift to inspire others. At the moment there is a group of Hindu missionaries in the city, singing [the Hare Krishna chant] and playing a few musical instruments."

Is there a strong relationship between religious faith and national identity? [laughs] "For the moment the relationship is very strong. National aspirations have helped the church very much."

What is the relationship between the various churches? "It is rather official. The warmth we hear about in the West we don't have here, at least not yet. When it is necessary we meet and talk. We exchange congratulations. There is no anger. On the whole we each go on our own way."

Do you think the Orthodox Church receives better treatment from the political authorities than the Catholic Church? "I don't feel any difference. More Catholic churches were closed, but in general the Orthodox faced the same difficulties."

I mentioned some Catholics in the West who have come to prefer the Eastern-rite Liturgy. "We see that here as well. Some of our young Catholics are attending Liturgy at the Holy Spirit [Orthodox] Cathedral. They like the service even though it is very long — or perhaps because it is very long! They like the form of service."

What about the role of Catholics in charitable work? "Before *perestroika* we were not permitted to take any role in social life. Now we have lost the habit! [laughs] We have to learn all over again how to do it. Now we have Caritas, started by Catholic women, and we have a Charity Society. We have a special movement to help alcoholics. Various special groups are coming into existence. Priests are busy responding to requests and new possibilities — going into hospitals and prisons to hear confessions and celebrate Mass. We are free to do this now whenever there is an invitation. But we haven't yet the chance to start church-sponsored hospitals, children's centers, or old-age homes."

Do you feel secure about the changes that *perestroika* has brought about? "Perhaps the time has come. Everywhere the thirst for spiritual things is getting stronger. In history it happens from time to time that people can't go on living as they did."

Is the burden very heavy on priests? "In Vilnius we have only twenty-five priests — not nearly enough. We all celebrate Mass every day. There are so many baptisms, marriages, confessions, funerals. I have two funerals today. I am also a notary and that takes time. I am responsible for a lot of correspondence. Yes, it is a bit heavy."

I noticed people lining up in the cathedral to sign a petition. What is it about? "Sorry, but I don't know. There are so many petitions these days. I can't keep track!"

The next day in Kaunas, Lithuania's second largest city, I met the women who had founded Caritas. Launched the previous summer, by May 1989 there were more than six hundred Caritas groups operating in forty-four regions. Members were engaged in charitable work, religious education, preparation of couples for marriage, and efforts to repair family life. The movement's facilities were still quite modest. Caritas's office was a one-room ground-floor flat that included a narrow bed, old couch, and a small refrigerator. A table in the center of the room was surrounded by wooden chairs.

"Caritas began last summer with the awakening of the nation," explained founder Albina Pajarskaite, a silver-haired woman in a grey sweater. She had a quiet voice and shy manner that only amplified her quality of deep conviction. "We realized that with only political means, the country wouldn't awaken. A movement of spiritual life is needed as well. Last August we held a session, prayed together, attended Mass, and signed a covenant concerned with restoration of the family, education, and the revival of society. We were eight people. We addressed the covenant to the cardinal and to *Sajudis*. The cardinal blessed us. Everyone supported it! On the eve of the *Sajudis* congress in October, in the second issue of the *Sajudis* newspaper, *Awakening*, we addressed an appeal to all the women of Lithuania. There was a big response. Caritas groups began to form in every part of the country, and we have been working hard ever since.

"Militant atheism almost destroyed the family, the village, the parish. Our first concern is to repair the status of women and to repair the family. The family is the root of the nation. If you restore womanhood and motherhood, you do much to repair the family, and if you repair the family, you restore a healthy situation to our society. But in our present society, women are forced to get paid jobs — the family can't survive financially otherwise. Children are sent to centers where there is no love or faith. We want to create a healthy situation for the family and restore the dignity of woman.

"Our second area is education. We understand education in the Catholic way, which stresses that personality can best be developed by respecting human nature, culture, and religious virtues. We are concerned about the education of the child from birth and even before birth. We need to pay attention to the first three years. Most mothers, because of jobs, aren't available to their children in the first three years, so there is the problem of nurseries and kindergartens. We are concerned about educational methodology, but also the religious factor."

What about religious education in public school? "We hope to get permission to lead voluntary classes in school to introduce young people to the church, the Gospel, and Christian morality. Yesterday a few of us met some officials at the Ministry of Education in Vilnius. They didn't have a clear idea of how to respond to us — what to allow, what to forbid. But at least they are willing to meet and talk. Eventually it will get somewhere. In the meantime we are starting youth clubs where discussions can be held and religious literature made available. The discussion topics will be up to the young people — it can be marxism or anything they want. We are not afraid of any subject. The first such club opens next month here in Kaunas. Our goal is that every parish — there are 640 parishes at present — should have such a club. This will make a big difference for our young people. At present they are crippled due to a one-sided education. You can only stand firmly when both sides are developed. Our aim is that each person should have the chance to be happy and strong in his beliefs, his faith, his ideals. Lithuania is a very small nation — we need a big soul!

"We are starting programs for young people preparing for married life, to help them to live a Christian life and raise believing children. In our society, the understanding of marriage is very superficial. One project already finished is a 380-page guide book on marriage. This was published by the Catholic Church. The paper is poor but the content is good. In June we will start our first school for those who are planning to marry. It will meet on Saturdays and Sundays.

"We are concerned about old people and the sick that no one notices or cares for. There are many. They have been abandoned. There are also many younger people with alcoholism or drug problems. But at this moment there are few people who know how to care for others.

"We are working to make the parish into a community once again, not only a place where people come for the sacraments. We want to revive the Lithuanian language — it used to be a good language, not the jargon we have now. We want to restore the landscape of Lithuania, which has been so damaged by contempt for beauty and for ecology. We are promoting a return to a human scale in architecture — smaller buildings such as we used to build. It is spiritually destructive to be surrounded by ugly, huge structures. Often these were built where there were beautiful buildings. We also want to restore customs, traditions, and the symbols of our faith and of the spiritual life."

She showed me a book of photos of the high wooden crosses that once dotted the Lithuanian countryside. "Part of our work is to promote the reconstruction of standing crosses. We have started to do it. The crosses were a vital expression of our culture and history. Many used to stand in a place where czarist soldiers executed those who took part in the uprising in 1863. Some crosses stood near a certain pine tree where prisoners were hung. Most were destroyed. Some were put in museums. Lithuania will be a land of crosses once again."

Can church volunteers get into public institutions? "We feel no obstacle now except at prisons and schools. We are trying now to get access to a women's prison. Some of the prisoners invited us to come at Christmas. It wasn't allowed. They said our request didn't come early enough. We tried again for Mother's Day. Again they said we weren't in time. We are still trying."

Is each Caritas member involved in all these different areas of interest? "No, we ask each person to concentrate in one direction. Perhaps you have a gift to help sick people — to help at home or in a hospital. Perhaps you can do educational work. Perhaps you can help prepare young people for marriage. Perhaps you can help children whose parents are not able to look after them."

Is Caritas attempting too much? "We are working for a miracle. Sometimes we feel like ants. It is only possible to achieve results with the strength of everyone. We are women, and women are half the nation. It is a good place to start. Take us as we are! We believe in God and we have hope."

What gives you inspiration? "For many years we have seen what was going on. Every Lithuanian woman has had it in her heart. But we felt we couldn't do anything, or very little. We did what little we could — a kind of underground work. But it was this that gave birth to Caritas and *Sajudis*. These things seem new but they have deep roots. There were many seeds in the ground. Then *perestroika* gave us the possibility we were waiting for and the seeds began to bloom."

Behind nearby walls reminiscent of a monastery, we met the vice rector of Lithuania's Catholic Seminary, Father Algis Baniulis. Ordained in 1974, he had been on the seminary staff since January 1987 as a teacher of moral theology and ethics. He was a big man with an athletic build.

I asked what led him toward a priestly vocation. "I felt it from childhood, even before starting primary school. There are strong religious traditions in my family, which is a large one — nine children. One brother is also a priest. But we didn't feel pressured toward the priesthood. In fact I didn't tell my family I was making this step until I had been accepted into the seminary program."

Did you experience atheist indoctrination growing up? "There was atheist teaching in the school and a lot of pressure not to attend church. Children who openly showed their belief were persecuted.

In the early sixties, the Khrushchev time, it was declared that soon there would be no churches, no priests and no believers."

What about political restriction of the seminary in earlier years? "It used to be that before a candidate could be accepted his name had to be submitted to the Council for Religious Affairs in Vilnius, which meant that the KGB would check the names to see if there was any relative abroad or someone in the family sent to Siberia. Or perhaps the person had in some way been politically active in an unapproved manner. Perhaps he had been brave enough to sing a forbidden song. Perhaps his name had been mentioned in a *samizdat* publication. Perhaps he had signed a petition. There were many reasons for removing a candidate's name. Under such conditions it wasn't easy to find anyone who could be approved. Even once you were accepted there was the chance that the authorities would demand your expulsion. Two students were dismissed because they tried to arrange for the publication of a book that a professor had received from abroad. I hardly dared believe I might be one of the few able to study here. In 1963 the seminary had only twenty-three students in the entire seminary's five-year program. It was our lowest ebb. In that year only five were permitted to enroll. In 1969 I was one of eight accepted — altogether there were only thirty students."

And now? "Now the situation has changed. Last year the enrollment limit was forty, but the cardinal nominated forty-six and all were accepted. This year it was publicly declared that we could accept anyone we wanted and that there was no longer a limit on numbers. The only limit we face now is space and facilities. Now there are 163 students. We are ready now to go from a five- to a six-year program."

Do you have the study material you need? "Not enough but the situation is much better. We receive material from Rome, Poland, Canada, and the United States."

Are there enough priests to meet the need? "Far from it. We have about 650 priests, but many are very old and can hardly move. There are presently 160 parishes without priests. Our hope is that in the new conditions the number of priests will increase little by little and there eventually will be no parish without at least one priest. Right now we don't have the time we want to be with people. When I was a parish priest, it was normal to work seventeen or eighteen hours a day. There was no time for meals. I was afraid of anyone asking for my time."

What about the formation of monasteries? "There are unofficial monasteries but still those in them are careful. Who knows the future of *perestroika*? Our monks hesitate to draw attention to themselves. Perhaps it will happen in the near future. There were talks last year about reopening monasteries that were closed. The discussion showed that many people have very little understanding of monasticism. Some wondered how a monastery would fit under the existing law. Perhaps it could be considered some kind of cooperative that grows vegetables. But we are not founding economic cooperatives. So we are waiting for *Perestroika* Two."

Is the basic attitude of Communists toward religion changed or is this just a tactical withdrawal? "I think it is a change of heart. Attitudes have changed. In the recent pre-election period we even had party officials asking priests to help them get the votes of believers."

How is it that religious faith remains so deep and that so many believers seem so forgiving? "Our faith owes a great deal to atheist propaganda. It was so vulgar and went on for so many years. What the authorities did stirred up a lot of hatred. Many priests were sent to prison or labor camps — for teaching children or just because they were priests. But the Lithuanian people are faithful by nature. As Christians we cannot accept revenge or hatred. But it is not easy to forgive."

Has atheist education changed? "Completely. It is nothing like it was. The Atheist Museum in Vilnius has been closed. We now see religious programs on television while atheist programs have disappeared. Mass is shown live on television on major feast days. Religious articles are being published. Bishops and priests are regularly in the press."

What will happen to those who made their living promoting atheism? [laughter] "Their activity was state financed. I suppose the state can find something more useful for them to do. It was not such happy work. Most of them weren't very skilled in what they did — they didn't know much about religion. Their methods were primitive. Mainly they were blackmailing the young. Now the blackmail is over, and we find a lot of students coming here from nearby institutes. They want contact with our students — to talk, to play football or basketball, to sing together. A number of folk music groups have asked to come here — they want to show us what they can do, but also they want to learn from us."

What are your hopes for Lithuania's future? "It has been our tradition to be on friendly relations with all our neighbors. We are hard-working people, very democratic. We want to be as independent as is possible."

Chapter 6

Protestants

ONE OF THE MANDATES OF THE CZARS had been to safeguard the Orthodoxy of Holy Russia. Non-Orthodox religions were kept — at times driven — outside the borders. But from the time of Peter the Great onward religious isolation gradually ended, partly due to territory gained in war, partly due to modernization and commerce.

In the late 1700s Catherine the Great invited German-speaking pacifist Mennonites to form an agricultural colony on the Dnieper. They introduced not only more productive methods of agriculture but a Bible-centered way of life that impressed their neighbors. In the same period, with the acquisition of Latvia, a large Lutheran population came within the Russian Empire.

In 1812 Czar Alexander I discovered the Bible, read it with passion, and opened the way for the British and Foreign Bible Society to set up a Russian Bible Society. Bible reading was taken up in countless homes throughout the empire.

During the nineteenth century dissatisfaction with the Orthodox Church increased. Under Peter the Great, Orthodoxy had been stripped of its independence and become a closely regulated department of government, a condition that remained until the abdication of Czar Nicholas II in 1917. The local clergy were badly educated and overburdened while the higher clergy were often remote from the people. Fewer young men were choosing a priestly vocation: in 1840 there had been 117,000 Orthodox clergy while in 1890 the number had shrunk to 97,000. There was a thirst for something more vital and intimate. The climate was ripe for the activities of Protestant missionaries, yet the attempt to convert those who were nominally

Orthodox was a criminal offense. Protestant preachers risked severe penalties.

Despite all the dangers, the missionaries sought converts and found them. On August 20, 1867, Martin Kalweit immersed Nikita Isaevich Voronin in a stream near Tbilisi, marking the start of the Evangelical missionary movement. More baptisms followed, many occurring at labor camps. "It was a time of horrible persecutions," one Baptist leader recalled. "Exiles, arrests, fines and beatings of believers rained down upon the audacious followers of the Gospel... [yet] the brothers nevertheless did not cease their meetings, holding them in basements, in the woods, in the cemetery, in ravines...."[1]

Protestant fervor and courage brought results. By 1905 there were nearly twenty-three thousand Baptists and more than twenty thousand Evangelical Christians. "Every Baptist a missionary!" was the motto, and many took up the call despite the penalties that might be imposed.

Following the October Revolution of 1917, a "golden age" began for Soviet Protestants. With the abolition of a special status for the Russian Orthodox Church, Protestants were free to publish and evangelize freely. At their height in 1929, their number was about five hundred thousand, but that fall one hundred Baptist preachers were arrested and all regional Baptist offices closed following the arrest of their officers. By the mid-thirties, staggered by the blows of Stalin, the number of Evangelicals had been halved and the church driven underground.

Only after the Second World War, in a period of limited toleration, did slow growth resume. Even then, a significant section of Protestant believers refused to be registered by the local Councils for Religious Affairs. Many paid the price of years and even death in the *gulag*.

Within the Russian Empire, Protestantism acquired a special character that has not been lost in the Soviet period. As Sir John Lawrence has observed, "The danger of every strict religion is that it will end in hypocrisy, but that danger is not so great among the Russians as in the West. Many Russians tell lies, but they do not generally deceive themselves; and when a Russian is honest, his integrity goes deeper than the conventional morality which may pass for honesty in other countries. Many Russian Baptists [the main Protestant group

---

[1]Walter Sawatsky, *Soviet Evangelicals* (Scottdale, Pa.: Herald Press, 1981), p. 35. Also note Francis House, "Non-Conformists in Pre-Revolutionary Russia," in *The Russian Phoenix* (London: SPCK, 1988), pp. 43–51.

in the USSR] combine this deep integrity with some of the delightful qualities of the Orthodox spirituality that surrounds them."[2]

Kiev

On Monday nights the Seventh-Day Adventist House of Prayer in Kiev is shared with one of the city's five Baptist congregations. The building was rapidly filling up with Baptists when I arrived in January 1989. The light green hall was brightly lit by neon lamps. "God is love," read one text high on the right wall. The Ten Commandments filled much of the front wall of the hall.

There was about the same ratio of women to men — two-thirds — as one would usually find in an Orthodox church in Kiev. The older women were wearing scarfs and shawls; the scarfless younger women were colorfully and smartly dressed. Children were plentiful, especially in the balcony. One of them put a handkerchief on her head, grinning broadly at her neighbor until an adult hand pulled the handkerchief away and waved a scolding finger at the child. A choir of forty people, most in their twenties, sat in front. Christmas hymns, among them "Silent Night," alternated with texts from the Bible, the reading of poems, prayer, and preaching. I was surprised at how much Mary was emphasized. Orthodox piety has left its stamp on Soviet Baptists. Protestants in the West would have been alarmed.

Late in the two-hour service a young woman stood before the pulpit and, in a broken voice, confessed that she had made some serious mistakes in an effort to try to convince a friend to live differently. "I got involved with the wrong kind of people," she said, tears running down her face. "Trying to get her out of that crowd I just got myself into it." During the prayer for her that followed, the whole congregation got down on its knees. "Sin is the cause of all mischief and errors," Pastor Dukhonchenko responded, "but Jesus Christ has been born to show the way to become free of sin." He embraced her.

After the service, many members of the congregation crowded into a small adjacent room to meet me. This quickly turned into an amiable dialogue in which there was not a moment of silence. One man showed me the manuscript of a book of poems. "It is sometimes said in propaganda that believers are ignorant people," he said, "but many are cultured people — poets and musicians. The

[2]John Lawrence, *A History of Russia*, 6th rev. ed. (New York: New American Library, 1978), p. 135.

poems you heard in the service tonight were read by their authors. We are planning to publish a collection of Christian poems." "Most of our songs," said a member of the choir, "are typical Ukrainian folk songs. Did you like them? Now we are singing them in public squares."

I asked what *perestroika* has meant for them. "The first change," said an older man, "is that previously our state called itself atheist. Now it is described as a state of believers and nonbelievers. That's a big change!" A younger man spoke up. "*Glasnost* has meant access to information. It has been amazing for many people to discover that seventy percent of the population are believers — Christians, Jews, Moslems, and Buddhists. Kharchev said this in public when he talked about the rights of believing people. This surprises a lot of people and it makes us rejoice."

"It is easier to get Bibles," said the pastor. "There was an edition of 110,000 copies in our own language! And there are more Ukrainian Bibles coming to us soon from our brothers in Canada. We can see the time coming when whoever wants a Bible can have it. More people than ever want a copy. They are willing to pay money just to read the Gospel."

"And we are going to have a Ukrainian hymnal," said the choir director. He showed me the hand-copied text he was using. "People are more open," said a young woman. "You ask them if they want to come to church and they say yes." "The press has stopped printing articles distorting facts about believers," said a teacher.

But are there still problems? "Believers are praying for Gorbachev," said a man in a blue windbreaker, "but there is still a lot of red tape. Bureaucracy is still thriving. Also we have not yet been able to get permission to have our own place of worship. They allow it in Moscow, but we still have our local problems. The local authorities are at odds with *perestroika*."

What is special about Ukrainian Baptists? "First," said a smiling old man with raised eyebrows, "we are very open, friendly, and musical people. We have our own language and our own songs. But on the other hand believers are alike no matter where they are."

The next evening the same church was used for worship by Kiev's Seventh-Day Adventists. I sat next to Galina Gritsuk and her eight-year-old son Yuri. Galina had come despite her youngest son's grave illness. Galina whispered a translation of the service.

The service centered on a sermon by Pastor Alexander Pankov about the conversion of Mary Magdala. "Can a human being really be changed in a moment? Can sin be removed instantly? Look what happened to Mary. When Jesus was in Magdala, she was changed. But when Jesus left, Mary returned to her old ways. We are told that Jesus pulled her out of the devil's jaws seven times before the sin finally was removed from her heart. She abandoned her former way of life."

The sermon was followed by a collection, a time of prayer, a hymn, a blessing, and announcements. After the hour-long service I met with leaders of the congregation in an office across a courtyard.

"Officially there are 180 registered Adventist churches with 14,000 baptized Adventists in the Ukraine — and about 32,000 Adventists and 418 churches throughout the USSR," said Pastor Pankov. "In fact there are more. Not every congregation is willing to register itself. Now that we are in the phase of *perestroika*, perhaps the day is coming when we will know the real numbers. Nineteen churches were opened in 1988. We have 178 ordained ministers plus many Bible workers being prepared for ordination."

How did this congregation of Adventists come to share their church with the Baptists? "Originally our church was a private home. We bought it in 1954 and rebuilt it. The idea that the building should be used by the Baptists as well came from the state authorities. It looked better this way on their report to Moscow, uniting different denominations under one roof. Neither the Adventists nor the Baptists agreed, but we had no choice. Both are now asking permission for the Baptists to have their own building. They plan to build a new structure, and we want to reconstruct this one. It used to be that the authorities said to us, 'You are married until the second coming.' But now we hope for a positive response."

What divides Adventists and Baptists? "Like Baptists, we believe that salvation is in Christ only. We seek to present Christ in our life, to reflect his life, his character, his obedience. We differ with Baptists in keeping Saturday rather than Sunday as a day of rest. The seventh day, the Sabbath, is Saturday. In following Jesus, we are keeping his commandments, trying to obey them and live them in our heart. We stress leading a healthy life — no drinking, no smoking, no drugs. We abstain from all food prohibited in the Bible. We also differ in our way of preaching. The Baptist preaching style stirs up the emotions. The Adventist style is more deliberate. We avoid manipulating emotions. We try calmly to convert the mind and heart. Feelings are temporary. Faith is constant."

What effect did the Revolution have on Adventists? "In Lenin's time, it was wonderful. For the first time we faced no obstacles. We could preach and publish freely, hold open-air meetings and speak where we pleased. We met in the House of Columns in Moscow. Though it was a hard time for the country — civil war, foreign invasion, and hunger — it was a time of rapid growth for our church. Before the Revolution the Russian Orthodox Church dominated the country. It was difficult for all other denominations to survive. We had a lot of reasons to feel offended by the Orthodox. But then under Stalin all Christians suffered together, Orthodox and Protestant. We became friends in our suffering. Now the situation is healthy among the churches. No church is oppressing another church. This is good for us but it is also good for the Orthodox. It is salvation to them no longer to be an oppressor."

How is the present relationship with the local Council for Religious Affairs? "We have cooperation from the council even though we don't always get what we ask for. But the Gospel teaches us to be humble and meek and to be content with what we have. Patience is always rewarded."

Still, isn't facing bureaucrats a hard test of faith? "We have faced a lot of them and still face them. Not all of them like *perestroika*, as you know, but others understand. From our side, we go higher if we have to. On some questions we have gone to Kharchev himself in Moscow. He is a man we respect. We praise the Lord that he is making a real effort to help religion in the Soviet Union. The Council for Religious Affairs no longer works only for the atheists but for the believers as well."

What happens if the local council doesn't accept what they say in Moscow? "Then we have to be patient. We pray that what we asked for will be given, and we wait for the new law on religion."

Are believers helping to write the law? "The special commission working on the law consults with believers. The president of our Adventist association has been among those who gave advice."

What do you hope for from the new law? "Our great hope is that the Gospel can be preached throughout the USSR. We are made hopeful by what Kharchev says. All we ask for is what we had after the Revolution. Whenever they speak of Lenin's Law of Freedom of Conscience, we know what this means and we look forward to it."

But if your hopes aren't met? "A lot of people are skeptical about *perestroika*. If someone doubts *perestroika* can do what it should, we say God can restructure what needs to be restructured. We know that there are still a lot of enemies of religion. There are those who think of *perestroika* only in terms of material welfare, who don't consider the spiritual hunger of the people. Perhaps we still face hard times. But the Gospel reminds us of the woman suffering in labor before the joy of birth. We have been through Stalin and Khrushchev. We know about suffering. But we are ready to be tortured to give birth to new life."

Did members of your family suffer? "My great-grandfather went through all the persecutions before the Revolution. My grandmother tasted that golden age that followed the Revolution and then she suffered the repression. In the thirties believers met secretly at night. One grandfather died in the prison camps sometime between 1938 and 1940; the other grandfather was shot by the Nazis in 1942. My father was a pastor in the Khrushchev time. I have been through the Brezhnev 'stagnation period' — a very complicated time, doing Gospel work on the one hand and trying to have good relations with the state authorities on the other. You needed wisdom to do it. It was hard."

What about the prison camps? "Many of our pastors remained in the camps forever. Our church was beheaded. The best were martyred — they never returned. They suffered equally with all the Soviet people. No different."

Do you see positive developments today? "Many! We are publishing Bibles and other publications again. We were given permission to build a seminary near Moscow. We have built it at our own expense and by our own labor. People got permission to leave jobs and farms to take part — and where they had trouble with their employer, the Council for Religious Affairs helped. We didn't expect that. We already have first-year students. After so many years of difficulties, it has to be said that we still are somewhat apprehensive in our relations with the authorities, and they with us, but in the course of time we will leave our prejudices behind. We are living in a time when God is doing miracles even though we didn't expect them."

Irkutsk

When I arrived at the Baptist Church in Irkutsk later in the month I found a log building half-buried in snow. We sat in an austere dining room decorated with texts from the Bible: "Blessed are the pure in heart" and "I have set watchmen upon your walls, O Jerusalem, who must never be silent. Those who are mindful of the Lord must take no rest."

"We have just celebrated the seventy-fifth anniversary of our church's founding," Victor Georgievich Sitnikov said, adding that it had been closed from 1937 until 1945. The church had four hundred members.

Are Baptists widespread in Siberia? "In practically every city."

Has *perestroika* had much impact for Baptists? "There have been remarkable changes," said Deacon Genadi Ivanovich Abramov, a much younger man who divides his time between the church and work as a plumber. "We are no longer treated like third-class people. Kharchev, the head of the Council for Religious Affairs in Moscow, has said in the press that there must be equality between believers and nonbelievers, that both believers and atheists should have the same opportunity to preach their beliefs."

And here in Irkutsk? "With the Millennium celebration last year we were able to hold a concert in the House of Dramatic Arts. The choir sang. We read religious poems. It was two hours long. All the eight hundred seats were filled and people were standing. The theater was filled to the limit. A year ago, something like this was unthinkable — a religious event in a public hall! Formerly we were allowed to preach the Gospel only in church, nowhere else. Our choir also went to Chita [a city several hundred miles to the east beyond Lake Baikal] to take part in a similar concert. Two months ago we had a public meeting on the topic of morality for young people in the hall of the city library. This was announced beforehand in the press. There were three hundred seats available. About five hundred people came. The atmosphere was very friendly."

What was the discussion like? "We were talking about the moral state of young people now and what we should do, how to get out of the condition we are in, how to take the path to purity. We Baptists presented the Bible and what it teaches. We read some passages and sang a few psalms."

Are these events having an impact on church attendance? "Fresh people are coming. In fact our church is too small. We have just been given permission to build a larger one nearby."

What about the demand for religious literature? "We are also getting many requests for copies of the Gospels and the Bible. We are getting copies from abroad so we are able to meet this need, at least for now."

I asked the deacon how he became involved in the church. "My father and mother are believers so I grew up in church, participating in services and feasts. In 1976, when I was twenty-one, I confessed that I was redeemed and was baptized and was received as a believer."

I asked Victor Sitnikov how he came to be a Baptist. "I was born in Irkutsk. Now I am retired, but for twenty-five years I was the operator of an excavation machine. My relatives were believers and my father and mother had been in the church, but they loved civic life too much and gave it up. Now recently they have returned. I became a believer when I was twenty-six. The Lord had to fight hard for my soul. In December 1957 it became a bitter fight whether or not to come to church. My soul was a real battlefield. It was so severe that I couldn't say even a two- or three-letter word. I couldn't say yes or no. I asked myself, 'Am I not lord over my own word? If I say yes I will go and if I say no I won't go.' I was in the tram and finally I said yes to the Lord. Right away I felt like iron bars had been lifted from my shoulders. It seemed as if the sun was shining much brighter. I started visiting churches and then became a member of this one. Now I am chairman of the church council."

Are Baptists involved in local charity work? "It used to be impossible but now this has changed. There are five orphanages near us. We decided to get involved with one where the children are deaf and dumb. We met with the chief doctor who told us what their needs were. We collected eight thousand rubles and bought furniture — tables, wardrobes, dishes, cooking utensils, games. We also want to offer voluntary service, but they aren't yet prepared. We hope to be able to take care of a few wards. We are asking the regional party committee to give its approval. We could start with just one ward. Perhaps this year we can start. This is our hope."

As I left I made a gift to the church, a box of *matzo* bread just given to me by local Orthodox Jews. "It's ecumenical bread," I said, "the kind that Jesus ate."

Archangel

Archangel's Baptist House of Prayer is in the timber-processing area of the city. Transformed internally into a church, it was an ordinary house surrounded by similar wooden houses. Sidewalks in the neighborhood are made of boards. It was spring but there were still patches of snow on the ground. On the yellow walls inside were several texts from the New Testament. "Christ is Risen!" said the sign in front, identical to signs hung in Orthodox churches during the Easter days.

The pastor, Nikolai Devyatkin, was preaching when I arrived. "The life of Christ is an example for everyone. Today we must prepare ourselves for eternal glory. We must practice tolerance, console each other, and love each other. Christ is risen! You may go to Jerusalem and see the empty tomb. He is not there. He is among the people.

Not everyone knows of the existence of Christ. Not everyone knows who he really is. Not everyone knows about his resurrection. But more and more are coming to know. And we who know, we must redeem our sins in this life so that we will be given joy in the future life."

The congregation sang the traditional Orthodox Easter hymn: "Christ is risen from the dead, trampling down death by death, and upon those in the tomb bestowing life."

I was invited to an Easter meal at the pastor's home. "This section of Archangel was built up in the fifties," Nikolai Devyatkin told me. "The church is fifteen years old although the community of Baptists in Archangel goes back all the way to 1918 when Baptists from Leningrad came here. They preached in different parts of the city, and some people responded. A small group took root, which gradually grew to a congregation of a hundred. We weren't the only Protestants. In another district there was an Anglican church. So it was until 1920. Then came the time of purges. We lost the right to exist. Believers had to congregate underground. Many were exiled. But in 1947 our group started expanding. We were able to start holding regular meetings. In 1974 we officially registered and found our Prayer House, only a very shabby place at that time."

Why didn't the church register sooner? "The main problem before 1974 was that the authorities were unwilling. There were also different opinions within the church. The act of registration caused a split in our congregation. Some didn't agree and they left. They are still in Archangel. Because the reasons for the split are now gone we hope there can be a reconciliation."

What publishing work is being done by Baptists? "We don't attempt that in Archangel. Our national publication, *Bratsky Vestnik* (Fellowship Herald), which came out every two months, will now be monthly. Also our office in Moscow will publish a weekly newspaper, *Evangelskaya Vest* (Evangelical News)."

What about education of clergy? "In the late twenties we lost our Bible School. For many years our only educational program was by correspondence, although a few candidates were sent to Baptist schools in Germany. Just recently, in February, permission was given to open a seminary to train ministers and preachers — probably it will be in Moscow. We will have a four-year program. There is a hope that we will also be allowed to open a seminary in the Ukraine."

How many Baptists are there in the Soviet Union? "About 250,000. The number is growing steadily. Our All Union Council [of Evangelical Christian Baptists] in Moscow reports that baptisms are up by 25 percent. I don't know about the figures for the Ukraine, but in the Russian federation there are nearly six hundred registered churches and almost that many nonregistered. Probably there are twice that number in the Ukraine."

Over a meatless lunch with some of Archangel's Seventh-Day Adventists the next day, I heard about the Adventists' history. "The Church of Adventists of the Seventh Day was founded in the United States in 1863," said the pastor, Vyacheslav Petroberg. "We have no creed but the Bible. Membership is open to adults and young people who have accepted Jesus Christ as their personal savior and who have been baptized by immersion. We observe the seventh day, Saturday, as the Sabbath, and are awaiting the second coming of Christ.

"In 1886 the Adventist message was brought to the Crimea by Germans and then went up the Volga. In the czarist times it was difficult because only the Orthodox Church was permitted. The Adventist church came to Archangel only ten years ago. In the beginning the local attitude to our church wasn't easy. We didn't understand them and they didn't understand us. But now, by God's grace, we are witnessing wonderful changes. We opened a center for training pastors last year in Zaokski, in the Tula district. This combines part-time residential periods with correspondence courses. We will be opening a printing shop to publish both religious literature and material to make society more healthy. Land for it has been given in the Tula territory."

What is distinctive about Adventists? "We stress a healthy way of life, both moral and physical. We spread information about the harm done by tobacco and alcohol. We advocate healthy food grown in the right way. We now have permission to start a Soviet-American joint venture for food production, a factory to process vegetarian food for children. The food will be distributed throughout the system of child care. American Adventists are experts in vegetable production and we are learning their methods. In the territory where the theological school has been started the local authorities have given us land for agricultural use. The first greenhouses have now been built there. We will supply vegetables and greens for the settlement as well as local orphanages and hospitals. It's a small beginning but significant. We have the potential to do a lot more."

What do you hope for? "We expect that the opportunities churches had in the time of Lenin will be restored. In Lenin's time all religious communities had the chance to work for the benefit of the whole society. Before the Stalin purges began we had an eye-healing clinic. We believe in the new conditions our church can contribute positively to the improvement of health care and medicine in this country. We could help reduce smoking. Adventists in America have developed a remarkable system for giving up smoking. We have published an article about it in our magazine. We plan to launch campaigns to combat drunkenness and drug addiction."

I mentioned the consequences of Prohibition in the United States. "Prohibition is not the remedy. The evils causing addiction can't be solved that way. We haven't had prohibition here but the semi-prohibition we experienced [the campaign Gorbachev launched shortly after assuming leadership of the Communist party] caused many other problems. What we can do is show people how to stop. Also we have experience in operating detoxification clinics in East and West Germany, institutions served entirely by Adventists. These have been quite successful. We also have done a lot of educational work. Many people have no idea what the physical consequences are of using alcohol and other drugs. But it is not just a question of therapeutic methods. You have to care for both the body and the soul. First Christ healed the soul, then the body."

Are local Adventists able to engage in charitable service? "We are participating in actions of mercy in hospitals and asylums for the mentally ill. It is noble work, but difficult. In your country actions of mercy by believers were never suspended, but we faced quite a different situation. There was a mistake on the way and this is why *perestroika* is needed. Now we have started a regional Union of Charitable Societies. This embraces the Red Cross, the board of the health care agency, and believers. It is a remarkable achievement. On May 27 there will be a charity concert to raise money for the children's fund. Through charity work people are learning more about the church. Many knew nothing about it. There is a huge interest in religion in general and the variety of churches.

"In the time of suffering we lost our specialists. We didn't have the chance to send our young people for higher education. Now the situation is different. We will have the chance now, for example, to prepare people who will specialize in treatment of the heart diseases of children."

Is the present change irreversible? "We think so. We have the magnificent revelations from Saint John the Divine, who prophesied that at the end there will only be two forces, or three or four, that resist global evil. One of them will be this country, the USSR. Gorbachev confirms this prophecy. We will have the kind of freedom in this country that has never before existed in the entire world. Therefore we are thankful to our church and the national leadership. We are confident that our Lord God is running these developments. The emergence of the United States was an act of God that was prophesied by Saint John. The Soviet Union was also predetermined and we believe will be used by God. So we believe in the irreversibility of the *perestroika* process."

Petrozavodsk

The Lutheran church in Petrozavodsk is in a village-like suburb of traditional wooden houses. The church was full and the congregation singing a hymn as we arrived. A wooden altar was in the front of the church under a big wooden cross. Many people had Bibles, but all the hymn books appeared to be hand-written copies.

I was present for a service on Wednesday morning. When the hymn was finished, an elderly woman came forward and offered a prayer of thanksgiving: "We thank you, Lord, for helping us survive the winter and we thank you for the warm spring. We thank you for meeting our daily needs. We thank you for our bread. We thank you for this beautiful church to pray in. Most of all we thank you for your son Jesus Christ. We thank you for everything."

A hymn followed, then a reading from the Bible. Maria Kayava came to the front to speak. She began with prayer: "You are our God and you have always been our God and you have always shown us your love. You have spoken to us through your Son. I am always grateful for your words and for telling us what to do. We all have to follow your words no matter what. Without you we wouldn't have strength. You said, 'Go and teach all nations.' We are trying to do it. If we commit any sin, we turn to you for forgiveness."

She paused and then spoke to the congregation: "It used to be we had no right to practice our religion. Now we are living a new life. We prayed for this and it is happening. Isn't it wonderful? Isn't it a miracle? We thank God for *perestroika* and freedom of conscience. We feel we are free. How happy we are. Jesus is making all things new. He is making a road for us in the desert. We should go down that road without looking back on old evils. We don't have to remember what happened before. We must look ahead to see what God has in store for us. God is the God of love. We cannot comprehend such love. We cannot understand it with our brains, only in our spirit.

"Jesus was sent to earth to teach us how to love each other — not to fight each other. He taught us to love our neighbor no matter what his faults. If I have hatred and sorrow in my heart I must ask God to take it away. We must forgive. If someone pretends to be higher than God, God will punish him. That is not for us to do. We are taught to forgive. I have sinned but God has forgiven me. We must also forgive those who sinned against us. We have to love our neighbors no matter what. Restoration is happening now. Everything is developing beautifully. We can buy Bibles. More churches are opening. Let us pray that it will continue forever. In any event we know that God has only good things in store for us. We won't allow anyone to shake our belief in God. Let us help those who are stumbling get to their feet. Pray for those who are misguided. Let us serve Jesus from the bottom of our hearts. We only have to go the way he tells us. God is supporting us. Who can stand against us?"

She ended the sermon with another prayer: "We thank you for calling us your children. Help us spread your word so we can help anyone who is not at peace. We bless the government of this town for giving us the chance to pray freely. We appreciate our freedom. Help our youngsters to be free from the abominable manifestations of these times. If someone has been led astray, help him find his way back. Let us help anyone in dire need, as Jesus helped us. Bless us, God, and forgive us."

Her sermon kindled a request to speak from the local representative of the Council for Religious Affairs, Boris Feodorovich Detshuev. He spoke from in front of the altar: "Dear friends, it is an important time. *Perestroika* is going on in our country, and not only here but in other countries. You Lutherans too are upholding this process, helping us do away with the mistakes of the past. Crimes were committed against believers. We are guilty of this. We speak of it openly because we don't want the mistakes to be repeated. Our society is supposed to protect both believers and atheists. This is in our constitution. We are going to put the principle into practice."

After the service, Maria Kayava showed me a scrap book of photos of the church's construction. Many of the builders were women. "Having a church had been our request to the local authorities when we arrived here, but it took many years before we got permission. We could pray only in our homes. At last permission was given. Construction began just after Easter 1983. Our church warming occurred eight months later, on December 18. The Orthodox Church helped us. Also we have had help from Lutherans in Finland — they sent us our Bibles. Now we are building a reception room and a priest's house. We were given building permission and have received the material and the work is started. We will have our own priest this coming winter."

The congregation was founded by people of Finnish ancestry who once lived in villages near Leningrad. "We were peasants, not rich but living comfortably. We supplied most of the dairy goods to Leningrad. We were honest workers and had a good life — no one was drunk, no militia was needed to keep order, we never had to lock our doors. I am old enough to remember before the Revolution. I once saw Czar Nicholas II taking part in a parade. I was sitting on my mother's shoulders, and the czar was standing in the back of a car with his arms outstretched. I never saw Lenin but we were for him. The Finns put great store in the Revolution. We thought it would make life better and help us develop our culture. Some good things happened while Lenin was alive. In the beginning it was wonderful. 1918–19 were crisis years, but by 1925 there was a surplus of products. With Lenin's New Economic Policy, you could find what you needed and everything was cheap. If it wasn't in the stores, you could order it from abroad. But Lenin died and Stalin took over and it all came to an end. On the 7th of April 1931 at 2 A.M. they came and took us all away. We were dangerous people, they said. We were put in cattle cars and taken east. I worked in the gold mines for many years — I was a specialist in gold washing! I have held seven-gram pieces of gold in my hands. It was very hard for us. We were warned not to speak Finnish. We didn't dare to speak at all in the mines. Now they teach Finnish in the schools and use it on television. In those former times you would never have found your way to us. Never. In fact we wouldn't be here either."

I asked Maria what became of her husband. There was a pained look in her face and a prolonged silence. "My husband was sent to another place. I never found out when he died, only that he had been sentenced to ten years and had no right to correspond. When the ten years were over I wrote to him and then got a notice that he had died. My hope now is that we can find out where he is buried. Millions of others died like him. I am not alone in my sorrow. My lot was no harder than anyone else's."

I asked how she had come back to the western part of the country. "In the Khrushchev time we were allowed to move back to the west. Many of us came to Karelia. Here there was a welcome and we could live a new life. Let the dead bury the dead. God helps us."

Her face was free of any trace of bitterness — beautiful eyes, a gentle expression.

I asked her how such evil could have been possible. Her answer was brief: "Fear, fear, fear."

I asked her, "How did you maintain your hope? How do you

forgive those who took your husband's life and caused you such suffering?"

"It is the gift of the Holy Spirit. The spiritual values that the church gives cannot be compared with any other. I don't even want to lay the blame at Stalin's door. We are not alone in our sorrow. We are a piece of the nation, a piece of the world. We hope that our grandchildren will see another life and that such things will never be repeated." She talked about her children and grandchildren — where they were, what they were doing.

"Many people still cannot forgive," she added, "like my son-in-law Yasha. He saw his mother shot when the Germans came and took a vow to avenge her. He saw many terrible things. I tell him to forget vengeance — the German nation suffered just as much as we did."

I asked if her children had the chance to move across the border to Finland, would that be better for them? "No! The spiritual level here is much higher. In Finland they have accumulation fever. Our young people here are very independent and good workers. We have a lower rate of divorce than in Finland."

Baku

On a Sunday in May we drove into a residential district of Baku, capital city of the mainly Moslem republic of Azerbaijan in the Soviet Union's deep south, to participate in the Baptist morning worship service. The church was once a private house but had been enlarged. There was a vase full of flowers on the upright piano in front of the pulpit and a grand piano further back. In the center was a long table with six chalices. Women sat on one side of the church, men on the other. Only the older women were wearing scarves. Everyone appeared to be of European origin.

The pastor, Nikolai Pavlovich Grubich, preached about love with many hand gestures. There were two mikes on the pulpit but no amplification was needed. After the sermon, during a period of spontaneous prayer, many of the older women cried. A communion service followed. Only those who stood up received the blessed bread and wine. The piano played softly while the bread and chalice were passed. The men serving communion were the last to receive.

Meeting with Pastor Grubich in a side room after the service, I asked about the communion service. "We usually have communion on the first Sunday of May," he said, "but because Easter was on April 30, we decided to move it back two weeks. For us communion is a memorial service. Jesus Christ said to do this in his memory. When he said this bread was his body, he was comparing the bread with his preparation for suffering. This is why the bread should be treated firmly when it is broken into pieces. Christ's body had to pass through breaking and suffering. We look on the bread as food but it reminds us of the suffering of Christ. The same for the wine. It is made from pressing grapes. The grape has to be wounded, but its juice can wash away our sins."

How do Baptists prepare for it? "If we judge ourselves, no one can pass judgment. We see our need for purification and forgiveness, and this depends on Jesus Christ. Each person has to prepare, to forgive others, and to seek Christ's forgiveness."

How did you become a believer? "I was baptized in Poltava [in the eastern Ukraine]. After my army service I came to Azerbaijan and joined the local church and started teaching the word of God and visiting the sick. I was a deacon. In 1975 I was elected presbyter."

Have *perestroika* and *glasnost* had any impact on religious life? "They have had remarkable impact on the life of believers, but the situation is still tentative. The old law is being reconsidered and a new one being prepared. When the new law is published, then we can judge the real depth of *perestroika*."

What do you hope to find in the new law? "We look for the right to preach the Gospel to everyone who wants to hear it. We want to have this possibility anywhere. Now we are working within the framework of the old law. We can respond to anyone who comes to us with questions, but there are many people who still do not dare to come to church. We need to come to them. We want the same rights people have in England. At Hyde Park, a public place, anyone can speak. One person can speak for God, another against. We want the chance to speak for God."

What about your relations with the Council for Religious Affairs? "We have friendly relations. We always understood that it is appointed to carry out its assigned duties and that these are not of their own making. But the process of *perestroika* is going on and both sides understand what it means. We are on the way."

Is there atheist education going on in Azerbaijan? "It has been going on for a long time and is still going on."

How would you compare Azerbaijan with the Ukraine? "I lived twenty-one years in the Ukraine. Believers there were regarded as closed-minded. It is better here. I think Azerbaijan is a more religious area than many other regions, because of the Moslems. There isn't the same hostility toward believers. The antireligious education is not so militant. There is more respect for believers. People show more interest in faith."

Do you sense that Moslems here have an advantage over Christians? "No. The law is balanced. All believers have an equal opportunity."

And yet you said that there are still people afraid to come to church. "Yes, I think so. It is still hard to become a believer. If you are in a family of five or six, other people in your family may object. They think you will compromise the family. But a new law that equalizes both believers and nonbelievers, so that neither has more rights, will change the situation. Then belief will be no disgrace to the family."

Sergei commented that there will still be problems in the work place with functionaries who don't accept reform for believers and who can do harm to those who identify themselves as believers. "Yes, there will still be problems but the social climate will be better. The main question the functionary should think about is what kind of person you are. Are you a good worker? An honest person? Your religious belief should not be held against you. But for the believer what other people think of you shouldn't matter. If they oppose you, it may even encourage your faith. Jesus said that just as he was persecuted, his followers will be persecuted. We have seen it happen over and over again in history."

Will it present a problem to Christianity in the Soviet Union *not* to be persecuted? "We have to leave this in the hands of God. He knows best. You shouldn't try to take charge of events. Whatever happens, we will face the problems that come. The changes now going on in some way benefit us but they bring other problems."

For example? "Freedom is not a good thing in itself but only good if we point ourselves toward God. If we point ourselves away from God, it isn't a desirable freedom. If this freedom will give us more faith, we are asking God to give it to us. But if it will drive people further from God, then we do not need it."

Chapter 7

Jews

IN 1738, BARUCH LEIBOV, a Jew who had tried to establish a synagogue in a village near Smolensk, was burned to death after being convicted of attempting to convert a retired naval officer.[1] In those years, Jews were still rare in Russia. It wasn't until 1772, with Russian annexation of eastern Poland, that a large Jewish population came under Russian rule. In the nineteenth century their number was more than five million — the largest Jewish community in the world. Today it has shrunk to two million, the third largest Jewish population.

Czar Nicholas I regarded the Jews as "an anarchic, cowardly, parasitic people, damned perpetually because of their deicide and heresy... best dealt with by repression, persecution, and, if possible, conversion."[2] In 1827 he ordered that each Jewish community deliver up a quota of military conscripts. Jewish recruits were to serve twenty-five years in the army. Considerable efforts were made to bring the recruits — often twelve or thirteen years old — into the Russian Orthodox Church. A Yiddish song from those days expresses Jewish anguish:

> Tears flow in the streets
> One can wash oneself in children's blood
> Little doves are torn from school
> And dressed up in goyish clothes.... [3]

---

[1] Benjamin Pinkus, *The Jews of the Soviet Union* (Cambridge: Cambridge University Press, 1988), p. 10.

[2] Michael Stanislowski, *Tsar Nicholas I and the Jews* (Philadelphia: Jewish Publication Society, 1983), p. 10.

[3] Zvi Gitelman, *A Century of Ambivalence: The Jews of Russia and the Soviet Union* (New York: Schocken, 1988), p. 6.

From 1835 until the Revolution in 1917, Jews were mainly confined to the Pale of Settlement, a wide strip running along the western border of the Russian Empire from the Baltic to the Black Sea that centered on Kiev, though Jews were barred from the city itself unless given special residence permits.

In 1882 laws were passed further limiting Jewish rights of residence so that the country might be "cleansed" of Jews. Jews were forbidden to do business on Sundays or Christian holidays. The number of Jewish students allowed into Russian schools was limited to 10 percent in secondary schools within the Pale, 5 percent elsewhere, and 3 percent in Moscow and Saint Petersburg. In 1890 Moscow's chief of police ordered that the signs of Jewish shops must carry the full Hebrew name of the owner. The following year, at Passover, the Jews were altogether expelled from the city.

In cities and towns where Jews were allowed, they lived in constant danger. In 1903, one pogrom reached world attention when the fifty thousand Jews of Kishinev were attacked by mobs stirred up by anti-Semitic articles in a local newspaper. In the course of two days forty-five Jews were killed, eighty-six gravely wounded and hundreds injured. More than fifteen hundred houses and shops were destroyed. In a pogrom in Odessa that same year, three hundred Jews died.

Many Jews presented themselves for baptism, but often it was only an act of grief by those who despaired of survival and opportunity except as Christians. Hundreds of thousands of Jews packed up what little they could carry and went to far away places like America that promised a better life. Others, motivated by Zionism, managed to get to Palestine. Still others, more hopeful of the possibilities for change in Russia, joined movements for reform and revolution.

Once the Revolution occurred, Jews who continued to follow traditional religious life were as much victims as any other group of believers, at times even more, given pervasive anti-Semitism. (Nor were the anti-Bolsheviks any better. A poster published by the Whites during the civil war showed the giant figure of a diabolic Leon Trotsky, naked except for a star of David around his neck, sitting on the Kremlin wall, looking down with satisfaction on a field of skulls.)

In response to the continuing Zionist movement among Jews, the Soviet government established a number of Jewish settlements. In the twenties a "Jewish homeland" was created in the far east in the thinly settled territory of Birobidzhan. It was no promised land.

During the Second World War, the areas of the most concentrated Jewish settlement, the former Pale, were occupied by the German army. Countless thousands of Jews were shot and hanged. In one place alone, a ravine west of Kiev called Babi Yar, between one and two hundred thousand people, mainly Jews, were executed by the German army. Nor was the killing always done by the Germans. In Lvov, Ukrainians carried out a three-day pogrom in the days immediately following the German occupation. An Organization of Ukrainian Nationalists was set up that pledged obedience to Hitler in building a Europe "free of Jews and Bolsheviks."

In 1961 Yevgeni Yevtushenko, revolted with the resurgence of anti-Semitism, wrote a poem that began with the comment that there was no monument at Babi Yar. He identified with the victims:

> I seem to be a Jew.
> Here I plod through ancient Egypt.
> Here I perish crucified on the cross
> and to this day I bear the scars of nails....
> I seem to be Anne Frank
> transparent as a branch in April....
> The wild grasses rustle over Babi Yar.
> The trees look ominous, like judges.
> Here all things scream silently, and, baring my head
> slowly I feel myself turning grey."[4]

In 1962 Shostakovich set the poem to music in his Thirteenth Symphony, but it was suppressed shortly after its debut by authorities who insisted that anti-Semitism had been eliminated in the USSR. In 1976, in belated answer to the poem and symphony, a monument was erected at Babi Yar.

Though the Soviet Union voted in favor of the creation of the state of Israel, in later years Zionists were persecuted. Officially sanctioned anti-Zionism provided a fresh opening for anti-Semitism.

While Yiddish was accepted as the national language of Jews, many of those learning and teaching Hebrew were sent to labor camps. One young Zionist, Anatoly Shcharansky, was accused of treason in 1978 and spent eight years in prisons and camps before finally being permitted to move to Israel.

Despite all their sorrows, Jews persist in the USSR and the majority have no plans to move. Some dare to hope that a page is being turned in Soviet history and that at last they need not hide their faith, live in fear, or envy those who have left the country. But all Jews look with alarm at renewed public expressions of anti-Semitism occurring

---

[4] *The Poetry of Yevgeni Yevtushenko* (London: Marion Boyars, 1981), pp. 145–49.

due to the removal of censorship and the emergence of such nationalist movements as *Pamyat* in which anti-Semites receive a warm welcome.

Kiev

At Kiev's Jewish synagogue January 12, 1989, dawn was beginning to color the grey sky. Women were clustered outside the synagogue doors. Rabbi Isaac Fuchs greeted us with "Shalom" and brought us into a large hall with a balcony.

The walls were mainly blue with clouds and stars painted on the ceiling. Over the place where the Torah scrolls are kept was the Hebrew text: "Thou shalt make no graven image." Several men were in conversations in back while in the front a dozen men in prayer garments were reciting the Kaddish, each person praying independently, at his own speed. The sound was a quiet, warm babble. One old man with a medal on his jacket read his prayer book with a magnifying glass, reading slowly, giving each word the attention a jeweler might give a diamond. One man stopped in the aisle and stared at me warily, but another man took me under his wing. Rabbi Fuchs, in his forties, was the youngest member of the weekday congregation.

In the rabbi's office afterward, Elia Levitas told me of the founding in Kiev of a Society of Jewish Culture on November 22, 1988. "This is a consequence of radical changes going on right now. Finally we have the chance to communicate our culture. Practically everything is possible. Nobody seeks to govern us, to instruct or impede. In fact they even give us help."

What will the Society do? "We are preparing to open a Jewish Cultural Center in Kiev, and we also hope to establish a Jewish Museum in the building where the author Sholem Aleichem lived. We have requested it but the authorities have not yet responded to our proposal."

What about religious education for Jews? "We have asked permission to open a two-year school to prepare teachers of Yiddish and Hebrew. Also we have applied to talk to the Ukrainian Ministry of Education about offering a course for those who want to learn about Judaism. We want to ask teachers to talk to the parents of children about this. We have a Yiddish publication in which there will be a series of articles on teaching Hebrew to yourself."

What about anti-Semitism in the Ukraine? "It is not right just to accuse the Ukraine. My studies remind me that unfortunately many places are distinguished by anti-Semitism. I am compiling a bibliography of books on the history of Jews and Jewish communities in Russia in the period from 1700 to the present. So far I have described fourteen thousand books from libraries all over the Soviet Union as well as in a number of other countries — Israel, France, and Spain."

I asked Rabbi Fuchs about the synagogue's history. "It is old. The building dates from the eighteenth century. According to tradition, Peter the Great laid a stone in the foundation. It has been used continuously except during the German occupation. It was reopened in 1946. Another synagogue has opened in Lvov, and the Jewish population in Harkov wants to open a synagogue there. There are also some Jewish preaching houses in towns near Kiev. The Kiev synagogue is second in rank after the synagogue in Moscow. On weekdays normally twenty take part in the prayer service, mainly retired people. On Saturdays about a hundred come. On feast days the synagogue is filled and surrounded — if the weather is good, perhaps twenty-five thousand come. We have a second hall that we open for feast days. Also we have a *mikva* [for ritual baths], a bakery where we make *matzo* — twelve hundred kilos a day, and a room for slaughtering chickens in the *kosher* way. We receive support from Jews in other countries — thirty thousand tons of special flour for *matzo* has been given to us by Jews in France."

Irkutsk

The synagogue in Irkutsk includes a small factory where I found seven people making *matzo* bread. At one end of the room the dough was made and passed through rollers before being cut into rectangles on a long table and put into the wood-fired oven for quick baking. The smell of fresh-baked *matzo* brought back memories of the years I lived on the Lower East Side in New York where many of my older neighbors were Russian and Ukrainian Jews.

In an adjacent room a large photo hung on the wall commemorating the 1,667 Jews from the Irkutsk Oblast who fought and died in the last world war. "Nobody is forgotten, nothing is forgotten," said the text over the picture.

My visit happened to coincide with a day of remembrance for the dead. "Many people from the synagogue will visit our two Jewish cemeteries," said the vice-chairman of the Synagogue Council, Mordecai Levenson.

We walked to the front of the synagogue to the cabinet where the Torah scrolls are stored, a practice similar to the Catholic custom of having a place behind the altar for the consecrated bread that has become Christ's body. The Torah is a sign of God's living presence. The warden gently kissed the Torah as he lifted it out, just as Orthodox Christians kiss the Bible.

"Our synagogue is 108 years old," he said, "though there were seven years when it was closed, 1937 to 1944. We succeeded to stay open in the Khrushchev years, a time when 8,600 places of worship were closed."

I asked how it was that Jews first came to Irkutsk. "Mostly as prisoners, people sent into exile, but for a long time we couldn't come to Irkutsk. Only Christians. Irkutsk was a city and the Russian law used to be — before 1917 — that Jews couldn't live in a city except by permission. To get permission you had to be a doctor, a merchant — not some common person. So Jews lived in villages and towns. Not only could you not live in a city, you couldn't even go to a city without permission. If your child was sick, before you could take it to the doctor, you had to have permission to enter the city. If more treatment was needed, more permission was needed. If you were one of those few Jews permitted to live in the city, you had to do it discreetly. Otherwise you would be sent away."

He introduced me to an elderly woman, Leah Isayevna Eseyona, whose grandparents were exiles. I asked how it happened. "Grandfather was a soldier in the army," she said, "very tall and handsome! One day he went to a restaurant with his friends. As a Jew he wasn't supposed to go inside but he didn't look Jewish. An officer saw him and knew he was Jewish. He came up to the table and said, 'Jews are prohibited.' My grandfather was a temperamental person. He knocked the officer down. For this he was sent to Siberia. My grandmother came with him. She was pregnant at that time. There was another child she couldn't bring. That boy grew up in Russia with his uncle. My grandparents never left Siberia. It was permanent exile. They had six sons and two daughters born in Siberia. Until the Revolution, they lived in a village. It was better in some ways than it would have been in Russia. No troubles, except Jews weren't allowed to attend school. After the Revolution our family moved to Irkutsk, and the children went to school."

"But Jews also came here more recently," another woman said. "My family was evacuated to this region during the war. I was fourteen. The war was terrible and we had a lot of trouble getting here. It was a very hard life. At first we didn't live in the city, but then I got a job at a factory in Irkutsk and worked there for forty years, my husband for forty-seven. He was an engineer and I was a designer."

Rabbi Mordecai Cohen came to sit with us. "But in the earlier time, you couldn't even change your village," he said. "They sent you to a certain village and you had to stay there. It was like a prison. We didn't have the right to trade or to own land. A Jew could only rent land."

Given the restrictions of the nineteenth century, how could a synagogue be founded in Irkutsk? "Gradually things changed. One by one certain Jews got permission to live here. Finally they allowed the Jews to have a place to pray and so our synagogue was started."

"When they were building the Tikhvin church," said a bearded man who joined the conversation, "they needed someone to do the windows. My great-grandfather was a craftsman living in Zima, northwest of Irkutsk, and he was good at glasswork. Someone said to the priest in Irkutsk there was this Jew in Zima, just the right man to do the church windows! [laughing] So he was hired and came to Irkutsk to do this job. He did it perfectly, so well that the priest asked what reward he wanted. He asked for the remains of the glass, but the priest said no, this was too valuable. So he made a second request, to have permission to live in Irkutsk. The archpriest was willing. He wrote to the governor and the governor signed the paper and our family came to Irkutsk."

How is the situation today? "Today we have five thousand Jews in Irkutsk and the situation is good for us," the rabbi said. "We get a higher education. We get good jobs. We can make *matzo*. We can pray."

"My son is a journalist," said Leah Isayevna with great pride.

But, I pointed out, a lot of Jews seem to be having serious problems. Many are anxious to leave the country for Israel or the United States. "How can they leave their motherland?" Leah Isayevna asked. "How? I couldn't. I read the newspapers and I understand. I know one Jew who was forced to leave. But I don't want to leave. You only travel from one trouble to another."

Are the current changes making life better for Jews than before? "Jews are able to study Hebrew — it used to be forbidden," said Mordecai Levenson. "We are getting prayer books from the United States." He showed me a copy. "In some places there are synagogues being reopened. Jewish cultural centers are beginning. There is a Jewish museum being started in Moscow and a Jewish theater named Shalom. It is better."

What about religious education? "We don't want to teach religion in public school," said the rabbi. "You cannot teach someone to believe in God. The will of each person is cultivated in the family. But we want the chance for religious studies for those who wish it. We think this is starting now."

On the way out Mordecai Levenson gave me a carton of *matzo* still warm from the oven. "Just in case you get hungry."

Baku

The morning service was over when we arrived at the synagogue in Baku in May. The rabbi and members of the synagogue council were awaiting us at a table in the back of the synagogue set with tea, soft drinks, fruit, cookies, and candy.

One of the council members was a teacher of English. "I am one of the few members of the synagogue actually born in Baku," he said. "Most come from the Ukraine."

The rabbi, Israel Moiseyevich Berchick, introduced himself. He was born in 1909 in Bogoslav, near Kiev, and moved to Baku in 1930. He was unshaven and had a round, lined face. "The congregation on a typical Saturday is about fifty people," he said, "but on feasts the synagogue is full and more than full."

I asked if there were many Jews in Azerbaijan. "According to the last census, there are three hundred thousand Jews in Azerbaijan. Most are in Baku but there are two synagogues elsewhere in the republic."

What effect has *perestroika* had on Jewish life in Azerbaijan? "It is first of all a change of atmosphere, something you feel. But it shows in other ways. We are getting the books we need, the Torah, prayer books, a history book. Now we have a secondary school where we teach Hebrew — both youngsters and middle-aged people are coming to study. There were people from religious communities elected as deputies. In the years of stagnation no one could imagine such things. Still I want to stress that we had our synagogue long before the *perestroika* process. Faith is faith. But now it is easier for people to come who were hesitating before. More people come."

The chairman of the synagogue council, Mark Isaakovich Gartsman, also Ukrainian, was born in 1910. He was a thin man in a tidy grey suit. "It's strange," he said, "but the celebration of the baptism of Russia was something that was good for Jews. After that there were a number of positive events, even big changes. I visited the

Council for Religious Affairs, and we had good talks. They said that the former restrictions would be gradually removed."

What problems existed in the past? [long pause] "Synagogue-goers felt that they were somehow under supervision. There was a feeling of control. The international climate was tense. Relations with other countries were a factor. Whatever the cause, you could feel it in your skin. Now a believer can feel at ease, not like before."

How did it happen that so many Ukrainian Jews came to Azerbaijan? "The Ukraine was a hard place for us. It was a hard environment. There were pogroms and there wasn't enough food. I was the oldest child in my family. I had five sisters. We came to Baku in 1931."

Have there ever been pogroms here? "Never. Throughout all my years living here, I always felt that the local people respected Jews. It can't be compared to the Ukraine or Russia. And after the war, it got even worse in those places, especially the Ukraine."

We were interrupted by a desperate woman who asked if I could help her get medicine for her son, three years old, who has leukemia. The prescribed drugs weren't available in Baku. She had gone to Moscow for two months but couldn't obtain them there either. Could I send them from the West?[5]

"You see the problems we face," said Maria Bakun, the synagogue bookkeeper and cashier, "Jews along with everybody. But Jews were never mistreated here. Never. Many Azeris marry Jews. There are some things Jews and Moslems have in common, so we often marry. My sister is married to a Byelorussian. In my family we celebrate all the religious feasts — Jewish, Moslem, and Christian."

"But now," said Mark Gartsman, "you see a new wave of anti-Semitism, not here but in Russia and the Ukraine. When there is more freedom, it is also used by evil people."

Do your children share your attachment to the synagogue? "Not yet. I have three sons, all married, three granddaughters, and one grandson. My sons show their respect. But they don't understand the service. They don't know Hebrew. In other countries Jews have not only the synagogue but many programs to hold them together — social centers, cafes, schools. So far we don't have such things. But now it is possible to study Hebrew and we think this will help."

---

[5]I passed her request on to a Dutch organization, the Solidarity Committee for Jews in the Soviet Union, which took responsibility to assist her.

Chapter 8

Moslems

BEGINNING WITH THE VICTORY of Grand Prince Dimitri Don-
skoi against the Golden Horde in 1380 at the Battle of Kulikovo
Field, Russia's borders were outward bound. In the fifteenth century Moscow had its first czar, Ivan III, under whose rule Russia
became the largest state in Europe. By the sixteenth century, with the
incorporation of Siberia, Russia stretched to the Pacific. In the seventeenth century the eastern Ukraine was annexed, bringing Russia
to the Black Sea. In the eighteenth century, Peter the Great fought
his way to the Baltic, while in other battles he pushed the border
south to the Caspian Sea into the world of Islam. In the nineteenth
century the empire captured huge Moslem territories: Azerbaijan,
Kazakstan, and Turkistan and with these Baku, Bukhara, Tashkent,
and Samarkand, famed centers of Islamic studies.

Along with other religions, Moslems fared badly under Soviet
rule. In the thirties most mosques were confiscated and many were
destroyed. Islamic schools were closed and thousands of Moslem
leaders sent into the *gulag*.

Following a rebellion against Soviet rule in the north Caucasus
in the winter of 1940–41, Stalin transferred a million Moslems to
Siberia and Kazakstan. In the process the entire Chechen-Ingesh
Autonomous Republic was dissolved and all the mosques within it
destroyed.[1] (After Stalin's death the republic was restored, though it
was not until 1978 that any mosques were opened.) In 1942 Stalin
agreed to meet the mufti of Ufa, Abdurrahman Rasulaev, one of
the few Moslem leaders to have survived the purges that occurred

---

[1] Marie Broxup, "Islam and Atheism in the North Caucasus," *Religion in Communist Lands*, vol. 9, nos. 1–2 (Spring 1981).

in the period 1932–38 when Moslem clerics were hunted down as foreign agents and saboteurs. Afterward relations between the government and Islam were "normalized." As a result of the meeting four spiritual directorates[2] — later called boards — were established, one for Central Asia and Kazakstan, another for European Russia and Siberia, a third for the North Caucasus and Dagestan, and a fourth for Transcaucasia. All working mosques are under the supervision of the respective boards. All Moslem clerics are registered with them and paid by them.[3]

One staff member of the Council for Religious Affairs admitted to me in 1988 that, before Gorbachev came to power, the main direction in Soviet policy in regard to Moslems "was to eliminate Islamic consciousness." As late as 1986, when Gorbachev was in his first year in power, the first secretary of the Uzbekistan Communist party, addressing the Communist Party Congress in Moscow, spoke of "old prejudices and harmful customs" still surviving. He attacked "class enemies" who utilized the "Islamic factor" to undermine Soviet power. In Tashkent, he registered alarm at the growing number of unregistered Islamic associations providing religious education.[4]

Tashkent

Arriving in the central Asian republic of Uzbekistan in January 1989, I discovered not one Tashkent but two — one old, traditional, and Moslem, the other new, European, and secular. The European Tashkent had wide avenues dominated by high concrete apartment buildings similar to those in every Soviet city except there were screens built into the facades to provide some shelter from the sun. The traditional Tashkent beyond the Ankhor and Bozsu Canals was a city of winding, narrow streets and low rambling buildings squeezed together. Each house had its own yard, vines, and a few fruit trees.

In earthquake-prone Tashkent, the modern city was not only less attractive but dangerous. The last major earthquake, a monument at the epicenter indicates, was on April 26, 1966. Three

[2]As with so many institutions that seem peculiarly Soviet, this too had its model in czarist Russia. A Central Spiritual Moslem Directorate, analogous to the government-controlled Holy Synod of the Russian Orthodox Church, was established by Catherine II in the eighteenth century.

[3]Alexandre Bennigsen and Chantal Lemercier-Quelquejay, "Official Islam in the Soviet Union," *Religion in Communist Lands*, vol. 7, no. 3 (Autumn 1979).

[4]John Anderson, "The Islamic Factor in the Soviet Union," *Religion in Communist Lands*, vol. 14, no. 23 (Summer 1986), pp. 212–14.

hundred thousand people where made homeless and 35 percent of the buildings were destroyed. Those were the days of minimizing catastrophe — the number who died isn't indicated. Though new buildings are earthquake resistant, should there be a quake of 1966 proportions, there is the danger that many will die in the modern buildings. But the old city will again survive and those inside the traditional one- and two-story wood and mud buildings walk out alive. Walls will disintegrate and windows will break but the wooden structure will remain.

"Our ancestors were better architects," commented my host, Hassan Aka Turabekov, translator as well as chief editor of Uzbekistan's Literature and Art Publishing House. He resembled the old city more than the new — a large man in rumpled clothes, his tie loose and off center. He had a face round as the moon, black hair beginning to grey, light brown skin. "The old houses are nicer to live in, more humane, cooler in the summer, and better for earthquakes. The old architecture is also better for making community. In the *mahala* [neighborhood] everyone knows each other. Everyone takes part in weddings and funerals. But in these high-rise buildings you don't even know who lives in the next apartment. It is an architecture of disconnection. It is also uncomfortable. Concrete holds the heat. In the summer it is like an oven inside. But the new buildings go up and people are forced to live in them. They feel grief. They can no longer eat and sleep outside.

"On the other hand, there is the problem of being the capital of Uzbekistan. Tashkent has grown rapidly. When I was a boy, about six hundred thousand people lived here. Now it is about two million. We Uzbeks like to have children. Our birthrate is one of the highest in the USSR."

I asked if the city was mainly populated by Uzbeks. "In the city it is about 40 percent Russian and 40 percent Uzbek. The rest includes Tatars, Jews, and Ukrainians. But in the countryside it is mainly Uzbeks."

How do the different nationalities relate? "Usually very well. Uzbeks have a strong culture of hospitality. Our tradition requires a fence between neighbors but always a door in the fence and the door is never locked."

What else is traditional in Uzbek life? "It is very simple, good life. There is little furniture in the home. There is much singing. In the city people keep birds — it is nostalgia for life close to nature. But now life is threatened. Quail near the cities are dying of chemical pollution. There was a particularly dangerous defoliant being used on the field — it was supposed to make the cotton leafless for machine picking. It has done much harm to people and the environment. Only last year was this substance banned. Because of *glasnost* journalists were able to interview scientists and write about it. Public opinion became a factor."

Over lunch in a rambling country restaurant, Hassan Aka explained that Uzbeks believe the place in which one eats should resemble paradise. "This is why it is usual to have plants and birds near the table," he said. I counted sixteen birds in cages between windows, including a nightingale, several canaries, and a quail.

I asked how he had become a translator. "In my third year at the university I began a translation of Tolstoy's *War and Peace*. After graduation I was invited to teach literature at the university. A year later, in 1962, I had the chance to join the editorial board of the one publisher in Tashkent. Since then my time has been divided between translation, editing, and publishing. We are doing some important books. The most important was the annotated Koran we issued earlier this year. Seventy-five thousand copies were printed. The edition sold out in a couple of days."

Is religious education needed to overcome so many years of atheist indoctrination? "It is needed, but not in a classroom. No one can put religious truth on a plate and serve it to us. We each have to dig it out of the earth with our own hands. Unfortunately most people don't understand this. If you try to educate your children in the morality of happiness but you fail to teach them to pay attention to the happiness of others, it is no morality at all, and no true happiness either. If my happiness is selfish, I condemn my children to unhappiness. It is an endless chain. My personal happiness is connected to my wish for the happiness of all."

What changes are needed in readjusting local practices in Uzbekistan to respect Moslem tradition? "One problem that Moslems face in any secular society is that there is no provision to go to the mosque on Fridays. Friday is just another work day. But here provisions are made for Moslem feast days — for example special buses to assist people coming to the mosque. On a feast day, we would have a hard time getting near the mosque, the crowds would be so big."

What impact is *perestroika* having locally? "It was largely because of the family contract team that the last cotton harvest was so big. Each team gets a piece of land — how big it is depends on the size of the family. The family unit can be quite big when you start adding in aunts and uncles, brothers, sisters, cousins. People in them earn more than they did in the past and can provide for themselves better than before. There is also a form of family contract team for certain businesses — food service and catering cooperatives, for example, cafes and snack bars where you can sit down and eat the national food. In this area Uzbekistan is in the front rank. It is our tradition. We descend from famous traders. Uzbek traders have spread all over the world. Tashkent was the a main intersection of the Silk Road, a meeting place of East and West.

"But I think the main result of *perestroika* so far is that we are beginning to know happiness, not the happiness of paradise, but the happiness of not having to live a two-faced life — one face for the rostrum, another for the corridor. It is the happiness of being able to speak openly and honestly."

Back in the city, we stopped at the Kook-cha Mosque, one of the oldest in Tashkent. In the cemetery a funeral was in progress. We watched from a distance while Hassan explained the Uzbek funeral customs. "The Moslem funeral tradition is to be buried with your head toward Mecca. There is no coffin. A cloth is put over the body and then the hole is filled with earth. The imam reads from the Koran, 'May your grave be full of light and may you be received by Allah in heaven.' Everyone present takes part in the prayers. Then the son or brother or a close relative stands in front to take responsibility for any debts of the deceased, but I have never heard of anyone making a claim for payment of debts. With death all debts are forgiven. *Allah akbar!* [Great is Allah.] Then three days after the funeral friends come to the home. There are readings from the Koran and then a big meal. Then every Thursday for twenty days, just before sunset, there is a similar gathering and then another twenty days later there is a big commemoration where *pilaf* is served. They cook forty kilos of rice and add meat, carrots, and spices. There will also be pancakes, fruit and other things to eat, and of course bread and salt. Perhaps fifteen hundred people come, or two thousand.

"When I was more ignorant, I was put off by the custom of a common meal after a funeral. When someone is dead how can you rejoice? But one of the seven deadly sins is to be gloomy in your heart. If I become gloomy, perhaps you will become gloomy too. But if I smile, perhaps you will smile. My joy can become your joy. And joy is the major gift we can give to each other."

In the old part of Tashkent near the bazaar, in an office adjacent to the city's main mosque, Tillya-Shaikh Jami, we were received by Sheik Abdulghani Abdullah, editor of *Moslems of the Soviet East* and deputy chairman of the Moslem Religious Board for Central Asia and Kazakhstan. We sat around a table laid with fruit, bread, and nuts. Tea was served in orange porcelain cups. Sheik Abdullah was wearing a white turban and green jacket.

"This is the center of Moslem administration," he said, "not only for Uzbekistan but the four surrounding republics — Kazakstan, Kirgizstan, Tadzhikistan, and Turkmenistan. There are three similar boards in other regions. Except in Azerbaijan where there are Shi'ites, our Moslem population in the Soviet Union is mainly Sunite."

How many mosques are there in Tashkent? "Seventeen plus many places of prayer in private homes. In Central Asia, there are now about 260 mosques registered and in the USSR altogether about 600. It is impossible to say the exact number because so many are now being registered."

I asked about his past. "Both my grandfather and father were Moslem clergy. My father studied at several Moslem institutes but made his living as an agricultural worker. When I was fifteen I was sent to Bukhara to study and remained there for nine years, until 1954, except for the time of my army service. I later had the chance to study in Cairo and then was teaching at the Moslem school in Bukhara. For the last twenty years I have been editor of the magazine of the Moslem Religious Board for Central Asia. Since 1975 I have been the board's vice chairman."

What is the effect of *perestroika* for Moslems? "Quite a lot is happening. Two mosques are reopening here in Tashkent and similar events are going on wherever Moslems are living. We have about five hundred mosques now and hope to have a thousand. How soon depends on the local people and how effectively and quickly they promote the possibilities."

What about theological education? "We have a *madrassah* [a Moslem college] with a seven-year program in the Uzbek city of Bukhara. The basic course includes the study of Arabic, the Koran and its interpretation, traditions concerning the Prophet, Islamic law and history, as well as courses you would find in any college — language study, history, geography, literature, science, and so forth. From Bukhara a smaller number comes to the Islamic Institute here in Tashkent for an advanced four-year program. Also we send students to Egypt, Jordan, Syria, Libya, and other countries for study."

What about publishing activities? "Now we are preparing a new edition of the Holy Koran."

A large enough edition to meet the demand? "With more than 50 million Moslems in the Soviet Union, it will take a long time to fill the gap. There was too long a time when the Koran was not published —

the stagnation years. But we are also receiving copies of the Koran from outside, especially from Saudi Arabia. They are sending some in Uzbek translation as well as in Arabic."

Fifty million Moslems? "If you count all those with Moslem names, in fact it would be about 60 million, but at present the majority do not follow Moslem traditions."

How would you compare the situation of Moslems in the Soviet Union with that of Moslems in other parts of the world? "In some ways it is better. There is a higher educational level here than in much of the Moslem world. Though there are problems, still we don't know poverty, unemployment, and hunger. Now with *perestroika* there is a much better possibility to provide religious education. Articles about Islam are in the press. There are religious programs on television. These are remarkable events. The state doesn't fear more people becoming Moslem. In fact we even have the impression that the state wants more believers."

Was the repression of Moslems in former times severe? "Yes. Many honest people — peasants, workers, teachers, clergy — were sent away and never came back. Mosques were closed. Some were blown up — remarkable places, monuments of culture. It was a test on behalf of Allah. This is what we believe. But people persevered in their faith. They did not surrender their souls."

How extensive was the social damage? "Severe, and yet the culture has survived. For example the Uzbek tradition of respect for older people, including nonrelatives, has been preserved. We still prefer to live in our one and two-story houses. We like to be close to nature and have the sky over our heads. People are still building such houses."

Are Moslems engaging in charitable work in hospitals? "Not yet, but on the other hand, because of our tradition, old people are kept within the family. We consider it shameful to neglect a father or mother. The Moslem view is that if you do not care for the aged as the Koran commands, then it is no good to pray five times a day. So we take care of our relatives in our homes. But if someone must be in the hospital, relatives provide so fully that there is no need for the mosque to establish any program of further assistance. Our responsibility is not only for relatives but for anyone. It is our tradition to share our food with the stranger."

How is the ferment in the rest of the Moslem world being felt in the Soviet Union? "There are fundamentalists and sectarians here but not many."

We walked across the street to the Islamic Institute to see the new library, a place of such beauty that I was reminded of the Alhambra palaces Moslems built in the south of Spain. The display cases contained Korans produced in Tashkent over the centuries.

"All the books in the library have come to us as gifts. Not only our students but many others are coming to use the library — scholars, scientists, scholars of Arabic. All are welcome. The preparation of the library took one year with no days off. It was a work of love."[5]

Samarkand

Samarkand, among the oldest cities of central Asia, was one of the paradises of the world, according to Jules Verne. It has been ruled by Greeks, Persians, Arabs, Mongols, and Uzbeks. In the fourteenth century, it was taken by the Tatar warrior king, Tamerlane, who intended to make it the capital of the world. For centuries it was a major center of Moslem scholarship. With the decline of the Silk Road, the city too fell into such decay that it was uninhabited for half the eighteenth century. When the region was incorporated into the Russian Empire in the late nineteenth century, Samarkand became the provincial capital.

The heart of the city is Registan Square, enclosed on all but one side by three *madrassahs*, each with its own mosque. The buildings are presently a museum complex. One *madrassah* was founded by Uleg Beg, the scholar and astronomer who ruled Samarkand after Tamerlane's death. The mosque of the Tillah-Kari *madrassah* in the center is not only the most beautiful in Samarkand but is among the

---

[5]In early February 1989, shortly after this interview, there was a demonstration in Tashkent organized by a new movement, Islam and Democracy, in which an estimated twenty-five hundred people called for "purification of the Moslem establishment" whose "reputation had been destroyed by close alliance with the state." Soon afterward the mufti resigned.

On February 23 *Pravda Vostoka*, the regional newspaper, reported that the first secretary of the Communist party in Uzbekistan, P. N. Nishanov, criticized "forceful methods" used in the past "to break up peoples' traditions and to forbid centuries-old rites and customs." He called on party committees to "refrain from the administrative, bureaucratic approach to religious questions." At the same time he stressed that Communists and Komsomol members "should not participate directly in religious rites" because "a true affirmation of the new political thinking in relation to religion does not mean ideological compromise with it."

At an extraordinary congress of the Moslem board on March 15, Muhammad Sadiq Mamayusupov was chosen as the new chief mufti. Born in 1952, he was head of the Higher Islamic Institute in Tashkent. While previous conferences of the board had involved only carefully selected delegates, the congress was open to all imams in the region. In an interview in *Pravda Vostoka*, the new mufti expressed satisfaction in the new atmosphere with regard to church-state relations and the return of many mosques, including Bukhara's famous Kalyan mosque (Keston News Service, nos. 321, 323).

world treasures of religious architecture. The pattern of ascending gold leaves in the mosque's ultramarine dome seemed like an opening to heaven.[6]

The most vital spot in the city was the bazaar with its miles of round bread, apples, melons, pomegranates, dried fruit, milk balls, and many kinds of raisins and nuts. Still more impressive were the faces, many of them old: men with silky white beards, women with round faces sipping steaming tea.

We drove to the mosque and mausoleum of Abu Al-Bukhari at the village of Khartang, a place of pilgrimage for Moslems from many countries. Our host, Imam Hatib Alimov Usman Khan, was a man of thirty-eight with a short black beard, thoughtful face and calm manner. He wore a deep blue robe, fur hat, vest, and multicolored shirt.

"To understand why our mosque is so important to Islam you must learn about Al-Bukhari, revered by the entire Moslem world because his collection of the sayings of the Prophet is buried here. His great work was the *al-Jami as-Sahih*, second only to the Koran. Two years after his birth in Bukhara in 809, his father died. His mother, a scholar and scientist, gave him his initial education. When he was seven he knew the entire Koran by heart. At age ten he had memorized several thousand speeches of the Prophet. When he was sixteen, with his mother and older brother, he undertook the *hajj*, the pilgrimage to Mecca. For forty years, travelling from Cairo to central Asia, he studied sayings and actions ascribed to the Prophet, accepting for inclusion in his encyclopedia only those traditions he judged most reliable. This is arranged according to subject, allowing the reader to study accounts of the Prophet's teachings and actions on points of law and religious doctrine. Al-Bukhari also wrote a commentary on the Koran and the biographies of persons forming the living chain of transmission of traditions back to the Prophet. He finally returned to Bukhara but, for refusing to provide private tutoring for the children of the governor, was sent into exile. On his way to Samarkand, he died in 869 among his relatives at Khartang. Now many come to this holy place to show their respect to this great person. In the last three years pilgrims have included the prime ministers of several Moslem states."

I asked about his background. "My parents are believers. My father is not a clergyman but he knows the Koran very well. I have

---

[6]The April 10, 1989, issue of the international edition of *Time* magazine, in captioning a photo of the Registan Square, reported the return of one of the Registan mosques, presumably the Tillah-Kari mosque, as a place of worship.

three brothers. One is a driver, the second a team leader on a state collective farm, the third is head of a secondary school. All of us can read Arabic easily. Two are believers. I wanted to go to the *madrassah* either in Bukhara or Tashkent. At the time it was very difficult to do this. I made several vain attempts to enter. It took seven years but finally I was able to enter the *madrassah* in Tashkent. Now the outside obstacles are gone, although there is still a limited number of places within the schools."

I asked about home mosques. "On Friday, our day of prayer and rest, every Moslem is obliged to come to the mosque to pray. If you were here on a Friday, you would find a big crowd, in the summer especially, when they come not only from Samarkand but from distant countries. But there are many people living too far away from a mosque so a place is arranged in someone's house, a convenient place of prayer that is nearby. You find these home mosques in practically every neighborhood and village."

What changes are occurring locally? "We have a more positive response when we meet officials from the Council for Religious Affairs. We are able to open more mosques. Some have already opened, and we expect many more to open in the coming years. It is much easier for us to do our work. At this mosque we used to have two imams. Now we have nine. We serve several outlying parishes. It is much easier for us to meet the peoples' needs for weddings and funerals done according to *shari'ah* [Moslem law]."

Are people who were not religiously active beginning to follow the practices of Islam? "Yes, although this is something that happens little by little. A Moslem should pray five times a day — before sunrise, just before noon, in the late afternoon, just after sunset, and before going to bed. Before prayer you should wash your hands, your face and your feet. You should pray in the direction of Mecca. But if you are a young person working in a factory, how can you stop and pray? It is much easier for people who have retired. But we see that on feast days more people are coming to the mosque."

Many people associate Islam with intolerance and violence. Is this justified? "The Koran teaches us that God gave life to the earth and all people and that, no matter what tribe or nation we belong to, we all descend from the same parents, Adam and Eve. We are all leaves on the same tree and are required by God to live as one family. Whoever believes in God and the Last Judgment will never commit any evil against neighbors but will always help them. It is my experience that most Moslems are peaceful people. Whoever crosses the threshold of our homes is met with an open heart."

How has *perestroika* affected Moslems? "It means that the truth has triumphed. It is said in the Holy Koran that lies will be trampled under by the truth. We are seeing this happen. The truth has come, and now it is easier for people to live. They can tell the truth and live an open life without a mask."

Flying back to Tashkent, I saw huge, gun-studded planes on the ground. Presumably they had a role in the war in Afghanistan. Sergei drew my attention to a poem by Yevgeni Yevtushenko, "On Afghan Land a Russian Boy Lies Dead," just published in the January *Ogonyok*:

> A Moslem ant is crawling on his cheek.
> He says, You don't know why you have died, or where.
> You only know that Iran is somewhere nearby.
> What has brought you to this country
> with weapons in your hands?
> For the first time you have heard the word "Islam."
> What draws you to my Motherland, barefoot and poor,
> if in your own land people wait in long lines for sausage?
> Haven't you enough people killed?
> Do you need to add more to your 20,000,000 dead?
>
> A Russian boy lies dead on Afghan land.
> The Moslem ant is crawling on his cheek.
> The Moslem ant wants to ask the Orthodox ant
> how to raise this boy from the dead.
> On the ground of his Motherland of orphans and widows
> not so many ants of this kind are left,
> those who can tell how to raise him up.[7]

Irkutsk

I was welcomed to the mosque in Irkutsk by the imam and three other old men. The chairman of the mosque council, Gayaz Norgalievich Muhutdinov, did most of the talking. He was retired, living on a pension of 120 rubles a month. Imam Hatib was eighty-nine, very frail, also living on pension. The mosque paid no salaries.

The mosque — a stone building with Arabic script carved on the facade — was built a century ago but was closed in 1937. "Now it is ours again except for the basement," said Gayaz Muhutdinov.

---

[7]Translation by Sergei Afonin.

"The basement is used by the district party committee. Like many other centers of worship, it was returned to believers after the United States opened the second front in 1944. Our impression was that the reopening of churches, mosques, and synagogues was a demand U.S. President Roosevelt made to Stalin."

Like so many others, Moslems originally came to Siberia as prisoners and exiles, though others came for work. "The four of us all come from Kazan like most local Moslems. We worked on the railroad and also worked in construction of the hydroelectric dam on the Angara River just beyond the city. Now there are Moslems working on BAM [the new railroad project cutting a more northern route across Siberia to the Pacific from Irkutsk]. And most of us fought in the war." He showed me an impressive medal he was wearing, the Order of the Great Patriotic War.

I asked Imam Hatib how he came to Irkutsk. "I came here in 1916, voluntarily, just a young man looking for work. I got a job at a factory. I was a believer already. Later I studied at the *madrassah* in Ufa where I learned Arabic."

What about repression of Moslems? "In Central Asia it started earlier than here. Until 1937, in eastern Siberia, we didn't feel it. Then the purges started. Many imams and mullahs, many faithful people, were arrested and sent to distant places, as far away as Kamchatka."

What effect is *perestroika* having for Moslems? "In former times we weren't allowed to write in Arabic. We had to write with the Cyrillic alphabet. Now this is changed. We can use Arabic, publish books in Arabic, and teach Arabic to our children and any others who want to learn. More people can study in the *madrassah* and we expect to have more Moslem schools. And now mosques can be opened where believers want them."

What about services in the mosque on Friday? "For observant Moslems, even if you cannot get to the mosque, you can pray in your home after work. It is not essential for us to go to the mosque. But we hope that it will be easier for Moslems to come to the mosque. At the mosque you can be more open to Allah."

Can Soviet Moslems make the pilgrimage to Mecca? "It isn't easy but it is possible. People go every year, but you have to have the wallet for it! It costs four or five thousand rubles. To do it you write to the mufti, and he applies to the International Affairs Department at the Moslem Central Board office in Moscow. This office collects all the applications and sends the group."

What hopes have you for the new legislation on freedom of conscience? "First of all we want to teach our children in their native language. We don't mind that they learn Russian but we want them educated in our own language. We want our Moslem children to have access to the books of the Moslem world."

Are there enough Korans? "The mufti of Siberia, Talgat Dajetdinov, has been given permission to publish fifty thousand Korans and ten thousand copies of the Sayings of the Prophet. These are for the Siberian region. There are editions being published in the other three regions as well. So the situation is much better but still there is far to go."

Baku

Baku juts into the Caspian Sea like a hawk's beak. Despite the ethnic tension between Azeris and Armenians, in May 1989 the clues to the real state of things — tanks by the government house, the curfew in the small hours of the night — were few. Muscovites could walk down vine-covered streets into markets with abundant fruit and vegetables and think they had died and gone to heaven. On the other hand, the traffic was so loud and merciless that they might think they had died and arrived in purgatory.

The Russian connection with Azerbaijan dates back to 1804. In the course of wars with Persia (1804–13 and 1826–28), Russia annexed Baku plus a number of regional principalities. A treaty established the Aras River as the border, thus dividing the Azeri people. There is a large Azeri population in modern Iran. An independent Azerbaijan was set up in May 1918, but from August 1918 to August 1919, British forces occupied the city. In April 1920 the Red Army took control and created the Azerbaijan Soviet Socialist Republic. I noticed that the local portraits of Lenin make him look quite tropical.

Azerbaijan is the biggest producer of grapes in the USSR, a major exporter of cotton, citrus fruits, pomegranates, olives, tobacco, tea, and saffron. But oil is king. The world's first deep-bore hole was drilled at an oil field near Baku. Especially outside the city the air smells of oil. There are huge areas near Baku where oil derricks are more crowded together than any place in Texas — barren, battered land with nothing on it but oil rigs.

Baku's population is mainly Azeri — 56 percent — with 22 percent Russian and 14 percent Armenian, though the last statistic is now badly out of date. Following the ethnic riots, many Armenians fled. The rest of the population includes Caucasians, Jews, Tatars, and Ukrainians — nationalities first drawn to Baku at the turn of the century by the oil boom.

"Azeris tend to have large families," said Fikret Zarbaliyev, an editor with the Azerbaijan publishing department. "Three or four children is common. And we are a long-lived people — there were fourteen hundred people over ninety at the time of the last census. Even Russians tend to have larger families here than they do in Russia."

Fikret took me for a walk through the old city. Joining with us were several local writers: Fikret Akhundly, Zahid Khalil, and Tehran Veliev. It was a small literary parade.

At a café across from the Djuma Mosque, now a museum of carpets, we drank hot tea served in tulip-shaped glasses. "The tulip shape represents a flame," Fikret said. "Before Islam was accepted, the Azeri people revered fire. Some of the ancient fire traditions still survive, like leaping over fire on the New Year. But Islam has been here many centuries. Names from the Koran like Issa (Jesus), Myriam (Mary), Mussa (Moses), and Daud (David) are popular among us."

I asked about their marriages. One was married to a Russian, one to an Armenian, one to a Jew — and only one to an Azeri. "For us the family is the core matter," said Zahid. "You prove yourself for your family and with your family you show that you deserve to live on the earth. It is like our saying, 'The head exists not to provide life's necessities for yourself but for your family.' From your family the circle widens to include friends and finally — ideally — the whole world."

The whole world, it was admitted, is not in very good health. Locally this was exhibited in massive environmental damage caused by the oil and petrochemical industry.

"During the [Brezhnev] years of stagnation the only thing that mattered was what you were producing and how much," Zahid Khalil said, "not the impact on the environment. There wasn't a word about that. Brezhnev's slogan was only that the economy must be economical. Only after *glasnost* could we hold public meetings and begin to talk about closing factories and banning chemical discharges. Recently there was a television program about a dead zone, an area in which life is impossible. We see the cancers caused by these factories. The question is either to close these places or to find a way to make them safe. The first secretary of the Azerbaijan Communist party met with a group that wants to close certain plants. A beginning is being made — one percent of one percent. It will take many years to stop this destructive process, maybe centuries. Perhaps only our children will begin to see the results. May the mercy of God inspire us to do this."

Driving into the oil fields, we came to the fortress-like Ateshgah Temple, built by Parsees in the eighteenth century, a place of fire worship until 1883 when the natural fire went out. Now a museum, the fire is burning again from gas brought in by pipe. "The monks were fierce ascetics who saw the body as the soul's enemy," said the guide. "Islam is a higher form of religion as it sees body and soul in harmony."

We ate lunch in a town near the temple. "You should have bread on the table but you must have greens," said Zahid, concerned that I wasn't eating enough greens. After my hosts recited some of their own poems, we talked about recent changes in Azerbaijan.

"One of the differences between now and five years ago," said Zahid, "is that there are fewer boring meetings and the boring meetings we have now are shorter. More important, people are telling the truth. It used to be that people lied much more, even continually. While we cannot yet say that truth is victorious, still you hear it more often than before. People would lie and you knew they were lying and they knew you knew that they were lying but you pretended it was the truth — another lie. The lie of pretending belief was an essential courtesy. He pretended to be telling the truth and you pretended you believed him."

I asked if the Koran was easily obtained in Azerbaijan. "Still not, although a Russian-language edition of the Koran was published here last year. It was a small edition, however, only ten thousand copies. Now a translation of the Koran into Azeri is in preparation. It will be the first Koran to be published in our own language since the Revolution. Not all Moslems agree that the Koran should be translated. Some prefer that the people learn Arabic so that the music of the original can be preserved."

The following evening we ate at Zahid's home — a paradise-like meal of stuffed pepper, tomato, and eggplant followed by sweet pilaf and the local bread. "In Moslem culture we have a deep respect for bread," said Zahid. "After a funeral, the tradition is that people should gather to eat. Only when the bread and salt are taken from the table are you permitted to leave. Other food can remain on the table, but bread and salt are sacred. It is disrespectful to leave when these are on the table. We also have the custom that if you see someone throw bread on the ground, you have the responsibility to pick it up and put it on a higher place. In the villages, you kiss it first, but in the cities it seems we have lost that custom."

"One of our traditions," Fikret added, "is that we swear by a piece of bread. Also the sharing of bread is very significant for us. When you share bread with another, you are linked forever. To share bread is a sign of opening your soul. It means giving a piece of your heart."

After the pilaf we stood for a while on the apartment balcony. It was dusk. An open fire was burning across the street. Women were walking arm in arm as women do everywhere.

He showed me a children's book he had written, *Hello, Shertan!* "Shertan is a very tiny boy, finger-sized," Zahid explained. "When I think about him, I can see him. When I am absent-minded, he disappears. He is a living expression of the saying that with a small key you can open a big door or, as Shertan says, you can light a bonfire with a match, or, as I say, the small eyes of a child see the whole world."

I asked him about his religious beliefs. "I was not raised a religious person but I always felt respect for religion. Medieval literature, with its focus on beauty, love, the holiness of life, helped me to understand. I learned that life is not built on chaos and that there is something superior that evaluates and governs our life."

The next day we went to Baku's main mosque, Taza-Pir, a huge building erected in 1905. It was closed in the thirties and reopened in 1943 when the Moslem Board for Transcaucasia was established. Next to the mosque the *madrassah* was under construction. A television crew had arrived and was setting up their cameras for filming activities in the mosque compound.

I was the luncheon guest of Sheikh al-Islam Allashukur Pashazada, chairman of the Moslem Religious Board for Transcaucasia, a newly-elected deputy to the Supreme Soviet and chairman of the Deputies' Committee for Prisoners in Azerbaijan. A man in his forties, he wore a white turban and had a closely cropped black beard.

"In the past we always talked about freedom of conscience," he said, "but it was only words. Treasures were vandalized. There was barbarous destruction. Lenin's principles were ignored — he was in favor of believers having their rights and churches being used for their proper purposes. After the October Revolution, it was much better for religion than it had been before. But under Stalin Lenin's policies on religion were abandoned and the best people perished. There were the purges, the killing of believers and the destruction of mosques and churches. We cannot forget what Stalin did. Not only people but culture and tradition were killed. But only now can we speak freely about this tragedy. This is why believers support *glasnost* and *perestroika*. These have given us so much. Words and deeds are no longer at odds, or at least it is not normal for them to be at odds."

What are some of the deeds? "We have opened twelve mosques in the last six months and we are now preparing to open another six. We are building a theological school and we are publishing the Koran. It is much better for us, although there are still difficulties. There are decrees against red tape but there is still red tape. To get back the use of a mosque means relocating whatever the building was being used for — a club or some organization. What should be a simple matter takes a year or two or three. This is the red tape that we have to cut our way through. But my feeling now is that it isn't the top echelon that is to blame but the middle and low levels. There can be delays. But at least we are on the way."

What about publishing work? "We are beginning to get the Koran in quantities that will meet the need. Other books we need are being published. I am writing a book on the history of Islam that will be published here at the end of this year or early in 1990."

What does he expect from the new law on freedom of conscience? "Actually, if the old law had been properly observed, it would not have been so bad. Our main problem has not been law but bureaucrats who ignore the law."

He expressed distress that many people think of Islam as a religion of violence. "The fundamental principal of Islam is peace. We always greet each other with the word *salaam* — peace. In the Koran it is taught that to deliberately kill another is evil and that to kill one person is like killing all, but to save one life is like saving the life of all the people. Islam is a life-centered religion. Allah gave us the gift of life. We have this gift from the moment we are conceived, and it is our duty to guard this gift. This is the teaching of Islam."

Later we stopped at the Ajarbek Mosque in Baku where I had hoped to interview the imam, Ajund Gaji Ishmael, but mainly he interviewed me: "What is the divorce rate in the United States?" he asked. "Can religious leaders be elected to political positions? How many Moslems are there in the U.S. Congress? How many mosques in the U.S.? How many in western Europe? Why do they permit this Rushdie book in the West?"

I managed to ask if life was changing for Moslems in the USSR. "Yes, it is better. The atmosphere is completely different. We have a chance such as we haven't had since the Revolution."

Before catching a flight back to Moscow, I met the chairman of Azerbaijan's State Publishing Committee, Khanbabayev Azhdar Rzayevich. "There is," he said, "a basic problem of any society that denies God. Where there is no God, you can't sit down. How can you relax in a godless universe? How can you experience compassion?"

Then he told me a story about compassion: "An aged woman had a camel, her only source of income. But then the camel was stolen. There was a rich man. Among his thirty camels she found her camel. Everyone was surprised. Why would a rich man steal a poor woman's only camel? And how is it possible for you to know that a certain camel is yours? She insisted it was hers. But how can you prove it? I can prove it she said. How? Kill her, open her chest, and on her heart you will find a scar. The camel was killed and there on her heart was a scar! It could be easily seen. Everyone present was amazed. The rich man gave the old woman two camels as a gift. How, he asked her, did you know about the scar on her heart? It was simple, she said. Two years ago the camel's son was killed by a wolf. The camel was so sad that I knew it must have left a mark on her heart."

Chapter 9

Buddhists

BY THE TIME GENGHIS KHAN DIED IN 1227, his warrior horsemen had conquered a land mass that stretched from Peking to Baghdad. At its height, the Mongol Empire included all of China, Manchuria, Korea, Tibet, lower Siberia, the Middle East as far as the Euphrates River, the eastern Ukraine, and most of Russia including Moscow. In one of the surprises of history, many of the descendants of those ruthless warriors became peaceful Buddhists.

The coming of Buddhism in the eighteenth century and the arrival of the Trans-Siberian Railroad at the end of the nineteenth century were factors that led the Buryat people from a nomadic life as herdsmen dwelling in elk-skin tents to a settled agricultural life, though Buryats are still famed for their skill on horseback and traces of the old wandering life survive.

So profound was the impact of Buddhism on its converts that it made them a people who could not bear to kill. In the 1880s a Russian writer, G. N. Potanin, wrote of the Buryats' twins across the Mongol border: "Their ways are gentle. Brutal treatment of women and children is unheard of. Crimes, especially murder, are of rare occurrence. Russian merchants living among them assured me that during the seven years that they had inhabited the town, they had never heard of a murder.... They abhor violence to so great an extent that when [a certain man] was condemned to death for political offenses, no one among them would undertake the role of executioner. A heavy bribe finally induced one of them to carry out the sentence, but from that moment he was isolated by all and henceforth was obliged to wander as a beggar. All men kept him at a distance. When he stretched out his hand for alms, they gave, it is true, but at the same time they asked him to go away."

While Buddhists were regarded as infidels by the czarist government and were subject to state control under the Statute on Lamaist Clergy, the difficulties Buddhists suffered under czarist rule were minor compared to those that came under Soviet rule in the thirties when all the *datsans* (monasteries) were closed and many lamas (monks) arrested.

Ulan Ude

In Ulan Ude in late January, I was put up in the city guest house, a two-story mansion that a few months before had become the residence of the only American family living east of the Urals in the USSR: Jane and John Floyd and their sons, Floyd and Patrick, ages four and one. Formerly stationed at the embassy in Moscow, they were in the far east to provide a base for the U.S. On-Site Inspection Team set up under the terms of the INF Treaty. "Few people here ever saw Americans before," said John Floyd. "Now U.S. military planes land here at least once a month."

"The Buryats are still amazed when they see U.S. military personnel walking down the street," said Jane. She told me about one U.S. soldier who discovered he could communicate with a local Buryat child through the sign language of the deaf. Both have close relatives who are deaf.

Much of their food, down to the milk they drink, is flown in from Japan. "The local fruit and vegetables are okay," Jane explained, "but milk is delivered in what looks like a gas truck. You bring your bucket and fill it up from a hose. I'm not quite ready for that. But I like being here. We have made many friends. The kids too. Floyd is learning both Russian and Buryat in a neighborhood school." John showed me a video of a recent day spent ice fishing with neighbors on Lake Baikal. He was helping a local family enlarge their house.

The Buryat Autonomous Republic is about the size of New York state. The Buryats, traditionally Buddhist, form less than half the republic's population of nine hundred thousand. Though an Asian city, the dominant architecture of Ulan Ude, the capital, is Soviet. A massive snow-dusted head of Lenin grimly dominated the city's central square.

Many Buryats have adopted Russian names, like my host, Vladimir Radnayev, head of the Buryat Publishing Committee and a member of Ulan Ude's city council. With Mikhail Moesivich Mulonov of the Buryat Council for Religious Affairs, we drove out of the city, heading for the Ivolginsky Datsan, the center of Buryat Buddhism, reopened in 1946 after being closed ten years.

The countryside we were driving through reminded me of Wyoming: long rolling hills covered with snow, mountains in the distance, split-rail fences, no trees, few cars. An American cowboy would be at home. The Soviet version of the Marlboro Man would be a Buryat.

I asked Mikhail Mulonov if there was a school for Buddhist clergy in the Buryat Republic. "No. Until early in this century, their education was in Tibet. Currently candidates are sent to a school in Ulan Bator in Mongolia where there is a five-year training program. At the moment there are twenty-one Buryats preparing to become lamas at the Gandanchekchelin Datsan in Ulan Bator. There are another twenty or thirty Mongol students."

What happened to Buddhism after the Revolution? "Like other religions, it was persecuted. By the end of the thirties all *datsans* were closed. Lamas were arrested and sent to labor camps where it was hard to survive."

After half an hour we arrived in Ivolginsk. On one side of the road was a village of log houses, on the other the monastic compound of similar houses gathered around a temple. The temple — Gandan Dashi Choinkhorling — was of three stories, each of the upper stories half the size of the one below. The corners of all three roofs of the temple rose like wing tips. The roof of the third story was crowned with a small golden spire. Pillars and alcoves at each level helped create a climate of worship, playfulness, and mystery. The temple was vibrant with color, all the more intense for the bright snow and cloudless blue sky. The walls of the lower two stories were white, the third mustard yellow. The foundation and steps leading to the temple porch were forest green while the three doors the steps led to were blood red. Designs in gold, shining in the sun, were painted on the facade. The immediate visual impression was equivalent to hearing a loud gong. I felt as if only now had I truly arrived in Asia.

Inside, sitting along the center aisle, were twenty-five lamas, each at his own low table, all wearing wine-purple robes, reciting in a monotone chant and occasionally ringing silver bells. A labyrinth of forms, colors, and images all centered on the giant golden Buddha seated in the lotus posture at the front of the hall. Golden dragons encircled the tall red pillars. On either side of the great Buddha along the far wall were two tiers with smaller statues of *bodhisattvas* (awakened ones who renounced *nirvana* in order to save others), disciples of the Buddha, as well as a thousand small Buddha figures.

Though I had never seen anything like this in my life, still it was surprisingly familiar. While Russian Orthodox churches prefer slightly less brilliant colors, the wall of *bodhisattvas* had much in common with an Orthodox iconostasis. The *thang-ka* (painted scrolls) hanging on the temple's side walls between windows, while quite different, had something in common with Orthodox icons. Both Buddhist temple and Orthodox church reflect the conviction that every artistic gift and every sense faculty should be mobilized in the struggle to open the soul's eyes and bring each person to wakefulness.

Lama Syvan introduced himself at the end of the service and took us to the front of the temple to look more closely at the statues. "They are not old but very beautifully made. This temple was built only twelve years ago."

When we paused before the statue of Avalokiteshvara, the *bodhisattva* who embodies compassion, he explained the figure's many hands. "Each hand — what it is doing or holding — has meaning. The lotus symbolizes purity, the rosary is a sign of devotion, the wheel represents Buddhist teaching, the bow and arrow suggest the protection of faith, the mirror stands for sharp mind or omniscience, the vessel contains nectar — the sweetness of the Buddha's teaching. The center hands make the gesture of *andjali* associated with the *mantra*, 'om-mani-padme-khum.' The lower hands gesture giving."

Before the statues was a plate where pilgrims left offerings: ruble notes, kopeks, grain, butter, and beans. Among the gifts was a simple necklace carved from ivory.

I asked about the service that was under way when I arrived. "Today is a big feast, the celebration of the full moon. The Buddha was born on the day of the full moon, achieved enlightenment on the day of the full moon, and died on the day of the full moon. We were chanting the Heart Sutra. For feast days, we use this temple rather than our smaller temple close by."

How many lamas are in the community? "Now we are twenty-eight professed lamas. We each have our own small house on the temple grounds."

And how did you come here? "I was born in 1952 within a typical Buddhist family. Both my parents were believers. Wanting to become a lama was quite natural for me. I became a lama when I was twenty-eight."

How does one take the step to become a lama? "You write a letter to the head lama. He submits your name to the Council for Religious

Affairs. Both consider your request. If you have the permission of both, then you can train to be a lama. You cannot say that you rely upon heaven and heaven alone. You need approval."

How did Buddhism find its way to this part of Asia? "In the fourteenth century there was a Buddhist reform movement in Tibet, the Gelugpas, founded by a lama named Tsong-kha-pa. He was in the tradition of Atisha, a lama of the tenth century who wanted to unite all segments of Buddhism into one. Carrying forward this process, monks of this sect succeeded in finding a way to make the Buddha's teaching more accessible to ordinary people. It stressed the Three Treasures — Buddha, Dharma, and Sangha. Buddha is the teacher, Dharma is his teaching, and Sangha is his community of disciples. It was something anyone could understand, from the highest lama to a peasant child. Buddhist missionaries from Tibet spread this doctrine in several directions. It came to Buryatia 250 years ago."

Has *perestroika* had an impact on Buddhist life in the region? "It is beginning to. The *datsan* in Chita has been given back and is now under restoration, though it is in quite poor condition and much needs to be done. There is a *datsan* in Guzinoozyorsk that was closed but that we hope will be returned. We await the decision. Our request is under consideration by the Council for Religious Affairs. We also would like to open a *datsan* at Elista in the Kalmyk region."

Have you the possibility to publish religious literature? "We are going to publish a book of sutras translated from Tibetan into both the Buryat and Russian languages."

Do you have access to the mass media? "Recently a lama was on television to speak about the environment. We expect more opportunities."

What are the possibilities to teach Buddhism? "We do not hold public meetings but, as you see, many people come there, even some from the European part of the Soviet Union with no previous connection to Buddhism. We can talk with all our visitors and discuss any questions they have."

How many Buryats are Buddhist? [laughter] "How can anyone say? It's not hundreds of thousands. Perhaps it is seventy or eighty thousand people. Perhaps it is more. There is no census on such a subject."

Have you contact with Buddhists from other parts of the world? "Quite a lot. Two years ago the Dalai Lama came to visit us."

We walked to the smaller temple nearby where one of the older monks, Lama Dorji, was sitting before a drum, beating it slowly but with great force while praying. "I am praying according to the wishes of our pilgrims," he said. "They give us requests to pray for their needs. I am also praying that all people will understand each other and achieve agreements." He showed me how the drum should be struck. I was impressed by his enthusiasm and his drum-like voice. Was there something he could pray for on my behalf, he asked. I gave him a name.

One small building in the compound contained a lilliputian model of paradise. Up to our ankles in snow, we gazed through a window at a fabulous garden of flowers, fruit, and jewels — a world without suffering. Some of the tiny people were flying like birds.

Among the fascinated visitors studying the scene with us were several young Soviet soldiers. Seeing we had a lama showing the way, they joined us as we went on to the next stop, a greenhouse that provides refuge to a Bodhi tree. "It was under such a tree that the Buddha sat when he achieved enlightenment," said Lama Syvan. "This tree has that tree for its ancestor."

We visited the *datsan*'s library, as cold inside as outside. Unfortunately many of the library's manuscripts were lost during the years the *datsan* was closed, but still it is an important collection.

We arrived at the house of Bandido Kambo Lama Jimba-Jamso Erdyneev, president of the Religious Board of Buddhists of the USSR. He is a round-faced old man, stooped, gentle in his manner. Like the other lamas, his head was completely shaved. He invited us to have lunch with him, a real Buryat meal in which only the apples and mineral water were familiar tastes. The main dish was *pozi*, a steamed pastry filled with onion and meat.

I asked about his hopes for Buddhism in the USSR in the coming years. "The major challenge is to overcome the problem of training lamas. The future development of Buddhism here is linked to this. To reopen temples we need well-trained lamas. We hope that in the future we will have a center for training lamas within the Soviet Union. There are many young people who wish to be lamas. It used to be dozens had this wish. Now there are many more who think in this direction. We receive letters about this not only from Buryats and Kalmyks but also Russians. One day you will come here and meet a Russian lama!

"We have to reopen temples and *datsans* that were closed. There is presently only one other, the Aginkski Datsan in the Chita region. But in the Chita region we are re-opening the Tsugolsky Datsan. A temple has now been registered in Elista city in the Kalmyk region. We have two lamas there now but it is not yet functioning. We no longer face official opposition to reviving temples and *datsans* but the buildings themselves are often very deteriorated and in every case major restoration work is required. This is not easy to do and also it requires a lot of money. We also need many books and in several languages, Buryat, Tibetan, Classical Mongolian, and Russian. Our brothers in India [mainly Tibetan refugees gathered around the Dalai Lama] are helping us with literature in the Tibetan language."

Do you have close ties with the Tibetan Buddhists in India? "Yes. One of our lamas is now in India participating in a special series of ceremonies at which the Dalai Lama is describing the steps to holiness. The last such ceremony was held in 1913 in Ulan Bator."

Do you hope to teach the Tibetan language in the Buryat Republic? "Only to those training to become lamas. The books they must study are in Tibetan. But we see among young people here a fresh interest in learning Classical Mongolian, and we hope it will be possible for them to study it. The Buryat language is a dialect of Classical Mongolian. They are sister languages, like Ukrainian and Russian."

After the meal I was able to sit with the abbot on his couch. "Originally I was a lama at the Chita *datsan*," he told me. "I went there when I was ten and have been a monk ever since, though I was not able to live in a *datsan* from 1937 to 1945. I was fortunate in that period not to be a prisoner like so many others. I found a job in a factory. Now I am eighty-two. I am happy to have lived long enough to see Gorbachev and to witness these new events."

Outside we stopped near a large prayer wheel being turned by a newly married couple. The prayer wheel reminded me of the candles Orthodox believers light before icons — a similar integration of deed and symbol, tangible and intangible, unspoken prayer and physical action. "The Buddha taught the way for us to pass from suffering to *nirvana*," explained the abbot's secretary, Victor Mitypov, an English-speaking layman. "There are several ways but all involve movement, and this movement is symbolized by the eight-spoked wheel. At the center of the wheel is *dharmakaya* — the Buddha teaching. The spokes represent the eight-fold path: right seeing, right thinking, right speech, right action, right living, right effort, right mindfulness, and right meditation. The wheel's outer circumference shows that all these different forms are unified. In spinning the wheel, no one rod can be seen. We see only their oneness."

We encountered a Russian couple who had come to the *datsan* from Moscow. The man knew Lama Syvan and Victor Mitypov from an earlier visit. "I am Buddhist," he said. "My friend is Christian, but she wants to know more about Buddhism." I asked if there was a Buddhist temple in Moscow. "Not yet."

Before leaving Ulan Ude I met with Professor Regby Pubayev, a historian teaching in Ulan Ude, who described how Buddhism found its way to the Buryat people.

"The decisive event was a visit in 1725 by a group of 150 Tibetan lamas. By the end of the century there were many *datsans* in this region, and Buryat lamas were travelling back and forth to Tibet. It was mainly religious contact — there was little trade. Buryat lamas were deeply respected in Tibet. At the end of the last century, at the height of relations between Buryat and Tibet, a Buryat was teacher to the Dalai Lama. In this same period Buryat lamas tried to strengthen the relationship between Tibet and Russia. A Buryat delegation went to the court of Czar Nicholas II. On the whole their mission was not successful — in 1907 the British-Russian Treaty was signed that resulted in Russia abandoning relations with Tibet — but their effort had one positive result, construction of a Buddhist temple in Saint Petersburg in 1915.[1] One can say that there was a better understanding of Buddhism in Russia."

I asked about the doctrinal content of Buddhism. "At the heart of Buddhism is compassion. It is the red thread running through all the teaching. There is a list of Ten Virtues. Most of them have their basis in compassion — not to kill, not to steal, not to cherish an intention that could cause another harm, not to harm one's body with destructive substances, not to violate laws that protect the marital state. The Dalai Lama, head of this branch of Buddhism, is regarded as the reincarnation of the *bodhisattva* Avalokiteshvara who especially embodies compassion. It is because of compassion for those who suffer that a *bodhisattva* does not enter *nirvana* but chooses to help. The lama is primarily there to help the people. He is compared to a man guiding a ferry boat, carrying passengers from one side of the river to the other. People come to the lama with their problems, their worries, and the lama gives advice and prays. Believers show the highest respect toward lamas."

A Buddhist in Moscow

Eremey Parnov, president of the Science Fiction National Section of the Soviet Writers Union and vice president of the International Science Fiction Association, is also a Buddhist.

----

[1]On July 12, 1989, a Buddhist congregation was registered in Leningrad. The members anticipate the old temple will be turned over to them (Keston News Service, no. 336).

Parnov lives in the Sokolniki district in the northeast part of central Moscow. On the living room wall there are leopard and python skins, bow and arrow, and tribal wooden masks. The library is spread through several rooms and lines the main hallway. In areas not taken by books there were awards he has received, a photo of Boris Pasternak, exotic tropical shells, a large starfish, various kinds of coral, a cup imprinted with the label for Beefeater Gin, and a small Christmas tree standing in front of a Buddha statue.

We looked at photos of his trip to Hawaii and Buddhists he had met there. He pointed out a symbol, a circle on a square background. "This is a Buddhist icon. Within the circle is the leaf of the Bodhi tree, the tree the Buddha sat under when he achieved enlightenment. The circle represents the earth. The points where the cross intersects the circle are the four corners — north, east, south, and west."

He had a photo of Mother Teresa clipped from a Soviet magazine. "I was among those at the airport to meet her during her recent visit to the USSR. She wants to set up a section of her religious society here in Moscow to take care of victims of the Armenian earthquake who are brought to Moscow for treatment. She brought four nuns with her, nurses, who are staying in Moscow."

He is one of the lucky Russians who has had the chance to travel widely. "Travel in Asia is a pleasure to my soul," he said. "I have now been in all the Buddhist countries except China. A month ago I was in India. I have met the Dalai Lama two times, first at his retreat in the Himalayas and again in Mongolia."

He showed us a copy of his book on Buddhism, *Gods of Lotus*, published in Moscow in 1980, handsomely printed on glossy white paper with many color plates.

I asked what drew him toward Buddhism. "Perhaps it was fate — that is, perhaps I was genetically prepared for contemplation and drawn to the engagement of East and West. As a child I didn't know anything about the East but I knew fairy tales of the East like Sinbad the Sailor. It wasn't the only direction my interest went. I also liked Jack London and Edgar Allen Poe. Then in 1950, when I was fifteen, a friend gave me a little bronze Buddha statue. This was an impetus to find out what it meant and what it was linked with. After being given the statue I started reading books about eastern culture, sociology, environment, religion, and history. I found all this fascinating.

"There was an element of chance. Chance has played a big role in my life. In 1970, by the time I was a working writer, I went to Japan as part of a delegation from the Soviet Writers Union. I was *Pravda's* Vietnam correspondent in 1972–73. Living and travelling in Buddhist countries — this was my real university. I happened to be in certain places and happened to meet certain people, people who had never talked with 'specialists.'

"The next stage in my engagement was the consequence of symbolism opening its doors to me. I was drawn into the symbolism of the ancient world, from the pre-Buddhist period of human history, then Indian culture in the pre-Veda period, passing through the Gnostics to various forms of Christianity. I found that symbolism consists of rites and sacraments. It is a presentation of the invisible through the material world. You find that there are certain symbols that occur in every culture. Not only shapes but numbers have symbolic meaning. Three is a sacred number in many cultures. One represents the universe and God. Two represents all opposites — sun and moon, day and night, man and woman. Three, the trinity, is the triangle, three sides making a form of absolute stability representing the oneness of past, present, and future. This concept of oneness beneath all appearance of difference is fundamental to Buddhism. The number five has special associations. There are systems of five. There are five Buddhas of meditation each with five characteristic colors. There are five natural elements: earth, metal, fire, water, and wood. There are systems built on seven, especially in the Babylonian culture, with the Jews, and in Christianity: seven days, seven planets, seven colors, seven scents, seven metals, seven jewels, seven sacraments. We could spend months talking about symbols and the meaning of certain numbers. It's a big subject. Personally I have found it important."

I asked if his study of eastern religion and symbols had been of consequence in his writing. "I didn't include the oriental in my stories for a long time. Now there is a synthesis, and it happened 'without my participation.' A few years ago — 1983 — I wrote a novel, *Shambala*, which I think brings Buddhism into science fiction. Dreams are essential to the story. In dreams we create nonexistent worlds in which the dead are still alive. The line between ourselves and the dead is erased. In my novel the dream is not *in* us but rather *around* us. The dream is real. Our secret wishes and desires exist independently of us. The novel asks how would we live in that world in which our dreams are real? How would we adapt? How could we remain human?

"I named the world Famagusta after a port in Cyprus, but it has nothing to do with that city. The hero is John Smith, an American psychiatrist who took part in the Vietnam war. His wife and daughters have died. He has only his work. Suddenly he finds his wife and daughters are alive and with him again. It's impossible. He understands that this isn't 'reality,' not as a psychiatrist understands reality.

Yet he finds he can live in this other reality, but he has to be on his guard all the time. It's very seductive, this other reality.

"The story is partly about the European longing for knowledge of things. In the story the doctor tries to reach the center of the Shambala land, this dream world he is living in."

Does John Smith find the center? "No, naturally not. The art of the writer is to convince the reader that there is something above, something higher, but the writer cannot take you there. When you watch a horror film, you are frightened only until the source of the horror is shown on the screen. Then your terror disappears."

Has horror been a factor in your religious development? "The history of this country is horrifying. You cannot consider our history without being presented with the dilemma of good and evil. It isn't hard for us to believe in the devil. In fact it often seemed that *only* the devil existed, no power of goodness. But you can learn from suffering that the way taken by many people is not the best way. You learn that the path to follow is the way of nonparticipation in evil. This is fundamental Buddhist teaching — the noble truth that the source of suffering is desire but that it is possible to live a life not dominated by desire. The control of desire prevents evil."

How has Buddhism mattered in your own life? "It's difficult to say. There has never been a religious revelation. Rather Buddhism has led me into conscious meditation about life. This reinforces my life. What was sensed intuitively was proved. It has meant a deeper sense of connection with the universe. Buddhism has been a way of understanding. But I can't say anything extraordinary has happened."

Does Buddhism have much in common with other religions? "The majority of teachings exist in each religion. The differences that exist are around the points of agreement, not at the center. The differences mainly have to do with what comes of trying to describe a world beyond our limits, the content of the 'other world.'"

Chapter 10

The Council for Religious Aæairs

P ETER THE GREAT saw the patriarch of the Russian Orthodox Church as a competitor. "Dazzled by the shining virtue and splendor of the supreme pastor," Peter declared, "the common people imagine that he is another sovereign, equal to the autocrat in power and even greater than he is." When Patriarch Adrian died in 1700, Peter chose no successor, instead appointing an archbishop to serve under his direction as "Exarch of the Holy Throne of the Patriarch." In 1721 Peter officially abolished the patriarchate, replacing it with a department called the Holy Synod. Its members were several archbishops selected by the czar whose work and decisions were monitored by a procurator exercising veto power. In no case was the procurator to be an ecclesiastic. The first person Peter appointed to the job was a colonel of the dragoons.

State control ended only with the abdication of Czar Nicholas II two centuries later. In 1917, at a council in Moscow's Savior Cathedral, the patriarchate was restored with the election of Tikhon.

On January 23, 1918, Lenin signed a decree separating church and state. In some ways it was a step forward from the arrangement of the previous two hundred years. The decree prohibited any law or regulation that would "put any restraint upon, or limit freedom of conscience or establish any advantages or privileges on the ground of the religion of citizens." Citizens were free "to confess any religion or none at all."

Religious rites could be performed so long as they did "not disturb the public order or infringe the rights of the citizens of the Soviet Republic." In years to come the very existence of a church, not to say the performance of religious rites, would be seen as disturbing public order.

As the government was determined to raise a new generation of children "free of superstition," churches were barred from any role in schools, public or private. Religious instruction was permitted only on a private basis. Some believers saw this ruling as a blessing in disguise. Religion would no longer be a subject that one passed or failed before a blackboard.

The most aggressive aspect of the decree concerned property ownership: "No ecclesiastical or religious association shall have the right to own property.... All property belonging to churches and religious associations... shall become public property. Buildings and objects intended especially for religious worship shall be handed over by special decision of local or central authorities, free of charge, for use by the religious associations concerned."[1]

It was at this time that the cathedrals within the Moscow Kremlin were taken away.[2] A few months later, with the adoption of the first Soviet constitution, clergy — along with capitalists, criminals, and imbeciles — were deprived of the right to vote.

It was Lenin's view that the church was one of the principle agents of oppression: "Autocracy cannot do without its twin agents: a hangman and a priest," he wrote. "The first suppresses popular resistance by force, the second sweetens the fate of the oppressed by empty promises of heaven." The priest was simply a "policeman in a cassock." In a letter to Gorky, he wrote, "Every religious idea, every idea of God, even flirting with the idea of God causes unutterable vileness of the most degrading kind, a contagion of the most abominable type." With such convictions, it is hardly surprising that Lenin put great stress on the role of the Communist party to undertake atheist education, yet for tactical reasons he opposed an all-out frontal attack on religion, preferring a step-by-step approach.

The initial response of the Orthodox Church to the October Revolution, which occurred during the council, was to declare the Bolsheviks anathema. In an encyclical to the faithful, Patriarch Tikhon excommunicated all those "open and secret enemies of [Christ's]

---

[1] Trevor Beeson, *Discretion and Valour: Religious Conditions in Russia and Eastern Europe*, rev. ed. (London: Collins; Philadelphia: Fortress Press, 1982), pp. 34–35.

[2] For the first time since the confiscation of the Kremlin's Dormition Cathedral in 1918, the Holy Liturgy was celebrated there on October 13, 1989.

Truth" who engage in "persecutions... and in sowing the seeds of hatred and... fratricide."[3] The letter was not, however, a call to armed resistance.

In 1918, fifty-four clerics, having resisted state efforts to confiscate chalices and other objects used at the altar, were tried for inciting civil strife. Several were executed, among them the saintly young bishop of Petrograd, Metropolitan Benjamin. Perhaps in response to the shock many felt at such bloody actions, in 1919 Lenin warned party workers to "strive to avoid all offense to the religious feelings of believers, because such offense may lead to intensifying religious fanaticism." The same year he signed a decree exempting conscientious objectors from military service, and in 1920 a law was passed transferring certain areas of farm land to religious communities.

In 1921, however, a decree declared sermons were legal only if limited to purely religious subjects. In 1923 two decrees legalized the closure of churches if the buildings were needed "for other uses" or the religious association was found to be "politically unreliable and anti-Soviet."[4]

In the course of the civil war and for several years afterward, acts of violence were frequently committed against believers. Between 1917 and 1923, it is estimated that in the Russian Orthodox Church alone twenty-eight bishops and twelve hundred priests were killed.[5] These killings mainly occurred during the civil war in situations where clergy had openly backed the opponents of Soviet power or were assumed to be supporters of the Whites.

With the end of the civil war in 1920 and the launching of the New Economic Policy, certain groups of believers — notably Protestants and "renovationist" Orthodox who supported the Revolution — enjoyed a period of freedom that some still remember as "a golden age." They could publish freely, organize meetings, and start new churches. But the period of toleration was short-lived, and even during these few years believers were under many restraints.

On Easter Sunday, 1925, with Lenin dead and Stalin on his way to absolute power, the League of the Militant Godless had its founding congress in Moscow.[6] Three years later Stalin's first Five Year Plan

---

[3]In 1919 another encyclical warned clergy to stand aloof from politics of any kind. In 1923, after a term of imprisonment, Patriarch Tikhon published a confession regretting that he had succumbed to a "negative attitude to Soviet power."

[4]Dimitry Pospielovsky, *The Russian Church under the Soviet Regime* (Crestwood, N.Y.: Saint Vladimir's Seminary Press, 1984), vol. 1, p. 32.

[5]Beeson, *Discretion and Valour*, p. 37.

[6]In 1935 it claimed five million members and fifty thousand local groups. Under its auspices children between eight and fourteen were enrolled in Groups of Godless

called for "the unification of thought of all Soviet citizens." In 1929 the oppressive Law of Religious Associations was passed. Churches, seminaries, and Bible schools were closed and many thousands of Bibles and liturgical books confiscated. The church had indeed been separated from the state, but not been freed from state control.

The state agency established for control, the Council for Religious Affairs, is invested with the power to oversee religious life and to be certain that national policies in regard to religion are being followed. Over the decades it has grown into a huge structure. There is the All-Union CRA in Moscow, attached to the Council of Ministers, whose large staff requires several buildings. There is a CRA in each Soviet Republic with local offices in major cities.

Councils at the local level registered churches, approved particular persons being sent to seminary, decided whether or not an exception to a particular rule might be allowed (an outdoor rather than indoor funeral or a priest from another church presiding), permitted repairs and restoration work, saw to it that the local congregation was "contributing" at an adequate level to the Soviet Peace Fund, and followed the activities of every local religious association. They were also responsible for the "political education" of religious leaders and made regular reports that were funnelled through to Moscow. A myriad of decisions by religious bodies could only be made with the approval of the CRA. Often a CRA appointee was designated a member or even chairman of a parish council. When a given believer was seen as dangerous or ignored orders restricting religious life, the CRA initiated actions that ranged from fines to prison terms.

A tentative change in government policy toward believers could be noted in 1983 with the return to the Russian Orthodox Church of the Danilov Monastery in Moscow, but it was not until the Gorbachev period, most notably following the April 1988 meeting with Orthodox bishops in the Kremlin, that the CRA began, still within many limits, to espouse believers' rights.

Moscow: Konstantin Kharchev

In a widely read interview published in December 1988, Konstantin Kharchev, CRA chairman since January 1985, talked at length about

Youth. A huge troop of "godless missionaries" were established to give lectures up and down the country. Prizes were given for the best "godless hymns." "Godless bibles" were published and museums of religion and atheism set up. In Moscow a thoroughfare was named Godless Street.

the oppression of believers, advocating many changes for which dissidents had been struggling for years.[7]

"I think we must," he said, "as quickly as possible, free ourselves of the [antireligious] legislation of 1929.... This legislation limits in a Stalinistic and bureaucratic fashion all independent and democratic activity.... Practically every line of that law underlines the dependence of the church on the power of the state. All kinds of arbitrary actions are admissible under such conditions."

Alexander Nezhny reminded Kharchev of the killing of bishops that had occurred in the early years of the Soviet state, mentioning by name Metropolitan Vladimir of Kiev, Archbishop Andronik of Perm, Bishop Germogen of Tobolsk, and Metropolitan Benjamin of Petrograd (now Leningrad). One of the lies often told against the Orthodox Church to justify acts of violence against bishops and priests, Nezhny pointed out, was that they were refusing to come to the aid of famine victims in 1921. "But then how are we to explain," he asked, "the church's creation of a Pan-Russian Committee of Aid Against Famine?... In fact, they [the state authorities] were simply looking for an excuse to let loose an attack on the church." It was a question all the more striking in that it concerned a period of Soviet history when Lenin was still alive.

Kharchev said that one "must not lose sight of the fact that [these killings] occurred in a period of open confrontation" when "leaders of the church did not accept the new power and fought against it." Then he added that a process was now under way "to seal for all eternity the memory of those innocent people who were victims of that war waged against our own people" including members of the church.

Changes at the top did not automatically mean change further down, he admitted. "The fact is that a battle is raging over many churches [which in the past were confiscated]. The believers demand that they be returned to them while the local authorities reply that they intend to make the church into a museum, a café, a concert hall, or a library.... Their reasoning is that it would be better to let the church fall down than to give it back to believers.... The Council for Religious Affairs [in Moscow] will have to ensure the suppression of such decisions on the part of local authorities." The principle should be, he went on, that churches belong to believers. "In general [the authorities] would be justified in transferring all the Orthodox

---

[7]*Ogonyok*, issue 50. The interviewer was the journalist Alexander Nezhny, respected in Russian Christian circles for his integrity.

churches to the patriarchate of Moscow, which should have complete responsibility for them."

More than five hundred Orthodox churches had been registered in 1988, Kharchev said, as contrasted with sixteen in 1987, but the number would have been still greater in 1988 had it not been for certain officials who still blocked the way. He reported that in 1988 the CRA in Moscow had reversed eighty-three refusals by local authorities to register religious societies, actions that occasionally had provoked calls from regional or republican leaders demanding to know the reason for such reversals. "I replied," said Kharchev, "on the basis of law. But some responsible comrades still have fresh in their memories the time of 'rule by telephone,' the times when you could close a church and disband a religious society by one telephone call." He expressed his view that in the future legal registration of churches should no longer be required, thus eliminating the main job of local Councils for Religious Affairs.

The problem still facing the church, Nezhny said, is that it is still like "a person living somewhere without a residence permit. This person may live, eat, and drink, but he is never free of the idea that at any moment the police may come and say to him, 'You have one day to get out of this place,' or again, 'Citizen, you are liable to a fine.'"

Kharchev found the analogy "a bit invidious." Did not the bishops' meeting with Gorbachev in the Kremlin in April suggest a status higher than that of a vagrant? He went on to discuss the need for religious groups to have the possibility to carry on publishing work, not only to issue Bibles and theological books but "why not a review that will handle seriously political and social problems as well as religious philosophy?" The state, he said, should provide paper for religious publications but "it is indispensable that the church should have its own printing press."

Asked about the situation of the draft law on Freedom of Conscience, Kharchev replied that, following instructions received from the Central Committee, "the Council for Religious Affairs, the Ministries of Foreign Affairs and of Justice, and the Judiciary of the Supreme Soviet...have all taken part in the elaboration of the project."[8] In addition, he said, "consultations have taken place with the representatives of religious organizations covering practically all confessions." With so many proposals put forward, the process "has

---

[8]During a subsequent visit to Britain, Kharchev said that the Soviet Academy of Sciences had also been consulted.

taken rather a long time, giving rise to questions and perplexity in our country as well as abroad."[9]

Kiev: Nicholai Kolesnik

The chairman of the Ukrainian Council for Religious Affairs, Nicholai Kolesnik, is a thin, cautious man in a grey suit. We met at his office in Kiev early in January 1989.[10] "Western nations have only slight information about the situation of believers in the Ukraine," he complained, "and what is said is often misinformation. But we are people interested in building up understanding."

I asked how he got his job. "I started in 1978. The opportunity came from the party apparatus, quite by chance, really. I had studied at the Academy of Social Sciences. My dissertation was on the subject of the application of Lenin's principles to church-state relations. I didn't expect to have such a major responsibility, but I am pleased with the job. These activities are important in the country's life."

What is the council's work? "We are required to see that the law in regard to church activities is observed. It is a big job. The Ukrainian territory has a population of more than 50 million people, fifteen religious denominations, and over sixty-five hundred active religious communities. Most are Russian Orthodox, forty-one hundred parishes — more than half of all the Orthodox parishes in the USSR; altogether there are about seven thousand in the Soviet Union. The second largest religious group in the Ukraine is the Evangelical Christian Baptists — they have eleven hundred congregations. Then come the Roman Catholics, Calvinists, Old Believers, Seventh-Day Adventists, Pentecostals, Methodists and Jehovah's Witnesses. To serve the needs of the Jewish population there are fourteen synagogues. We

---

[9]*Sourozh: A Journal of Orthodox Life and Thought*, Oxford, England, May 1989, translated by Benedict Roffey.

[10]In the *Ogonyok* interview with Konstantin Kharchev published in December, two weeks before this interview, Kolesnik was held up as an example of officials obstructing the rights of believers. He cited the attempt to register a church by villagers in Podgaichiki in the Ternopil region of the Ukraine. Local officials refused, said Kharchev, adding that Kolesnik, "who ought to have explained to these comrades that they were violating Soviet legislation, authenticated their refusal with his signature." The villagers, he said, had to come to Moscow to seek justice. Such actions, he said, were "a most harmful and dangerous thing for our *perestroika*." Kharchev added: "And what if a person can't find support in Moscow either? What if here too he comes up against a bureaucrat, an indifferent executive, a cold functionary? All this happens! Then he'll return and say to the people at home: there is no justice, don't look for it."

also have some Moslems but as yet no mosque, though there is now an application to open one."

Recently, he said, the Council for Religious Affairs has helped to improve relations with Jews in the United States. "There was the problem here of cemeteries in areas where Jews used to live but where there was no longer anyone to take care of the graves, including some tombs of famous people. A Committee on Preservation of the Values of the Jewish Culture in the Territory of the Soviet Union has been set up in the United States to provide support for maintenance of the graves and also arrange for Jews to visit the Soviet Union. It was started by Albert Reichman, head of the Olympia and York Company, and Noach Deer, a member of the City Council of New York and chairman of the Committee on Human Rights. A coordination committee has been organized in the USSR with Konstantin Kharchev the co-chairman for the Soviet side. This is a positive step in work to overcome one area of friction."

I asked about developments involving Christians. "The major event was the Millennium celebration last year. The first parts were in Moscow and Kiev but it continued in various cities and towns until the end of the year. This event inspired faithful people. There have been many new appeals to open or reopen parish churches. In the Ukrainian territory alone 450 churches were opened or reopened in 1988. Most were Orthodox, but there were fourteen Catholic parishes [Latin-rite Catholics, not the Ukrainian Catholic Church, which uses the Eastern rite] and fourteen Protestant. There has also been a surge of religious publishing. There has just been a new edition of 110,000 copies of the Bible in the Ukrainian language plus a large printing of the New Testament." He took examples of both out of his office safe — an unusual location for Bibles — and gave them to me. "There has also been a manual for preachers. These are examples, I think, of the positive way things are going."

What about the tension between Orthodox and Eastern-rite Catholics? "It isn't an area in which the council can have influence. It is between the churches. The strategy of the Moscow patriarchate has been to open its doors to the Vatican, but with one precondition, the principle of parity. The Vatican has considered itself the 'senior mother' in the church, though I think it is fair to say that there is more religious life in modern Moscow than in Rome! The Orthodox insist on equal footing."[11]

---

[11] In an interview published in *Izvestia* on February 1, 1989, Kolesnik said that 430 Orthodox churches had been registered in the Ukraine in 1988, mainly in western

What about the role of believers in social service? "Immediately after the earthquake in Armenia, churches in the Ukraine had a special collection. Believers gave 850,000 rubles. Within the Ukraine believers are socially active in many ways. For example, here in Kiev the Baptists are helping an orphanage. First they bought carpets. They want to make the orphanage a better one. There are eighty faithful people, all pensioners, helping in one of the city hospitals doing all kinds of domestic tasks from carpentry to assisting the nurses. The hospital manager is very pleased."[12]

Despite a civil conversation, I felt the chill of traditional Soviet bureaucracy. I wouldn't want to be a local petitioner facing Nicholai Kolesnik.

Archangel: Mikhail Ksenofontov

Mikhail Feodorovich Ksenofontov, head of the Council for Religious Affairs in the Archangel Oblast, got the job because of Gorbachev. "I have been thirty-two years in this region but only the last two working on religious issues," he said. "There has been a big turnover in personnel. The former functionaries in the Council for Religious Affairs were linked with persecution of the church and believers. It would be incredible to expect them to change their views and strategy. Another person was needed. The Regional Council of Deputies gave me the job of moving things in a new direction in conformity with the government's decision to undertake actions beneficial to the believing people, to respect them and seek a real dialogue. Our first task

---

regions that had been "a bulwark of Uniates." He said that his office had received statements signed by thousands of citizens living in these regions "requesting to register precisely an Orthodox society and not that of some other religion." It was his opinion that believers were not concerned whether the church near their home belonged to Rome or Moscow, but nonetheless he saw a trend toward Orthodoxy. "Even those who only yesterday made use of the services of itinerant Uniate priests are today attending an Orthodox Church." He said many disapprove of Uniates "because of their alliance with outspoken supporters of ideas of Ukrainian bourgeois nationalism..." (Keston News Service, no. 321, March 16, 1989).

[12] A local Orthodox priest took a critical view of the Ukrainian Council for Religious Affairs. He credited the return of the Monastery of the Caves and other churches to insistence from Moscow rather than local political will. He was frustrated with the local council's resistance to churches undertaking programs of social service. "Believers in Moscow and Leningrad are able to do volunteer service in hospitals. We want to do the same here, but lawyers of the council here say it is against the law. Kharchev in Moscow says the old law should be regarded as extinct, but here they say that until there is a new law, they have to make their decisions by the old law. This is how it is."

was to grant them rights that had been denied them before. The problem was never the clergy or the faithful people — it was the policy."

Mikhail Feodorovich is a short, grandfatherly man nearing retirement. Despite his many years of responsibility in the Communist party, he impressed me as unbureaucratic. By the time I left Archangel I was certain he was well liked and trusted by local believers. I sensed in him a genuine warmth to religion and even began to think he might be a believer himself. Not only he but his wife, wearing a scarf like any devout older woman, came with me to the Easter Liturgy. During our several days together, I noticed that whenever he met believers, he greeted them with the words, "Christ is risen!"

We visited a church across the Dvina River in the village of Zaostrovje. While the lower church was in good repair, the upper church and its icons were in an advanced state of decay.

"The icons are like our villages," said Mikhail Feodorovich, "hardly surviving. Everywhere villages are being destroyed by neglect and urbanization. My wife and I have a house here. Last year we grew a ton of cabbage! We sold a hundred kilos to the collective. We feel at home here but such villages are dying. Their only hope is a change in policy. At least here there is a church. Not many villages are so fortunate."

Knowing that in the old days many Old Believers had fled to the far north, taking distance from the czar, I had hoped to meet them in Archangel, but Mikhail Feodorovich's efforts to set up an interview hadn't worked out.

"There is one Old Believer woman I talked to but she refused to see you. If she did this, she said, people would curse her. Traditionally those dissidents who came here sought an isolated life in settlements with people who shared their convictions. Old Believers are not so talkative."

Personally, he was most at home with the Orthodox. "The smaller the church, the busier it is seeking converts, especially Adventists and Baptists. Sometimes they speak in buses. When I am forced to listen to a speech or sermon, I don't like it."

Was he convinced that the change under way would be durable? "It will come if we are patient. We are slow people in the north. We don't mind to wait in line so much. This isn't a bad quality. Patience is a virtue."

Baku: Rafig Abdullaev

While in Baku in May, I went to the Government House for a meeting with Rafig Abdullaev, head of the Council for Religious Affairs in Azerbaijan, and his assistant, Alexander Alexandrovich Kozlov. Like many working in senior positions in the council, Abdullaev used to work for the Ministry for Foreign Affairs. Kozlov, a younger man responsible for contact with Christian groups, had been a teacher working with physically handicapped children in Tashkent before starting his work with the council in 1985.

I asked Abdullaev if the Council for Religious Affairs was still needed. "In my own view, yes. It is not only in the USSR that religious organizations are registered. This is a common practice both in the East and the West. It is not unusual for states to have ministers responsible for religious bodies — their land, property, etc. In Russia, before the Revolution, there was the office of the Procurator of the Holy Synod. It was started by Peter the Great. In the Holy Synod, the Procurator's word was law. The Council for Religious Affairs does not have the right to interfere with the internal life of religious bodies. Our law is that the religious bodies are independent of the state. They should not interfere with the state nor the state with them. This is the basic principle. The role of the Council for Religious Affairs is to provide a point of contact between the state and believers. On the one hand we defend the rights and needs of believers before state bodies and assist believers when they have needs. On the other hand we are responsible to see that the interests of the state are defended among believers."

If this is the present situation, why is a new religious law needed? "A lot has been written about failures of the 1929 law. A new law on freedom of conscience has been drafted. We have read it and made an assessment. An ideological committee attached to the Politburo of the Central Committee of the Communist party of the USSR has considered it. The draft will be published in the mass media so that the public can participate in the discussion about it. About ten days ago it was discussed in the Politburo. I gather it will be published soon. I expect the new law to be adopted in the near future."

How has the work of the Council for Religious Affairs changed in the last two years? "Remarkably. We have been restructuring our practices, operating in many respects under what we assume will be the content of the forthcoming law. Formerly we had only sixteen mosques in the republic, six of them in Baku. Now the number of mosques has more than doubled — there are eighteen more. One of them is a very beautiful mosque that had been restored by the Ministry of Culture for use as a museum, but believers requested it and now it is a working mosque. Many old mosques are being restored and some will be returned to religious use. There are also more Christian churches. There are three synagogues. Altogether there are now four Russian Orthodox churches, one church for Old Believers, two Armenian Orthodox churches, twelve Molokan churches [Milk Drinkers, a Christian sect that grew out of the Dukhobors], six Baptist churches, and four Adventist churches. The principle is that wherever people want to have a place of worship, it is their right and we must help them. We have many requests to open more religious centers."[13]

Aren't these far too few mosques for such a huge Moslem population? "One stumbling block is the shortage of clergy. It was only in 1968 that Moslems were permitted to send students to the [Sunnite] Moslem theological institutes in central Asia, and then only two persons at a time. Sometimes not even two were sent. There was no such institute in Azerbaijan. Now a [Shi'ite] *madrassah* is under construction here in Baku. It will open with fifteen students this September. By 1994 there should be seventy-five students in the five-year program. When there are more imams, there will be more mosques. The Christians didn't face such a serious obstacle — Russian, Armenian, and Georgian seminaries were able to provide for the needs of their believers here. But in the former administrative system, the Moslems were somehow oppressed."

Why? "It is something like the problem faced by Catholics and Buddhists. In general everything connected with religion was disapproved, but this was even more the case for certain religions. Islam was regarded as a dangerous religion. Now that view has changed and the old strategy has been abandoned. We have come to realize that believers are also Soviet citizens working for the development of society. They are even more active in supporting *perestroika* than nonbelievers."

What are your hopes for the future? "It will take a long time to repair the damage done in the past. In the thirties various mosques and cathedrals were destroyed, places of worship that were also national

---

[13]In a letter to me dated October 27, 1989, Rafig Abdullaev updated the figures. Since we met, he said, the CRA in Azerbaijan had registered another three mosques, bringing the total to thirty-seven. He also noted two more Armenian churches, a Georgian church, one more Molokan church, and one church "for those between Molokan and Baptist." Altogether there were seventy-four registered religious communities. In addition, he noted "more than forty small Molokan and Baptist groups" not officially registered but known to the CRA. "Soon we are going to register more than thirty [additional] Moslem and Christian communities."

monuments. Many religious people were purged [the word often used in the USSR for those who were killed or sent to labor camps]. It was illegal but it happened. We must investigate what happened. Also we need to do all we can to make it possible for believers to participate in charitable work. This also was formerly prohibited. We hope that believers can act as supervisors for orphanages and old-age homes."

Are there those who oppose the change in policy in regard to believers? "Some can only think of believers as fanatics. They have heard about holy wars, torture of heretics, killing of dissidents, people beating themselves with chains — things of this kind. They think this is typical of religion. But our point of view is that particular excesses, if they occur, can be dealt with by law."

What about religious education? "Our view is that it should be done privately. To do it in the schools would violate the constitutional separation of church and state. But it can be done on a voluntary basis at mosques, churches, and synagogues. Parish schools will be a possibility under the new law."

What about atheistic indoctrination? Will this remain a standard feature of public education? "Atheist education is also being restructured with the idea to focus on materialism and not to abuse the feelings of believers."

Moscow: Yuri Smirnoff

Back in Moscow from Baku, I had hoped to interview Konstantin Kharchev, but he had been ill and remained in the hospital.[14] In Kharchev's absence I met Yuri Petrovich Smirnoff, director of the council's International Information Department. A doctor of economics, he had served in diplomatic posts in Thailand, Austria, and the German Democratic Republic before joining the CRA staff ten years ago.

"A lot has changed in the past year," he commented. "The big event that opened the gate was the meeting in the Kremlin in April 1988 when Gorbachev received Patriarch Pimen and several Metropolitans. Until then we talked and talked but nothing happened. After that things started to happen. *Perestroika* began to reach the churches. Now there is news about some new event supportive of religious life practically every day."

---

[14]In mid-June 1989 Yuri Khristorandov was appointed head of the Council for Religious Affairs.

Does the change face much resistance? "Of course there are people against it — some professional atheists. There are fights concerning every area of *perestroika*. You can see it on television and in the press or in debates on the street. But in the meantime religious development is going on continuously. One big event was the launching yesterday of the Orthodox newspaper. It is the first real newspaper in church hands since the Revolution."

What effect has *perestroika* had for the council? "The council's direction has changed. We still have the old 1929 law but practically we don't apply it. All the regulations and instructions the council had sent out between 1961 and 1983 have been officially invalidated.[15] Charity work is allowed. Churches are free to publish. There are still some difficulties on paper but in practice these are ignored. Formerly it was very difficult to register a local church — local authorities didn't want to do it and all sorts of obstacles were put in the way."

Why? "They were embarrassed. One event that helped to change attitudes was the editorial in the April 1988 *Communist* [official journal of the Communist party], which said that the registration of a church should not be considered a defeat on the ideological front. But there are still problems. Even the Central Committee hasn't yet fully succeeded in reorienting party members. It can be much worse in some regions. You may have heard about the case in Ivanovo where local believers have gone on a hunger strike because they weren't able to get back their church."[16]

What about the problem of the Ukrainian Catholic Church? "We are going to solve it. Millions of Soviet citizens are involved. We have to respect them. One problem is that the Uniates are practically under the Vatican — no state likes having its citizens obedient to someone outside the country. Also leaders of the Russian Orthodox

---

[15]Among regulations promulgated in this period were the prohibition of church engagement in charitable activity, the ban on church bell ringing, the order not to register certain religious groups (Jehovah's Witnesses, Pentecostals, Adventists, and others), and the requirement that a religious group can have a meeting only with prior approval and after listing the issues to be discussed and the number of participants to take part (*Moscow News*, no. 15, 1989)

[16]The hunger strike for the return of the Church of the Presentation of the Blessed Virgin in Ivanovo was begun in March 1989 by a dentist, a jurist, a cleaner, and a philologist, all women. Their campaign received considerable attention in the Soviet press. Anatoli Golovkov, chairman of the Ivanovo City Executive Committee, said to a reporter, "I, for example, am sickened, frankly speaking, between ourselves, by the expansion today of the number of believers" (*Ogonyok* no. 28, July 1989.) On August 14, *Izvestia* reported the church's return to local believers, but with several conditions: that tourists be allowed to visit the church, that the priest's house could be used for a museum exhibition, and — most peculiar — that there would be no funeral services at the church.

Church resist change. In the western Ukraine, my judgment is that the majority are Uniates. It will be hard for the Orthodox Church to let go of so many local churches. Probably the Orthodox recall what happened in Czechoslovakia in the Dubček time. Changes were made on behalf of the Catholic Church, but the situation didn't become better for the Orthodox. Catholics became even more aggressive in their efforts to obtain churches and monasteries from the Russian Orthodox Church. But for us [in the CRA] there is no reason to reject any group of twenty believers who want to register as a local church. It is their right. You cannot prohibit it. You see what is happening in Lithuania."

Why are *glasnost* and *perestroika* so much more successful in regard to religious matters than other areas of life? "It doesn't cost much. You can easily give back a church. You can say yes. It is easily done. Other problems are much harder to solve, more complex, and more costly."

Are you encouraged with the changes taking place so far? "Now we await the new law of freedom of conscience. Whatever will be achieved with this, a lot has changed just in the past year. You can also see the direction things are moving. You see it in the press, you see it on television, you see it wherever people meet. There is now a ten-minute sermon every week on All-Union Radio. We never had that before. And you can see it in Bibles. It used to be that it was a big trouble for a tourist just to try bringing a single copy through customs. In the coming months we will pass the two million mark for imported Bibles.[17] [He showed me a two-page letter from Britain's United Bible Societies listing recent shipments of Bibles.] Compare that with the 350,000 Bibles printed in this country since the October Revolution of 1917. Of course we still have a long way to go but we are on the way."

---

[17]In June 1989 Keston College calculated that 954,000 Bibles and 1,540,000 New Testaments had been imported into the Soviet Union since January 1988 and reported that permission had been given for importing a further 3,688,000 Bibles and 13,025,000 New Testaments by the end of 1995. Among major donor groups were the Taizé Community in France, Bibles for All in Sweden, Open Doors in England, and various national Bible Societies. In April 1989 the United Bible Societies reported that a "memorandum of understanding" had been signed with the Russian Orthodox Church that would open the way for printing large editions of the Bible within the USSR and the establishment of a Soviet Bible Society.

Chapter 11

Free at Last?

As THESE FINAL PAGES ARE BEING REVISED IN MARCH 1990, the long-awaited new religious legislation is still pending in the USSR.

Two draft versions of the legislation give indications both of what to expect and also reveal points of unresolved tension. One draft appeared in the February 1989 issue of *Sovetskoye Gosudarstvo i Pravo* (Soviet State and Law). The author, Yuri Rozenbaum, was a jurist involved in the field of religious legislation since Khrushchev's time. The same month a different draft, unpublished, was distributed for comment to Soviet religious leaders by the Council for Religious Affairs.

Both texts restore to religious organizations a "judicial personality" and thus the right to own property, to enter into contracts, and to participate in judicial proceedings. All this was taken away in Lenin's day in the 1918 decree on the separation of church and state.

Both draft texts support the right to profess any or no religion and to "propagate religious or atheist views" (in the Rozenbaum version, "to carry out religious or atheist education"). The CRA version notes that the basis of the new law is Article 52 of the Soviet Union's constitution, as revised in 1977, which guarantees the right of citizens to perform "religious rites or carry out atheist education." Rozenbaum finds Article 52 inadequate because it implies believers do not have the same right to public communication of their convictions enjoyed by atheists. The constitutions of 1918 and 1925, permitting "freedom of religious and antireligious propaganda," are preferred by Rozenbaum.

While the 1929 law limited religious education to the home, both versions of the new law open the way to organize Sunday schools, adult study groups, and catechism classes in homes, at churches, or at other facilities. The CRA version speaks of the parental right "to ensure the religious and moral education and teaching of their children in accordance with their own convictions." It also affirms the right of citizens "to teach or study religion, privately as individuals or with others, at home or at the religious society."

The CRA text permits performance of rites and ceremonies at home, banned under the old law, and suggests they can also be performed in hospitals, prisons, and old-age homes — *if* the administration is willing, quite a big if.

On the topic of charity work by religious organizations, formerly prohibited, the CRA version states that churches would have the right to set up charitable societies and that money used for charitable purposes would not be taxed.

Both versions assume that religious organizations will continue to be registered. In the CRA text, ten (it used to be twenty) adult citizens can apply to register a religious organization and the local Soviet is obliged to respond within one month (formerly no time limit was set). In the Rozenbaum version it is not the association that is registered but rather their *ustav* (statute).

In the CRA version the final court of appeal for registration would be the CRA — profoundly problematic in the event that the old-style bureaucrats one day recover their thrones. In the Rozenbaum version believers would be able to go to court.

Both versions bar discrimination on religious grounds.

The CRA version states that while religious convictions cannot be used as a means of avoiding civil obligations, "exceptions to this can be made in terms of exchanging one civic responsibility for another, with each case to be decided in court." In other words, there will be the possibility for those refusing military service to do alternative service, but the matter is referred to a judge.[1]

Whether there would still be local and regional Councils for Religious Affairs, or even a national CRA, and what form these would take, remains vague. The CRA text refers to "the state organ for religious affairs." Rozenbaum would leave the monitoring of religious

---

[1] For many years conscientious objection to military service was one of the Soviet Union's prohibited topics of public discussion. Lenin's decree of January 4, 1919, providing exemption from military service for conscientious objectors, became part of the Soviet Union's lost history after Stalin came to power. In 1984 I was one of several people from the International Fellowship of Reconciliation who presented a photocopy of Lenin's decree to leaders of the Soviet Peace Committee in Moscow. They suggested it was a forgery. It was a significant sign of the times that the Soviet Peace Committee published the decree in the January 1989 issue of its magazine, *XX Century and Peace.*

rights to local soviets and legal organs. He proposes that a new State Committee for Religious Affairs be set up attached to the Presidium of the Supreme Soviet.

The CRA version stresses the need to bring the application of "Leninist principles into line with the contemporary stage of development of Soviet society." The Rozenbaum text spells out in greater detail the right to atheist convictions and education.

While neither version specifically recognizes the right of religious organizations to publish literature, the text of a new publishing law, issued in draft form early in 1989, permitted publishing not only by official organizations but also by cooperatives, artists' unions, other groups, and ordinary citizens, so long as the material being published does not violate the law.

Both versions, comments John Anderson of Keston College, "go some way in meeting the criticisms of existing legislation made by believers.... [In] a climate where everything that is not expressly forbidden is permitted, the new law seems likely to be a significant improvement over its predecessor, especially as the last article of the CRA draft states that should the USSR accede to an international treaty whose provisions differ from the law of Freedom of Conscience, then the treaty shall be applied."

Responses were submitted to the CRA by religious associations. They refer only to the content of the CRA draft:

• The Russian Orthodox Church proposed removal of the reference to "Leninist principles." It called for direct participation of religious organizations in shaping any government decisions affecting the churches. Responding to the draft text's ban on religious education in school, the church proposed prohibition of compulsory atheist education as well. It asked for specific recognition of the right of churches to set up educational, charitable, youth, and other associations and stressed the right of minors to participate in religious communities. It advocated that churches should have the right to appeal in court if a matter cannot be resolved with the CRA. In the event a local church closes, it was proposed that the property be retained by the larger church organization and not revert to the state. It also proposed that money given to the church for restoration be exempt from taxation.

• Seventh-Day Adventists stressed "the right of religious organizations to engage in charitable activities, that is, to perform the service of charity at state-run institutions such as hospitals, orphanages, prisons, and so on."

• The All Union Council of Evangelical Christian Baptists asked that religious organizations "be given the preferential right to use previously confiscated religious buildings."

• The Moslem Board for the European Part of the USSR and Siberia advocated "pensions on a uniform basis" for those employed by religious organizations.

• The Catholic Bishops of Lithuania, noting that trade unions often refuse to register labor contracts of persons working for the church — organists, bell-ringers, and others — called for legal protection of the "right to social security of those in church employment."

• An Armenian bishop suggested that the law forbid the fomenting of ethnic hostility.

An independent response was submitted by a group of Orthodox believers, including Alexander Ogorodnikov, Vladimir Osipov, and a monk of the Danilov Monastery in Moscow. They advocated the total separation of both religion and atheism from the state and called for the return of all confiscated buildings and property. They proposed that rather than prohibit both atheist and religious education in school, both be available in schools on a voluntary basis. They went further than the CRA in calling for the new law to recognize the right of individuals to abstain from certain civic duties on the grounds of conscience. They proposed an article on the right of both religious and atheist organizations to have access to the media and to have their own media resources. The new law, they said, should prohibit punitive taxation of clergy and religious workers.[2] Neither should churches be pressured to make donations to the Soviet Peace Fund or other funds. Officials found guilty of infringing the law should be removed from their posts. Finally they suggested that representation of religious groups in state bodies should be on a proportional basis. If the principle were accepted, it would be a drastic change.

The proposal that churches should be returned was taken up in an appeal organized by the Public Commission for Giving Help to Christians, signed by thousands of Soviet citizens and submitted to the Congress of Peoples' Deputies in August 1989. The appeal noted

---

[2]A tax of 16 percent is imposed on clergy, full-time parish workers, and others paid for performing or assisting in religious rituals, teachers at theological schools, and workers engaged in church restoration or construction whose contracts were not concluded under the auspices of a trade union. The normal income tax is 4.7 percent. Persons in this higher tax category are not permitted the usual 30 percent discount for those with four or more dependents. An article on the injustice of this arrangement, written by a staff member of the Council for Religious Affairs, was published in *Sovetskaya Yustitsiya* (Soviet Justice) in January 1989. A summary was issued by Keston News Service, no. 320, March 2, 1989.

that, while the repression of believers and closure of churches is now in the past, "local authorities are not hurrying to return churches to believers despite many requests.... In many corners of the country thousands of people are stifling in overcrowded churches.... At the same time, huge cathedrals made into atheist and other museums are practically empty, their lonely attendants bored to death, receiving a tiny stipend for their enforced idleness." These churches "were taken away illegally and without compensation. For many years the state has made use, in whatever ways it wished, of church buildings, icons, religious utensils, and also the unpaid labor of millions of repressed [imprisoned] believers." Among the signers were Father Dimitri Dudko and Father Gleb Yakunin, former prisoners.

While in Moscow in May 1989, I asked Yuri Smirnoff, director of the CRA's International Information Department, to summarize the central elements of the new law.

"Religious bodies will have the status of juridical persons," he said. "The law will recognize the right to participate in charitable work. It will confirm the right to publish journals and periodicals. We hope it will provide equal taxation for all citizens, which would have positive consequences for clergy. It will assure the right to teach religion privately in whatever way religious bodies arrange. It will provide alternative service for conscientious objectors."

I asked why passage of such a law was taking so long. "The process has taken longer than any of us in the council expected. If you had asked me a year ago, I would have said that the law would be ready by the end of 1988. Six months ago we thought it would be ready by the end of January 1989, but then parts had to be revised as it didn't fully meet the terms of the Vienna Conference.[3] In March there was a meeting with religious representatives to get more responses from

---

[3]The 1975 Helsinki Final Act had affirmed "the freedom of the individual to profess and practice, alone or in community with others, religion of belief acting in accordance with the dictates of conscience." In January 1989, ending twenty-six months of negotiation, the Vienna Conference on Security and Cooperation, attended by representatives of thirty-five states, including the USSR, reached accord on a number of issues affecting religious rights. Participating states agreed to "take effective measures to prevent and eliminate discrimination against individuals or communities on the grounds of religion or belief... [and] to ensure effective equality between believers and nonbelievers." They committed themselves "to grant upon the request of communities of believers the right to practice their faith," to respect the right of religious communities "to establish and maintain freely accessible places of worship and assembly, to organize themselves according to their own hierarchical and institutional structure, to select, appoint or replace their personnel in accordance with their respective requirements and standards... and to solicit and receive voluntary financial and other contributions." The states also recognized "the right of everyone to give and receive religious education in the language of his choice, whether individually or in association

them and this meant more revisions. I expect the draft text will soon be published in the press so that there can be public debate about it. Work on the legislation is still going forward. There has just been the tenth meeting on the draft legislation by the commission set up in the Supreme Soviet. I don't know when the law itself will be passed — this summer, I hope, but in any event this year."

On September 19, addressing the Central Committee Plenum, Mikhail Gorbachev mentioned the new law in connection with the nationalities question: "The position and role of the church in relations between nationalities is something that affects the question we are discussing today. It is well known that in the past hostility and conflict between different nationalities were in part a consequence of religious intolerance. This factor also makes itself felt today. We appreciate the peacemaking position of the Russian Orthodox Church and Islamic and other religions groups, and we hope that they will use their influence and opportunities to help avert and overcome inter-ethnic conflicts. The churches today are being given the opportunity to pursue their activities in normal social conditions fully in keeping with their constitutional principles. This can be seen most strikingly in the fact that some of their most prominent representatives have been elected to the Congress of Peoples' Deputies. A law on freedom of conscience, now being drafted, should regulate the whole range of problems connected with the position and activities of church organizations in today's conditions."

Assuming that in the near future the new law will finally be passed and that it will be essentially as has been described, there are major problems still to be solved that, at least in the draft versions of the law, were not resolved.

First, there is the matter of the return of thousands of churches, synagogues, mosques, seminaries, monasteries, and other buildings as well as many items the buildings contained — icons, ritual articles, relics of saints, and vestments that are either on exhibition in museums or, more frequently, in storage.

There is the question of government responsibility for restoration

---

with others" and "the liberty of parents to ensure the religious and moral education of their children in conformity with their own convictions."

Other sections dealt with the right to train religious personnel, to acquire and publish religious books, and to manufacture religious articles. States were asked to "favorably consider the interest of religious communities to participate in public dialogue, including through the mass media." Participating states have the right to challenge other states if they consider that violations of rights have occurred.

A conference to review progress on human rights was scheduled to take place in Moscow in September 1991.

of buildings that were confiscated. Some were destroyed. Others are either empty and rotting or have been turned into storehouses, museums, offices, clubs, and libraries. None is in the condition it was when last used for worship.

There is the point of unambiguous withdrawal. Even in recent instances of property being returned, for example, the Monastery of the Caves in Kiev, adjacent buildings have been retained. In Leningrad, all the buildings within the walls of the former Alexander Nevsky Monastery except the cathedral are used either for museums or offices. No monastic community has yet been able to reestablish itself on the monastery grounds.

The problem of buildings that are in ruins is another issue. Is the government obliged to provide financial support for restoration and reconstruction? Or must believers pay for repair of what was stolen, vandalized, or destroyed?

In addition to the return of buildings, there is the matter of returning people. While the great majority of prisoners of conscience have been released, in February 1990 Keston College listed thirty-two persons serving camp or compulsory labor sentences due to the consequences of religious conviction. The majority were conscientious objectors. There were another thirty-five unconfirmed cases.[4]

The right for religious associations to establish libraries has yet

---

[4]The confirmed cases included seventeen Jehovah's Witnesses, five Pentecostals, one Georgian Orthodox, three Moslems, and four Yogis; the sectarian membership of two Christian prisoners was uncertain. The unconfirmed cases included one Russian Orthodox, two Eastern-rite Catholics, one Seventh-Day Adventist, six Jehovah's Witnesses, and twenty-four Moslems.

Twenty-three of the thirty-two confirmed cases were conscientious objectors. "Most Soviet COs are serving sentences under conditions similar to what in the West would be called 'open prisons,'" comments Keston's Michael Rowe. "They do compulsory labor — construction projects mainly, or sometimes industrial work in remote areas. On the unconfirmed list, two objectors are reported as serving their sentences doing 'community labor.' We are not sure whether this means compulsory labor or some kind of sentence served from home. One Pentecostal CO completes his sentence March 31. Another Pentecostal was sentenced for refusing to serve in the army, though he was never called up. At a pre-call-up interview, he declined to say whether he would serve in the army or not; he was apparently prosecuted out of spite, to delay the family's emigration."

Among the remaining prisoners, one was jailed on the charge of "hooliganism." A Seventh-Day Adventist leader, whose church has refused to be registered, was convicted of bribery and forgery, though Keston believes his religious activity was the real issue behind the charges brought against him. The cases Keston College was least sure of concerned the Moslems, most of whom were arrested for printing or selling the Koran. By now they may have been released.

Two of those listed on the unconfirmed list were in psychiatric hospitals, a dramatic change for the better in contrast with earlier times, but still, if the reports are true, two people too many.

to be recognized. The only books officially permitted on premises designated for religious use are books required for "ritual purposes."

There is an urgent need for religious education. In addition to allowing churches to erect community centers in which religious education can occur, there should be the possibility for voluntary study groups meeting in schools or other public buildings during hours when space is available.

Will there still be an institution similar to the Council for Religious Affairs? Konstantin Kharchev said in his *Ogonyok* interview in December 1988 that he considered government registration of religious associations, once a central task of the CRA, as "pernicious," but he did not advocate the CRA's abolition. Rather he saw it as "taking another shape," becoming instead a Commission of the Supreme Soviet rather than a body under the direction of the Council of Ministers. There would be identical commissions within the various Soviet republics, each under the authority of the local legislative body. "The council would thereby be transformed into a democratic instrument of the people," Kharchev said, "whose decisions, in a state ruled by law, would be obligatory for all."

While putting the CRA in a zone of democratic control would be a significant improvement over the old structure, the question arises: Why must there be anything like the CRA? Many states get along quite well without any equivalent body. In a state struggling to reduce bureaucracy, the CRA would be a prime candidate for complete evaporation. The only valid intermediate function would be to help undo the harm it did in earlier years: to facilitate the return of churches and other confiscated property and to provide assistance in restoration and construction work.

Another question still unresolved is the future place of atheism in Soviet life. What will become of what was the state religion? A number of "chairs" in atheism exist in Soviet universities. Are these to be maintained? Will students still be "expected," even if not required, to take atheist classes? So far only one atheist museum, the one in Vilnius, has been eliminated and the church in which it was housed returned to believers, but others remain, the most famous being the atheist museum in the former Kazan Cathedral in Leningrad. These are run at state expense and always lodged in places of worship to which the government has no legitimate claim.

The issues still outstanding, however, concern not only the state's duty to believers but the responsibility of believers to each other.

There is an urgent need for a more profound ecumenical movement within the Soviet Union. Despite the ecumenical content of many religious publications, especially those issued by the publishing department of the Moscow patriarchate, little has been done within the various religious communities to overcome religious prejudice. Catholic-Orthodox hostility remains sharp and dangerous. Protestants still remember vividly what it was like for them when only the Russian Orthodox Church was legal. One still finds little understanding of Orthodoxy and Catholicism among Protestants, while Orthodox and Catholic believers still tend to regard Protestants with condescension. Anti-Moslem views are as widespread in non-Moslem regions of the USSR as they are in general in the West. Few know anything about Buddhism.

The most extreme form of prejudice has been anti-Semitism. While there have been no pogroms in many years, the bigotry and hatred that gave rise to pogroms remain. Though not officially sanctioned, anti-Semitism is widespread among Soviet Christians. Will the churches work actively to overcome this heritage of contempt, as many churches in other countries have done, or will they continue to say that this is not their task?

An urgent question confronting the hierarchy of the Russian Orthodox Church is its future relationship with the Ukrainian Catholic Church. While the right of the Ukrainian Catholic Church to exist is at last being recognized by the state, many of its churches are in the hands of the Orthodox Church. Will the Russian Orthodox hierarchy return places of worship that were formerly Ukrainian Catholic, at least if the majority of the congregation requests the transfer? Will leaders of the Russian Orthodox Church express penitence for the ways in which the Orthodox Church allowed itself to be used in Stalin's time to suppress Ukrainian Catholicism? And will Ukrainian Catholic bishops be ready to offer their forgiveness if it is sought, or will they continue to carry on a verbal war against Russian Orthodoxy? As the great Orthodox ecumenist Nicolas Zernov noted shortly before his death, "Christians have on the whole regarded themselves as exempt from the necessity to love those who deviate so far from their tradition that they seem to blaspheme against God."[5]

Repentance is a question confronting many religious leaders. Bishops as a general category are not renowned as penitents. While bishops may occasionally take public responsibility for personal sins, it is rare for them to recognize guilt for sins committed on the collective level or in their official capacity. Can they repent of compromises

---

[5]Nicolas Zernov, "Some Reflections," *Sobornost* (London, Fellowship of Saint Alban and Saint Sergius), vol. 1, no. 1 (1979).

they deemed essential to protect the community of believers from utter destruction? The health of a religious community depends on each believer, not least those with great responsibilities, examining his or her conscience and repenting.

Connected with this is a willingness, even readiness, to forgive those in society who sought the destruction of religion and who caused believers to suffer. Is such forgiveness possible after such irreparable harm has occurred? Remembering those women in Moscow who broke through police lines to bring bread to German prisoners of war, I dare to imagine that it is possible. After all, what is happening in the Soviet Union has much to do with the countless prayers that believers have said in their hearts for the conversion of those persecuting them, prayers that were like those scraps of bread offered to the very soldiers who had killed husbands and sons. Whatever their creed, millions of people living within the borders of the USSR have in common a deep attention to the spiritual, and every tradition of spiritual life insists that each of us is called to be a channel of the mercy of God.

•

Are Soviet believers free at last?

Not yet. But events have happened in recent years that even five years ago no one dared to imagine. Whatever becomes of Gorbachev and his campaign for *perestroika*, he has freed immense spiritual energy that has touched everyone.

I recall a television broadcast about the national Cultural Fund meeting in Moscow that I happened to see while in Kiev in January. It was beautifully edited: church choir music alternated with extracts from speeches; during the speeches the camera often explored icons and churches.

"We need to hear the voices of past generations, their pain, their conscience, their love," said Metropolitan Pitirim. "All countries glorify the memory of those who brought them faith. May we glorify Saint Vladimir, Prince of Kiev and Equal of the Apostles."

The camera focused on an icon of Saint Vladimir as Metropolitan Pitirim described the process of evangelization that rapidly spread from Kiev in the tenth and eleventh centuries.

Vladimir Rasputin, the Siberian writer and environmental campaigner, spoke passionately of the influence of religious faith on Russian culture. "We have the richest literature in the world," he said, "a literature deeply imbued with Christianity. This reached its highest point in Dostoyevsky's *The Brothers Karamazov*, which gives the impression of not just being written by a human hand but by an angel.

His novels highlight the tragedy of the modern age — that we grew tired of fighting evil and failed to cherish truth, ignoring the commandments of God and doing violence to our brother. We should revive our ideals, not only earthly but heavenly. Then we shall find the understanding and reconciliation that we all need."

"It is wrong to believe that we were born in October 1917," said another speaker. "We were born from our ancestors long ago and shaped by their faith, but hostile actions have destroyed much of our national culture. Repeated blood-lettings made it difficult to survive."

The program closed with the camera following an old man in Novgorod carefully reassembling fragments of a destroyed fresco in which saints quietly peer out of the plaster. He and his wife have been repairing such war-shattered images since 1945. They expect to finish their lives still doing it. Patiently they were restoring the past, not only the past maimed by bombs but by those determined to destroy the very thought of God.

"I will forgive Gorbachev any mistake he makes just for the sake of one great deed," said my friend Sergei as the credits appeared on the television screen, "that he has ended the war against religious faith."

Index